AF560322

32

INTERNET MARKETING
HISTORY • CONCEPT • STRATEGIES

INTERNET MARKETING

HISTORY • CONCEPT • STRATEGIES

PROF. MUKESH BHATIA

REGAL PUBLICATIONS
New Delhi - 110 027

Contents

SECTION II
INTERNET MARKETING

SECTION IV
CASE STUDIES

Preface

These days, everything you need should be everything you find and search for. This everything can be easily bought on the internet. Our technology is now very advanced making things done at the fastest rate. And because of this, the competition arises between the businesses making the world become a compact global market. Businesses nowadays who are starting and for those who are in the market for a long time tends to make their websites where people can come visit them.

What is Internet Marketing? This type of marketing is some times referred to as On-line marketing, or can also be known as e-marketing. An explanation for this is the marketing of products or services by using the big World Wide Web and that's it in a nut shell. People often see marketing as selling, and this can be some times confuse people. Look at it like this, the majority of people who make a living from home, network marketing on the internet are not physically selling anything. To put it another way, they are actually trying to generate traffic to a product or service so that they gain prospects or email addresses to build up a list of prospects. Whilst you are gathering information, they get lead to a service or product that actually does all of the selling by itself *via* the sales pages, etc.

Having the internet has now exploded the work from home business opportunity. In the early days most internet users would generally use the net to search for items or research a topic, etc., but now this has been pushed aside and people are seizing the chance to make serious incomes online whether it is their primary income, part time, a hobbie or what ever, there is money to be made and plenty of it. After all making money as your own boss and from your own home has got to attract even the cynical of people this world and plant that seed of doubt that maybe they need to open their mind to the potential of making a lot of money is definitely possible.

Promoting and marketing online is popular now and people from all over the world tend to go to the online market rather than seeing their selves stuck in the traffic while trying to get to their favorite shopping malls. SEO plays a role in directing your website towards these people who are constantly making ways to increase their sales. Shopping for the internet brings a lot of benefits to the consumers. They just search on what they want, click on the websites that attract them, order the items and get it delivered to their doors. It is pretty easy for them to do so. But thing is that the constant battle between websites is getting tight now. Finding the right SEO provider will give you enough benefits for your online promotional too. The best thing about them is that they are highly trained and their experiences are above excellence to deliver you the right results.

When you think of an online marketing company you probably think of web design and website building but their services shouldn't stop there. Having a website, contrary to what some small business owners might naively believe, is no guarantee of online sales or even of visitors to the website. Any responsible online marketing company should explain to that your website will not automatically appear on page 1 of the Google search results when a user types in the name of one of the products you sell.

More and more companies have a presence on the big social media sites such as Twitter and Facebook. Whilst social media marketing isn't for every company in every business, many businesses can benefit from using it. An online marketing company is a good place to seek help and advice with your social media marketing. Facebook and Twitter allow companies the opportunity to enter into a dialogue with their clients, and in this respect it is very different from conventional forms of marketing. Already, businesses without a social presence are beginning to be left behind.

Digital and online marketing is growing at an unprecedented rate. Business owners' realisation of the rewards of online marketing has led them to divert over 50% of their marketing budget into this area. Not only is it targeted and cost effective but it can be monitored and measured to ensure success and the highest possible return on investment.

It is vital to know that whatever you decide and do concerning your web business is an important factor of yourself. Once you market online, you are exposing a whole lot about your identity, like what you are enthusiastic about and what type of merchandise you believe in. For that reason, you must focus on which facets of yourself are being published in your online marketing enterprise. Keep an eye on all relevant statistics and results that are crucial for your web work. You should always track the efficiency of your advertising and marketing initiatives. You do not want to keep on throwing money and possibly time into approaches that do not function, so make adjustments as necessary. You need to be informed of the amount of traffic that is returning to your web sites, and how nicely it's converting. Without right supervision, you cannot effectively handle your internet marketing company. The World Wide Web presents us a remarkable potential to monitor our development in countless ways and discover how our functionality can be bettered.

Internet Marketing is the best way to brand or promote your products or services. It helps you to make a strong impact of your business on Internet. This is the main reason why it has surmounted all types of traditional marketing techniques and is very fruitful. Not only it has more reach across the various sections but is also very cost effective programme. Advantages of web marketing have made this acceptable for all businesses that are looking to have some online influence.

This book has been written to help the students of marketing to understand the nitty gritty of internet marketing. It is the sincere hope of the author that the lessons learned here are beneficial, not only in the readers' career, but also in his or her personal life.

PROF. MUKESH BHATIA

SECTION I

Internet

CHAPTER

1

Introduction to Internet

The *Internet* is a global system of interconnected computer networks that use the standard Internet Protocol Suite to serve billions of users worldwide. It is a *network of networks* that consists of millions of private, public, academic, business, and government networks, of local to global scope, that are linked by a broad array of electronic, wireless and optical networking technologies. The Internet carries a vast range of information resources and services, such as the inter-linked hypertext documents of the World Wide Web (WWW) and the infrastructure to support electronic mail.

Most traditional communications media including telephone, music, film, and television are reshaped or redefined by the Internet, giving birth to new services such as Voice over Internet Protocol and IPTV. Newspaper, book and other print publishing are adapting to Web site technology, or are reshaped into blogging and web feeds. The Internet has enabled or accelerated new forms of human interactions through instant messaging, Internet forums, and social networking. Online shopping has boomed both for major retail outlets and small artisans and traders. Business-to-business and financial services on the Internet affect supply chains across entire industries.

The origins of the Internet reach back to research of the 1960s, commissioned by the United States government in collaboration with private commercial interests to build robust, fault-tolerant, and distributed computer networks. The funding of a new U.S. backbone by the National Science Foundation in the 1980s, as well as private funding for other commercial backbones, led to worldwide participation in the development of new networking technologies, and the merger of many networks. The commercialization of what was by the 1990s an international network resulted in its popularization and incorporation into virtually every aspect of modern human life. As of 2009, an estimated quarter of Earth's population used the services of the Internet.

The Internet has no centralized governance in either technological implementation or policies for access and usage; each constituent network sets its own standards. Only the overreaching definitions of the two principal name spaces in the Internet, the Internet Protocol address space and the Domain Name System, are directed by a maintainer organization, the Internet Corporation for Assigned Names and Numbers (ICANN). The technical underpinning and standardization of the core protocols IPv4 and IPv6 is an activity of the Internet Engineering Task Force (IETF), a non-profit organization of loosely affiliated international participants that anyone may associate with by contributing technical expertise.

Internet is a short form of the technical term internetwork, the result of interconnecting computer networks with special gateways or routers. The Internet is also often referred to as *the Net*.

The terms *Internet* and *World Wide Web* are often used in everyday speech without much distinction. However, the Internet and the World Wide Web are not one and the same. The Internet is a global data communications system. It is a hardware and software infrastructure that provides connectivity between computers. In contrast, the Web is one of the services communicated via the Internet. It is a collection of interconnected documents and other resources, linked by hyperlinks and URLs.

In many technical illustrations when the precise location or interrelation of Internet resources is not important, extended networks such as the Internet are often depicted as a cloud. The verbal image has been formalized in the newer concept of cloud computing.

HISTORY

The USSR's launch of Sputnik spurred the United States to create the Advanced Research Projects Agency (ARPA, later DARPA) in February 1958 to regain a technological lead. ARPA created the Information Processing Technology Office (IPTO) to further the research of the Semi Automatic Ground Environment (SAGE) program, which had networked country-wide radar systems together for the first time. The IPTO's purpose was to find ways to address the US military's concern about survivability of their communications networks, and as a first step interconnect their computers at the Pentagon, Cheyenne Mountain, and Strategic Air Command headquarters (SAC). J.C.R. Licklider, a promoter of universal networking, was selected to head the IPTO. Licklider moved from the Psycho-Acoustic Laboratory at Harvard University to MIT in 1950, after becoming interested in information technology. At MIT, he served on a committee that established Lincoln Laboratory and worked on the SAGE project. In 1957 he became a Vice President at BBN, where he bought the first production PDP-1 computer and conducted the first public demonstration of time-sharing.

At the IPTO, Licklider's successor Ivan Sutherland in 1965 got Lawrence Roberts to start a project to make a network, and Roberts based the technology on the work of Paul Baran, who had written an exhaustive study for the United States Air Force that recommended packet switching (opposed to circuit switching) to achieve better network robustness and disaster survivability. Roberts had worked at the MIT Lincoln Laboratory originally established to work on the design of the SAGE system. UCLA professor Leonard Kleinrock had provided the theoretical foundations for packet networks in

1962, and later, in the 1970s, for hierarchical routing, concepts which have been the underpinning of the development towards today's Internet.

Sutherland's successor Robert Taylor convinced Roberts to build on his early packet switching successes and come and be the IPTO Chief Scientist. Once there, Roberts prepared a report called *Resource Sharing Computer Networks* which was approved by Taylor in June 1968 and laid the foundation for the launch of the working ARPANET the following year.

After much work, the first two nodes of what would become the ARPANET were interconnected between Kleinrock's Network Measurement Center at the UCLA's School of Engineering and Applied Science and Douglas Engelbart's NLS system at SRI International (SRI) in Menlo Park, California, on 29 October 1969. The third site on the ARPANET was the Culler-Fried Interactive Mathematics center at the University of California at Santa Barbara, and the fourth was the University of Utah Graphics Department. In an early sign of future growth, there were already fifteen sites connected to the young ARPANET by the end of 1971.

In an independent development, Donald Davies at the UK National Physical Laboratory developed the concept of packet switching in the early 1960s, first giving a talk on the subject in 1965, after which the teams in the new field from two sides of the Atlantic ocean first became acquainted. It was actually Davies' coinage of the wording *packet* and *packet switching* that was adopted as the standard terminology. Davies also built a packet-switched network in the UK, called the Mark I in 1970. Bolt, Beranek and Newman (BBN), the private contractors for ARPANET, set out to create a separate commercial version after establishing "value added carriers" was legalized in the U.S. The network they established was called Telenet and began operation in 1975, installing free public dial-up access in cities throughout the U.S. Telenet was the first packet-switching network open to the general public.

The early ARPANET ran on the Network Control Program (NCP), implementing the host-to-host connectivity and switching layers of the protocol stack, designed and first implemented in December 1970 by a team called the Network Working Group (NWG) led by Steve Crocker. To respond to the network's rapid growth as more and more locations connected, Vinton Cerf and Robert Kahn developed the first description of the now widely used TCP protocols during 1973 and published a paper on the subject in May 1974. Use of the term "Internet" to describe a single global TCP/IP network originated in December 1974 with the publication of RFC 675, the first full specification of TCP that was written by Vinton Cerf, Yogen Dalal and Carl Sunshine, then at Stanford University. During the next nine years, work proceeded to refine the protocols and to implement them on a wide range of operating systems. The first TCP/IP-based wide-area network was operational by 1 January 1983 when all hosts on the ARPANET were switched over from the older NCP protocols.

In 1985, the United States' National Science Foundation (NSF) commissioned the construction of the NSFNET, a university 56 kilobit/second network backbone using computers called "fuzzballs" by their inventor, David L. Mills. The following year, NSF sponsored the conversion to a higher-speed 1.5 megabit/second network that became operational in 1988. A key decision to use the DARPA TCP/IP protocols was made by Dennis Jennings, then in charge of the Supercomputer program at NSF. The NSFNET backbone was upgraded to 45 Mbps in 1991 and decommissioned in 1995 when it was replaced by new backbone networks operated by commercial Internet Service Providers.

The opening of the NSFNET to other networks began in 1988. The US Federal Networking Council approved the interconnection of the NSFNET to the commercial MCI Mail system in that year and the link was made in the summer of 1989. Other commercial electronic mail services were soon connected, including OnTyme, Telemail and Compuserve. In that same year, three commercial Internet service providers (ISPs) began operations: UUNET, PSINet, and CERFNET. Important, separate networks that offered gateways into, then later merged with, the Internet include Usenet and BITNET. Various other commercial and educational networks, such as Telenet (by that time renamed to Sprintnet), Tymnet, Compuserve and JANET were interconnected with the growing Internet in the 1980s as the TCP/IP protocol became increasingly popular. The adaptability of TCP/IP to existing communication networks allowed for rapid growth. The open availability of the specifications and reference code permitted commercial vendors to build interoperable network components, such as routers, making standardized network gear available from many companies. This aided in the rapid growth of the Internet and the proliferation of local-area networking. It seeded the widespread implementation and rigorous standardization of TCP/IP on UNIX and virtually every other common operating system.

Although the basic applications and guidelines that make the Internet possible had existed for almost two decades, the network did not gain a public face until the 1990s. On 6 August 1991, CERN, a pan-European organization for particle research, publicized the new World Wide Web project. The Web was invented by British scientist Tim Berners-Lee in 1989. An early popular web browser was ViolaWWW, patterned after HyperCard and built using the X Window System. It was eventually replaced in popularity by the Mosaic web browser. In 1993, the National Center for Supercomputing Applications at the University of Illinois released version 1.0 of Mosaic, and by late 1994 there was growing public interest in the previously academic, technical Internet. By 1996 usage of the word *Internet* had become commonplace, and consequently, so had its use as a synecdoche in reference to the World Wide Web.

Meanwhile, over the course of the decade, the Internet successfully accommodated the majority of previously existing public computer networks (although some networks, such as FidoNet, have remained separate). During the late 1990s, it was estimated that traffic on the public Internet grew by 100 percent per year, while the mean annual growth in the number of Internet users was thought to be between 20% and 50%. This growth is often attributed to the lack of central administration, which allows organic growth of the network, as well as the non-proprietary open nature of the Internet protocols, which encourages vendor interoperability and prevents any one company from exerting too much control over the network. The estimated population of Internet users is 1.97 billion as of 30 June 2010.

From 2009 onward, the Internet is expected to grow significantly in Brazil, Russia, India, China, and Indonesia (BRICI countries). These countries have large populations and moderate to high economic growth, but still low Internet penetration rates. In 2009, the BRICI countries represented about 45 percent of the world's population and had approximately 610 million Internet users, but by 2015, Internet users in BRICI countries will double to 1.2 billion, and will triple in Indonesia.

USES OF INTERNET

The Internet is allowing greater flexibility in working hours and location, especially with the spread of unmetered high-speed connections and web applications.

The Internet can now be accessed almost anywhere by numerous means, especially through mobile Internet devices. Mobile phones, data cards, handheld game consoles and cellular routers allow users to connect to the Internet from anywhere there is a wireless network supporting that device's technology. Within the limitations imposed by small screens and other limited facilities of such pocket-sized devices, services of the Internet, including email and the web, may be available. Service providers may restrict the services offered and wireless data transmission charges may be significantly higher than other access methods.

Educational material at all levels from pre-school to post-doctoral is available from websites. Examples range from CBeebies, through school and high-school revision guides, virtual universities, to access to top-end scholarly literature through the likes of Google Scholar. In distance education, help with homework and other assignments, self-guided learning, whiling away spare time, or just looking up more detail on an interesting fact, it has never been easier for people to access educational information at any level from anywhere. The Internet in general and the World Wide Web in particular are important enablers of both formal and informal education.

The low cost and nearly instantaneous sharing of ideas, knowledge, and skills has made collaborative work dramatically easier, with the help of collaborative software. Not only can a group cheaply communicate and share ideas, but the wide reach of the Internet allows such groups to easily form in the first place. An example of this is the free software movement, which has produced, among other programs, Linux, Mozilla Firefox, and OpenOffice.org. Internet "chat", whether in the form of IRC chat rooms or channels, or via instant messaging systems, allow colleagues to stay in touch in a very convenient way when working at their computers during the day. Messages can be exchanged even more quickly and conveniently than via email. Extensions to these systems may allow files to be exchanged, "whiteboard" drawings to be shared or voice and video contact between team members.

Version control systems allow collaborating teams to work on shared sets of documents without either accidentally overwriting each other's work or having members wait until they get "sent" documents to be able to make their contributions. Business and project teams can share calendars as well as documents and other information. Such collaboration occurs in a wide variety of areas including scientific research, software development, conference planning, political activism and creative writing. Social and political collaboration is also becoming more widespread as both Internet access and computer literacy grow. From the flash mob 'events' of the early 2000s to the use of social networking in the 2009 Iranian election protests, the Internet allows people to work together more effectively and in many more ways than was possible without it

The Internet allows computer users to remotely access other computers and information stores easily, wherever they may be across the world. They may do this with or without the use of security, authentication and encryption technologies, depending on the requirements. This is encouraging new ways of working from home, collaboration and information sharing in many industries. An accountant sitting at home can audit the books of a company based in another country, on a server situated in a third country that is remotely maintained by IT specialists in a fourth. These accounts could have been created by home-working bookkeepers, in other remote locations, based on information emailed to them from offices all over the world. Some of these things were possible before the widespread use of the Internet, but the cost of private leased lines would have made many of them infeasible in practice. An office worker away from their desk, perhaps on the other side of the world on a business trip or a holiday, can open a remote desktop session into his normal office PC using a secure Virtual Private Network (VPN) connection via the Internet. This gives the worker complete access to all of his or her normal files and data, including email and other applications, while away from the office. This concept has been referred to among system administrators as the Virtual Private Nightmare, because it extends the secure perimeter of a corporate network into its employees' homes.

SERVICES

Information

Many people use the terms *Internet* and *World Wide Web*, or just the *Web*, interchangeably, but the two terms are not synonymous. The World Wide Web is a global set of documents, images and other resources, logically interrelated by hyperlinks and referenced with Uniform Resource Identifiers (URIs). URIs allow providers to symbolically identify services and clients to locate and address web servers, file servers, and other databases that store documents and provide resources and access them using the Hypertext Transfer Protocol (HTTP), the primary carrier protocol of the Web. HTTP is only one of the hundreds of communication protocols used on the Internet. Web services may also use HTTP to allow software systems to communicate in order to share and exchange business logic and data.

World Wide Web browser software, such as Microsoft's Internet Explorer, Mozilla Firefox, Opera, Apple's Safari, and Google Chrome, let users navigate from one web page to another via hyperlinks embedded in the documents. These documents may also contain any combination of computer data, including graphics, sounds, text, video, multimedia and interactive content including games, office applications and scientific demonstrations. Through keyword-driven Internet research using search engines like Yahoo! and Google, users worldwide have easy, instant access to a vast and diverse amount of online information. Compared to printed encyclopedias and traditional libraries, the World Wide Web has enabled the decentralization of information.

The Web has also enabled individuals and organizations to publish ideas and information to a potentially large audience online at greatly reduced expense and time delay. Publishing a web page, a blog, or building a website involves little initial cost and many cost-free services are available. Publishing and maintaining large, professional web sites with attractive, diverse and up-to-date information is still a difficult and expensive proposition, however. Many individuals and some companies and groups use *web logs* or blogs, which are largely used as easily updatable online diaries. Some commercial organizations encourage staff to communicate advice in their areas of specialization in the hope that visitors will be impressed by the expert knowledge and free information, and be attracted to the corporation as a result. One example of this practice is Microsoft, whose product developers publish their personal blogs in order to pique the public's interest in their work. Collections of personal web pages published by large service providers remain popular, and have become increasingly sophisticated. Whereas operations such as Angelfire and GeoCities have existed since the early days of the Web, newer offerings from, for example, Facebook and MySpace currently have large followings. These operations often brand themselves as social network services rather than simply as web page hosts.

Advertising on popular web pages can be lucrative, and e-commerce or the sale of products and services directly via the Web continues to grow.

When the Web began in the 1990s, a typical web page was stored in completed form on a web server, formatted with HTML, ready to be sent to a user's browser in response to a request. Over time, the process of creating and serving web pages has become more automated and more dynamic. Websites are often created using content management or wiki software with, initially, very little content. Contributors to these systems, who may be paid staff, members of a club or other organization or members of the public, fill underlying databases with content using editing pages designed for that purpose, while casual visitors view and read this content in its final HTML form. There may or may not be editorial, approval and security systems built into the process of taking newly entered content and making it available to the target visitors.

Communication

Electronic mail, or email, is an important communications service available on the Internet. The concept of sending electronic text messages between parties in a way analogous to mailing letters or memos predates the creation of the Internet. Pictures, documents and other files are sent as email attachments. Emails can be cc-ed to multiple email addresses.

Internet telephony is another common communications service made possible by the creation of the Internet. VoIP stands for Voice-over-Internet Protocol, referring to the protocol that underlies all Internet communication. The idea began in the early 1990s with walkie-talkie-like voice applications for personal computers. In recent years many VoIP systems have become as easy to use and as convenient as a normal telephone. The benefit is that, as the Internet carries the voice traffic, VoIP can be free or cost much less than a traditional telephone call, especially over long distances and especially for those with always-on Internet connections such as cable or ADSL. VoIP is maturing into a competitive alternative to traditional telephone service. Interoperability between different providers has improved and the ability to call or receive a call from a traditional telephone is available. Simple, inexpensive VoIP network adapters are available that eliminate the need for a personal computer.

Voice quality can still vary from call to call but is often equal to and can even exceed that of traditional calls. Remaining problems for VoIP include emergency telephone number dialing and reliability. Currently, a few VoIP providers provide an emergency service, but it is not universally available. Traditional phones are line-powered and operate during a power failure; VoIP does not do so without a backup power source for the phone equipment and the Internet access devices. VoIP has also become increasingly popular for gaming applications, as a form of communication between players. Popular VoIP clients for gaming include Ventrilo and

Teamspeak. Wii, PlayStation 3, and Xbox 360 also offer VoIP chat features.

Data Transfer

File sharing is an example of transferring large amounts of data across the Internet. A computer file can be emailed to customers, colleagues and friends as an attachment. It can be uploaded to a website or FTP server for easy download by others. It can be put into a "shared location" or onto a file server for instant use by colleagues. The load of bulk downloads to many users can be eased by the use of "mirror" servers or peer-to-peer networks. In any of these cases, access to the file may be controlled by user authentication, the transit of the file over the Internet may be obscured by encryption, and money may change hands for access to the file. The price can be paid by the remote charging of funds from, for example, a credit card whose details are also passed—usually fully encrypted—across the Internet. The origin and authenticity of the file received may be checked by digital signatures or by MD5 or other message digests. These simple features of the Internet, over a worldwide basis, are changing the production, sale, and distribution of anything that can be reduced to a computer file for transmission. This includes all manner of print publications, software products, news, music, film, video, photography, graphics and the other arts. This in turn has caused seismic shifts in each of the existing industries that previously controlled the production and distribution of these products.

Streaming media is the real-time delivery of digital media for the immediate consumption or enjoyment by end users. Many radio and television broadcasters provide Internet feeds of their live audio and video productions. They may also allow time-shift viewing or listening such as Preview, Classic Clips and Listen Again features. These providers have been joined by a range of pure Internet "broadcasters" who never had on-air licenses. This means that an Internet-connected device, such as a computer or something more specific, can be used to access on-line media in much the same way as was previously possible only with a television or radio receiver. The range of available types of content is much wider, from specialized technical webcasts to on-demand popular multimedia services. Podcasting is a variation on this theme, where—usually audio—material is downloaded and played back on a computer or shifted to a portable media player to be listened to on the move. These techniques using simple equipment allow anybody, with little censorship or licensing control, to broadcast audio-visual material worldwide.

Digital media streaming increases the demand for network bandwidth. For example, standard image quality needs 1 Mbps link speed for SD 480p, HD 720p quality requires 2.5 Mbps, and the top-of-the-line HDX quality needs 4.5 Mbps for 1080p. Webcams are a low-cost extension of this phenomenon. While some webcams can give full-frame-rate video, the picture is usually either small or updates slowly. Internet users can watch animals around an African waterhole, ships in the Panama Canal, traffic at a local roundabout or monitor their own premises, live and in real time. Video chat rooms and video conferencing are also popular with many uses being found for personal webcams, with and without two-way sound. YouTube was founded on 15 February 2005 and is now the leading website for free streaming video with a vast number of users. It uses a flash-based web player to stream and show video files. Registered users may upload an unlimited amount of video and build their own personal profile. YouTube claims that its users watch hundreds of millions, and upload hundreds of thousands of videos daily.

INTERNET COMMUNICATIONS TO RETAIN YOUR CUSTOMERS

Every company spends a lot of money to acquire new customers, so investing a bit more to keep them is well worth the price. It's widely acknowledged that the cost of acquiring a new customer can be upwards of five times greater than the cost of retaining an existing one. That means marketing tactics aimed at customer retention should be a priority. One smart, effective, and efficient customer retention tactic is an integrated e-mail communications program. There are many opportunities to communicate with customers via e-mail, and e-mail fits well into the communications methods engineers and other technical professionals prefer. To make internet work as a customer retention tool, you need to do two things:

1. *Get out of the promotional mindset and get into your customer's mindset*. Whether they are a loyal, long-term customer or have just purchased from you for the first time, your customers want to hear from you when you have something to say that's relevant to them. They don't want to be sold to again and again. They want useful information to help them do their jobs better. This will keep your company "top of mind" with them.
2. *Coordinate efforts among different departments who will use e-mail to communicate with customers*. This is where the integrated part comes in. Anyone who might be sending a customer an e-mail—customer service, marketing, accounts receivable, sales—must be on the same page. Their communication efforts should be coordinated and spaced apart so that the e-mails customers receive from you are relevant and timely. There's nothing like a barrage of similar or contradictory e-mails to turn an e-mail retention program into a mess of communications that backfires and turns your customers away.

Ideas for Internet Communications

The key to using e-mail for customer retention is to think in terms of having conversations with your customers. Stay away from the hard selling and limited-time offers and try cultivating your relationship by providing relevant information.

Here are some examples of relevant information:

- A simple thank you e-mail for purchasing a product with links to support information or other products that are related to the one they purchased.
- An e-mail with phone numbers, e-mail addresses, or links for support.
- E-mails containing technical articles or links to articles about their industry or job functions.

- E-mails announcing new versions of products they own.
- E-mails containing customer satisfaction surveys.
- An e-mail from the salesperson just "checking in" to see if the customer has any questions or needs additional help.

While none of these examples are promotional in nature, several of them still perform important cross-selling and up-selling functions. E-mails on new product announcements or related products can lead to additional sales for your company. A survey conducted in September 2006 by Alterian, a marketing software company, revealed that 90% of clients of marketing services providers use e-mail for customer retention and cross-selling.

What Format to Use for Communications

Many of the communications outlined above can be fulfilled by a regular customer e-newsletter. Remember that relevance is the key to a good e-newsletter. Larger companies that have a wide variety of customer types will want to segment them into appropriate groups and send each group an e-newsletter that pertains to their area of interest. If you are unable to do this or have a small customer list, you might consider personalized one-to-one communication from a sales or customer service representative. You can also make your customer retention communications look less like an e-newsletter and more like a personalized letter. This will enhance the relationship aspect of the communications and might decrease the chance your customers will opt-out of your e-mails. Speaking of opting out, although you have a business relationship with your customers and the right to send them e-mails to confirm orders and conduct business communications, you should adhere to all CAN-SPAM laws when working on your retention campaigns. A good summary of the spam law can be found here.

A Final Word on Integration

To get serious about using e-mail as a customer retention tool, representatives from every department that will send e-mails should form a team and plan out the e-mail strategy. It helps to have an executive sponsor. This way, communications will be properly spaced, relevant, and effective, which is exactly what you need to keep your customers in the fold.

Internet Marketing : Use the 3 C's of Communication

There's a tendency, particularly in a tough economy, to try to be all things to all people. So some businesses that do X advertise that they also do Y and Z. They cast a wider net in hopes of bringing back whatever business they can get. You actually stand a better chance of getting and keeping customers if you focus on what you do best and how it benefits them. Consumers are pickier than ever about whom they do business with, so you need to communicate your benefits if you want to stand out in the crowd. The way to do that is through the three C's of effective communication. Take a look at your recent marketing efforts and see whether they pass the test of the 3 C's:

Crisp and Clear

How do you describe who you are and what your business does for customers? Let's go back to that tried-and-true technique–the elevator pitch. Can you describe what you do to someone *not in your industry* in 30 seconds or less? When you go to a networking event and you meet a promising prospect, does your description of your business hold that person's attention? Or do his eyes glaze over or wander across the room? Being crisp is about telling people what you do in as few words as possible–and using that same crisp message in written marketing materials.

Customer-Centric

Tell customers not only what you do but *why* you do it. Make sure they know that they are the focus of your business. Promote your business in terms not just of your experience and expertise, but how *what you* do benefits them. For example: Let's say you're a style consultant. Your e-mail and other marketing communications could relate your experience in the industry and your fabulous style sense. Or you can tell your "value story" from your customer's perspective. Write something like, "I can help you stand out at a job fair and make a great first impression on an interview". That's your message. Make sure you illustrate it with a customer testimonial or case study that shows how your service benefits real people. People need convincing as to why they should spend their limited dollars with you. Your story should focus on how your products or services benefit customers–written from a "what's in it for them?" perspective. When you make your story your customer's story, your marketing materials practically write themselves.

Consistent

Once you've nailed down your crisp message, and you're telling your story from your customer's perspective, make sure you tell it consistently in your e-mails, on your website, in print materials, via the internet and in any other advertising and marketing media. Nothing is more disconcerting to prospects than hearing one story from one communications channel and then reading a different version of the story someplace else. They don't know which version to believe. Reestablish who you are with every customer interaction. Reinforce your story as often as possible.

Improve Your Next Campaign

If your last e-mail or other marketing communication fell short of the three C's, jot down a few ideas to improve the next campaign. Communications that are crisp, clear, customer-centric and consistent are more likely to bring in and keep customers during tough times and in the better days ahead. Following are some additional tips for more effective e-mail communications:

1. Communicate more frequently, but make a direct sales pitch less often.
2. Offer things of value for free. For example, offer hints and tips in your e-mail newsletter or a downloadable report when customers subscribe to your mailing list from your website. When you give expertise away for free, business usually follows.
3. Communicate from the heart. Use e-mail and surveys

to ask customers about how the economy is affecting their purchasing decisions and anything else that's on their minds. Tell them you're in this together and ask them to write about their positive success stories. Then share those in your newsletter.

4. Reinforce your commitment to customers with every interaction. And have faith. That's what entrepreneurship is all about.

Email Deliverability Tips: Ensuring requested opt-in email is delivered to subscriber inboxes is an increasingly difficult battle in the age of spam filtering. Open and click thru response rates can be dramatically affected by as much as 20-30% due to incorrect spam filter classification.

Permission: Confirming that the people who ask for your information have actually requested to be on your list is the number one step in the battle for deliverability. You should be using a process called confirmed opt-in or verified opt-in to send a unique link to the attempted subscriber when they request information. Before adding the person to your list they must click that unique link verifying that they are indeed the same person that owns the email address and requested to subscribe.

Subscriber Addresses: When requesting website visitors to opt-in ask for their "real" or "primary" email address instead of a free email address like Yahoo or Hotmail. Free emails tend to be throw away accounts and typically have a shorter lifetime than a primary ISP address.

List Maintenance: Always promptly remove undeliverable addresses that bounce when sending email to them. An address that bounces with a permanent error 2-3 times in a 30 day period should be removed from the list. ISP's track what percentage of your newsletters bounce and will block them if you attempt to continually deliver messages to closed subscriber mailboxes.

Message Format: Usage of HTML messages to allow for text formatting, multiple columns, images, and brand recognition is growing in popularity and is widely supported by most email client software. Most spam is also HTML formatted and thus differentiating between requested email and spam HTML messages can be difficult. A 2004 study by AWeber.com shows that plain text messages are undeliverable 1.15% of the time and HTML only messages were undeliverable 2.3%. If sending HTML it is important to always send a plain text alternative message, also called text/HTML multi-part mime format.

Content: Many ISP's filter based on the content that appears within the message text.

Website URL: Research potential newsletter advertisers before allowing them to place ads in your newsletter issues. If they have used their website URL to send spam, just having their URL appear in your newsletter could cause the entire message to be filtered.

Words/phrases: Choose your language carefully when crafting messages. Avoid hot button topics often found in spam such as medication, mortgages, making money, and pornography. If you do need to use words that might be filtered, don't attempt to obfuscate words with extra characters or odd spelling, you'll just make your messages appear more spam like.

Images: Avoid creating messages that are entirely images. Use images sparingly, if at all. Commonly used open rate tracking technology uses images to calculate opens. You may choose to disable open rate tracking to avoid being filtered based on image content.

Attachments: With viruses running rampant and spreading thru the usage of malicious email attachments many users are wary of attached documents. It's often better to link to files via a website URL to reduce recipient fear of attachments and reduce the overall message size.

CAN-SPAM Compliance: The January 2004 Federal CAN-SPAM law introduced a number of rules regarding the delivery of email. It's important you have your legal counsel review your practices and ensure you are in compliance. The two most important rules include having a valid postal mail address listed in all commercial messages and a working unsubscribe link that is promptly honored to remove the subscriber from future messages.

Reputation: Reputation services are often used by large ISP's as a way to vet email senders regarding their email practices and policies. Businesses listed with these services are then given less stringent filtering or no filtering at all. Several reputation services are:

http://www.isipp.com/iadb.php
http://www.bondedsender.com
http://www.habeas.com

Relationships and White listing: Contact with major ISP's and email providers is essential in letting them know about your requested subscriber email. Many large providers such as AOL and Yahoo have specific white listing programs and postmaster website areas to ensure your email is delivered as long as you meet their policies and procedures in handling your opt-in list.

CHAPTER

2

Server

Internet server (web server)-this is a special computer, which is constantly switched on and connected to the Internet so that each Internet user around the world can access your website at all times. This computer is built up with selected high quality components, which can endure incessant work and high load. Depending on the expected load and the type of services, which this computer will provide, different configurations can be set-up. As far as database hosting is concerned, for example, a multiprocessor solution combined with small-sized but very fast and stable hard disks would do just great, whereas a single processor configuration with many large size hard disks would be apt with file/image hosting. To ensure better Internet connectivity, the given server is stored in a data center, where it is mounted into a special rack, which offers good ventilation and easy maintenance.

Putting the machine itself in a data center and connecting it to the Internet do not automatically make it an "Internet server". For this purpose, specific web server software has to be installed on it and configured according to the given platform. After the installation and configuration of the web server software, FTP, E-mail, DNS, database, etc. software packages can be added as well.

In computing, the term *server* is used to refer to one of the following:

- a computer program running as a service, to serve the needs or requests of other programs (referred to in this context as "clients") which may or may not be running on the same computer.
- a physical computer dedicated to running one or more such services, to serve the needs of programs running on other computers on the same network.
- a software/hardware system (i.e. a software service running on a dedicated computer) such as a database server, file server, mail server, or print server.

In computer networking, a *server* is a program that operates as a socket listener. The term *server* is also often generalized to describe a host that is deployed to execute one or more such programs.

A *server computer* is a computer, or series of computers, that link other computers or electronic devices together. They often provide essential services across a network, either to private users inside a large organization or to public users via the internet. For example, when you enter a query in a search engine, the query is sent from your computer over the internet to the servers that store all the relevant web pages. The results are sent back by the server to your computer.

Many servers have dedicated functionality such as web servers, print servers, and database servers. *Enterprise servers* are servers that are used in a business context.

USAGE

Servers provide essential services across a network, either to private users inside a large organization or to public users via the Internet. For example, when you enter a query in a search engine, the query is sent from your computer over the internet to the servers that store all the relevant web pages. The results are sent back by the server to your computer.

The term *server* is used quite broadly in information technology. Despite the many server-branded products available (such as server versions of hardware, software or operating systems), in theory any computerized process that shares a resource to one or more client processes is a server. To illustrate this, take the common example of file sharing. While the existence of files on a machine does not classify it as a server, the mechanism which shares these files to clients by the operating system is the server.

Similarly, consider a web server application (such as the multiplatform "Apache HTTP Server"). This web server software can be *run* on any capable computer. For example, while a laptop or personal computer is not typically known as a server, they can in these situations fulfill the role of one, and hence be labeled as one. It is in this case that the machine's purpose as a web server classifies it in general as a server.

In the hardware sense, the word *server* typically designates computer models intended for hosting software applications under the heavy demand of a network environment. In this client–server configuration one or more machines, either a computer or a computer appliance, share information with each other with one acting as a host for the other. While nearly any personal computer is capable of acting as a network server, a dedicated server will contain features making it more suitable for production environments. These features may include a faster CPU, increased high-performance RAM, and typically more than one large hard drive. More obvious distinctions include marked redundancy in power supplies, network connections, and even the servers themselves. Between the 1990s and 2000s an increase in the use of *dedicated hardware* saw the advent of self-contained *server appliances*. One well-known product is the Google Search Appliance, a unit that combines hardware and software in an out-of-the-box packaging. Simpler examples of such appliances include switches, routers, gateways, and print server, all of which are available in a near plug-and-play configuration. Modern operating systems such as Microsoft Windows or Linux distributions rightfully seem to be designed with a client–server architecture in mind. These operating systems attempt to abstract hardware, allowing a wide variety of software to work with components of the computer. In a sense, the operating system can be seen as *serving* hardware to the software, which in all but low-level programming languages must interact using an API.

These operating systems may be able to run programs in the background called either services or daemons. Such programs may wait in a sleep state for their necessity to become apparent, such as the aforementioned *Apache HTTP Server* software. Since any software that provides services can be *called* a server, modern personal computers can be seen as a forest of servers and clients operating in parallel. The Internet itself is also a forest of servers and clients. Merely requesting a web page from a few kilometers away involves satisfying a stack of protocols that involve many examples of hardware and software servers. The least of these are the routers, modems, domain name servers, and various other servers necessary to provide us the world wide web.

SERVER HARDWARE

Hardware requirements for servers vary, depending on the server application. Absolute CPU speed is not usually as critical to a server as it is to a desktop machine Servers' duties to provide service to many users over a network lead to different requirements like fast network connections and high I/O throughput. Since servers are usually accessed over a network, they may run in headless mode without a monitor or input device. Processes that are not needed for the server's function are not used. Many servers do not have a graphical user interface (GUI) as it is unnecessary and consumes resources that could be allocated elsewhere. Similarly, audio and USB interfaces may be omitted.

Servers often run for long periods without interruption and availability must often be very high, making hardware reliability and durability extremely important. Although servers can be built from commodity computer parts, mission-critical enterprise servers are ideally very fault tolerant and use specialized hardware with low failure rates in order to maximize uptime, for even a short-term failure can cost more than purchasing and installing the system. For example, it may take only a few minutes of down time at a national stock exchange to justify the expense of entirely replacing the system with something more reliable. Servers may incorporate faster, higher-capacity hard drives, larger computer fans or water cooling to help remove heat, and uninterruptible power supplies that ensure the servers continue to function in the event of a power failure. These components offer higher performance and reliability at a correspondingly higher price. Hardware redundancy—installing more than one instance of modules such as power supplies and hard disks arranged so that if one fails another is automatically available—is widely used. ECC memory devices that detect and correct errors are used; non-ECC memory is more likely to cause data corruption.

To increase reliability, most of the servers use memory with error detection and correction, redundant disks, redundant power supplies and so on. Such components are also frequently hot swappable, allowing to replace them on the running server without shutting it down. To prevent overheating, servers often have more powerful fans. As servers are usually administered by qualified engineers, their operating systems are also more tuned for stability and performance than for user friendliness and ease of use, Linux taking noticeably larger percentage than for desktop computers. As servers need stable power supply, good Internet access, increased security and are also noisy, it is usual to store them in dedicated server centers or special rooms. This requires to reduce power consumption as extra energy used generates more heat and the temperature in the room could exceed the acceptable limits. Normally server rooms are equipped with air conditioning devices. Server casings are usually flat and wide, adapted to store many devices next to each other in server rack. Unlike ordinary computers, servers usually can be configured, powered up and down or rebooted remotely, using out-of-band management.

Many servers take a long time for the hardware to start up and load the operating system. Servers often do extensive pre-boot memory testing and verification and startup of remote management services. The hard drive controllers then start up banks of drives sequentially, rather than all at once, so as not to overload the power supply with startup surges, and afterwards they initiate RAID system pre-checks for correct operation of redundancy. It is common for a machine to take several minutes to start up, but it may not need restarting for months or years.

SERVER OPERATING SYSTEMS

Server-oriented operating systems tend to have certain features in common that make them more suitable for the server environment, such as :

- GUI not available or optional
- ability to reconfigure and update both hardware and software to some extent without restart,
- advanced backup facilities to permit regular and frequent online backups of critical data,
- transparent data transfer between different volumes or devices,
- flexible and advanced networking capabilities,
- automation capabilities such as daemons in UNIX and services in Windows, and
- tight system security, with advanced user, resource, data, and memory protection.

Server-oriented operating systems can, in many cases, interact with hardware sensors to detect conditions such as overheating, processor and disk failure, and consequently alert an operator or take remedial measures itself. Because servers must supply a restricted range of services to perhaps many users while a desktop computer must carry out a wide range of functions required by its user, the requirements of an operating system for a server are different from those of a desktop machine. While it is possible for an operating system to make a machine both provide services and respond quickly to the requirements of a user, it is usual to use different operating systems on servers and desktop machines. Some operating systems are supplied in both server and desktop versions with similar user interface.

The desktop versions of the Windows and Mac OS X operating systems are deployed on a minority of servers, as are some proprietary mainframe operating systems, such as z/OS. The dominant operating systems among servers are UNIX-based or open source kernel distributions, such as Linux (the kernel). The rise of the microprocessor-based server was facilitated by the development of Unix to run on the x86 microprocessor architecture. The Microsoft Windows family of operating systems also runs on x86 hardware, and since Windows NT have been available in versions suitable for server use.

While the role of server and desktop operating systems remains distinct, improvements in the reliability of both hardware and operating systems have blurred the distinction between the two classes. Today, many desktop and server operating systems share similar code bases, differing mostly in configuration. The shift towards web applications and middleware platforms has also lessened the demand for specialist application servers.

SERVERS ON THE INTERNET

Almost the entire structure of the Internet is based upon a client–server model. High-level root name servers, DNS servers, and routers direct the traffic on the internet. There are millions of servers connected to the Internet, running continuously throughout the world.

- World Wide Web
- Domain Name System
- E-mail
- FTP file transfer
- Chat and instant messaging
- Voice communication
- Streaming audio and video
- Online gaming
- Database servers

Virtually every action taken by an ordinary Internet user requires one or more interactions with one or more servers. There are also technologies that operate on an inter-server level. Other services do not use dedicated servers; for example peer-to-peer file sharing, some implementations of telephony (e.g. Skype), and supplying television programs to several users (e.g. Kontiki, SlingBox).

CHAPTER

3

World Wide Web

The *World Wide Web,* abbreviated as *WWW* or *W3* and commonly known as *the Web,* is a system of interlinked hypertext documents accessed via the Internet. With a web browser, one can view web pages that may contain text, images, videos, and other multimedia and navigate between them via hyperlinks. Using concepts from earlier hypertext systems, English engineer and computer scientist Sir Tim Berners-Lee, now the Director of the World Wide Web Consortium, wrote a proposal in March 1989 for what would eventually become the World Wide Web. At CERN in Geneva, Switzerland, Berners-Lee and Belgian computer scientist Robert Cailliau proposed in 1990 to use "HyperText . . . to link and access information of various kinds as a web of nodes in which the user can browse at will", and publicly introduced the project in December.

"The World-Wide Web was developed to be a pool of human knowledge, and human culture, which would allow collaborators in remote sites to share their ideas and all aspects of a common project".

FUNCTION

The terms Internet and World Wide Web are often used in every-day speech without much distinction. However, the Internet and the World Wide Web are not one and the same. The Internet is a global system of interconnected computer networks. In contrast, the Web is one of the services that runs on the Internet. It is a collection of interconnected documents and other resources, linked by hyperlinks and URLs. In short, the Web is an application running on the Internet.

Viewing a web page on the World Wide Web normally begins either by typing the URL of the page into a web browser, or by following a hyperlink to that page or resource. The web browser then initiates a series of communication messages, behind the scenes, in order to fetch and display it. First, the browser resolves the server-name portion of the URL into an Internet Protocol address using the global, distributed Internet database known as the Domain Name System (DNS); this lookup returns an IP address such as *208.80.152.2*. The browser then requests the resource by sending an HTTP request across the Internet to the computer at that particular address. It makes the request to a particular application port in the underlying Internet Protocol Suite so that the computer receiving the request can distinguish an HTTP request from other network protocols such as e-mail delivery; the HTTP protocol normally uses port 80. The content of the HTTP request can be as simple as the two lines of text.

DOMAIN NAME SYSTEM

The *Domain Name System* (*DNS*) is a hierarchical naming system built on a distributed database for computers, services, or any resource connected to the Internet or a private network. Most importantly, it translates domain names meaningful to humans into the numerical identifiers associated with networking equipment for the purpose of locating and addressing these devices worldwide.

An often-used analogy to explain the Domain Name System is that it serves as the "phone book" for the Internet by translating human-friendly computer hostnames into IP addresses. For example, the domain name www.example.com translates to the addresses 192.0.32.10 (IPv4) and 2620:0:2d0:200::10 (IPv6).

The Domain Name System makes it possible to assign domain names to groups of Internet resources and users in a meaningful way, independent of each entity's physical location. Because of this, World Wide Web (WWW) hyperlinks and Internet contact information can remain consistent and constant even if the current Internet routing arrangements change or the participant uses a mobile device. Internet domain names are easier to remember than IP addresses such as 208.77.188.166 (IPv4) or 2001:db8:1f70::999:de8:7648:6e8 (IPv6). Users take advantage of this when they recite meaningful Uniform Resource Locators (URLs) and e-mail addresses without having to know how the computer actually locates them.

The Domain Name System distributes the responsibility of assigning domain names and mapping those names to IP addresses by designating authoritative name servers for each domain. Authoritative name servers are assigned to be responsible for their particular domains, and in turn can assign other authoritative name servers for their sub-domains. This mechanism has made the DNS distributed and fault tolerant and has helped avoid the need for a single central register to be continually consulted and updated.

In general, the Domain Name System also stores other types of information, such as the list of mail servers that accept email for a given Internet domain. By providing a worldwide, distributed keyword-based redirection service, the Domain Name System is an essential component of the functionality of the Internet.

Other identifiers such as RFID tags, UPCs, International characters in email addresses and host names, and a variety of other identifiers could all potentially use DNS. The Domain Name System also specifies the technical functionality of this database service. It defines the DNS protocol, a detailed definition of the data structures and communication exchanges used in DNS, as part of the Internet Protocol Suite.

The Internet maintains two principal namespaces, the domain name hierarchy and the Internet Protocol (IP) address system. The Domain Name System maintains the domain namespace and provides translation services between these two namespaces. Internet name servers and a communication protocol implement the Domain Name System. A DNS name server is a server that stores the DNS records for a domain name, such as address (A) records, name server (NS) records, and mail exchanger (MX) records, a DNS name server responds with answers to queries against its database.

EMAIL

Electronic mail, commonly called *email* or *e-mail,* is a method of exchanging digital messages from an author to one or more recipients. Modern email operates across the Internet or other computer networks. Some early email systems required that the author and the recipient both be online at the same time, *a la* instant messaging. Today's email systems are based on a store-and-forward model. Email servers accept, forward, deliver and store messages. Neither the users nor their computers are required to be online simultaneously; they need connect only briefly, typically to an email server, for as long as it takes to send or receive messages.

An email message consists of three components, the message *envelope,* the message *header,* and the message *body.* The message header contains control information, including, minimally, an originator's email address and one or more recipient addresses. Usually descriptive information is also added, such as a subject header field and a message submission date/time stamp.

Originally a text-only (7-bit ASCII and others) communications medium, email was extended to carry multi-media content attachments, a process standardized in RFC 2045 through 2049. Collectively, these RFCs have come to be called Multipurpose Internet Mail Extensions (MIME).

The history of modern, global Internet email services reaches back to the early ARPANET. Standards for encoding email messages were proposed as early as 1973 (RFC 561).

Conversion from ARPANET to the Internet in the early 1980s produced the core of the current services. An email sent in the early 1970s looks quite similar to a basic text message sent on the Internet today.

Network-based email was initially exchanged on the ARPANET in extensions to the File Transfer Protocol (FTP), but is now carried by the Simple Mail Transfer Protocol (SMTP), first published as Internet standard 10 (RFC 821) in 1982. In the process of transporting email messages between systems, SMTP communicates delivery parameters using a message *envelope* separate from the message (header and body) itself.

There are several spelling options that occasionally prove cause for surprisingly vehement disagreement email is the form required by IETF Requests for Comment and working groups and increasingly by style guides. This spelling also appears in most dictionaries.

- e-mail is a form previously recommended by some prominent journalistic and technical style guides. According to Corpus of Contemporary American English data, this form appears most frequently in edited, published American English writing.
- mail was the form used in the original RFC. The service is referred to as *mail* and a single piece of electronic mail is called a *message*.
- eMail, capitalizing only the letter *M*, was common among ARPANET users and the early developers of Unix, CMS, AppleLink, eWorld, AOL, GEnie, and Hotmail.
- *EMail is a traditional form that has been used in RFCs for the "Author's Address", and is expressly required "...for historical reasons".*
- *E-mail, capitalizing the initial letter E in the same way as A-bomb, H-bomb, X-ray, T-shirt, and similar shortenings.*

RISKS AND LIABILITIES

Although instant messaging delivers many benefits, it also carries with it certain risks and liabilities, particularly when used in workplaces. Among these risks and liabilities are:

- Security risks (e.g. IM used to infect computers with spyware, viruses, trojans, worms)
- Compliance risks
- Inappropriate use
- Trade secret leakage

Security Risks

Crackers (malicious "hacker" or [black hat] hacker) have consistently used IM networks as vectors for delivering phishing attempts, "poison URLs", and virus-laden file attachments from 2004 to the present, with over 1100 discrete attacks listed by the IM Security Center in 2004-07. Hackers use two methods of delivering malicious code through IM: delivery of viruses, trojan horses, or spyware within an infected file, and the use of "socially engineered" text with a web address that entices the recipient to click on a URL connecting him or her to a website that then downloads malicious code. Viruses, computer worms, and trojans typically propagate by sending themselves rapidly through the infected user's buddy list. An effective attack using a poisoned URL may reach tens of thousands of people in a short period when each person's buddy list receives messages appearing to be from a trusted friend. The recipients click on the web address, and the entire cycle starts again. Infections may range from nuisance to criminal, and are becoming more sophisticated each year.

IM connections usually take place in plain text, making them susceptible to eavesdropping. In addition, IM client software often requires the user to expose open UDP ports to the world, increasing the threat posed by potential security vulnerabilities.

Compliance Risks

In addition to the malicious code threat, the use of instant messaging at work also creates a risk of non-compliance to laws and regulations governing the use of electronic communications in businesses. In the United States alone there are over 10,000 laws and regulations related to electronic messaging and records retention. The better-known of these include the Sarbanes-Oxley Act, HIPAA, and SEC 17a-3. Clarification from the Financial Industry Regulatory Authority ("FINRA") was issued to member firms in the financial services industry in December, 2007, noting that "electronic communications", "email", and "electronic correspondence" may be used interchangeably and can include such forms of electronic messaging as *instant messaging* and text messaging. Changes to Federal Rules of Civil Procedure, effective December 1, 2006, created a new category for electronic records which may be requested during discovery in legal proceedings. Most countries around the world also regulate the use of electronic messaging and electronic records retention in similar fashion to the United States. The most common regulations related to IM at work involve the need to produce archived business communications to satisfy government or judicial requests under law. Many instant messaging communications fall into the category of business communications that must be archived and retrievable.

Inappropriate Use

Organizations of all types must protect themselves from the liability of their employees' inappropriate use of IM. The informal, immediate, and ostensibly anonymous nature of instant messaging makes it a candidate for abuse in the workplace. The topic of inappropriate IM use became front page news in October 2006 when U.S. Congressman Mark Foley resigned his seat after admitting sending offensive instant messages of a sexual nature to underage former House pages from his Congressional office PC. The Mark Foley Scandal led to media coverage and mainstream newspaper articles warning of the risks of inappropriate IM use in workplaces. In most countries, corporations have a legal responsibility to ensure harassment-free work environment for employees. The use of corporate-owned computers, networks, and software to harass an individual or spread inappropriate jokes or language creates a liability for not only the offender but also the employer. A survey by IM archiving and security provider Akonix Systems, Inc. in March 2007 showed that 31% of respondents had been harassed over IM at work Companies now include instant messaging as an integral component of their policies on appropriate use of the World Wide Web, e-mail, and other corporate assets.

Security and Archiving

In the early 2000s, a new class of IT security provider emerged to provide remedies for the risks and liabilities faced by corporations who chose to use IM for business communications. The IM security providers created new products to be installed in corporate networks for the purpose of archiving, content-scanning, and security-scanning IM traffic moving in and out of the corporation. Similar to the e-mail filtering vendors, the IM security providers focus on the risks and liabilities described above. With rapid adoption of IM in the workplace, demand for IM security products began to grow in the mid-2000s. By 2007, the preferred platform for the purchase of security software had become the "computer appliance", according to IDC, who estimate that by 2008, 80% of network security products will be delivered via an appliance.

VOICE OVER INTERNET PROTOCOL

Voice over Internet Protocol (*Voice over IP, VoIP*) is one of a family of internet technologies, communication protocols, and transmission technologies for delivery of voice communications and multimedia sessions over Internet Protocol (IP) networks, such as the Internet. Other terms frequently encountered and often used synonymously with VoIP are IP telephony, Internet telephony, voice over broadband (VoBB), broadband telephony, and broadband phone.

Internet telephony refers to communications services—Voice, fax, SMS, and/or voice-messaging applications—that are transported via the Internet, rather than the public switched telephone network (PSTN). The steps involved in originating a VoIP telephone call are signaling and media channel setup, digitization of the analog voice signal, encoding, packetization, and transmission as Internet Protocol (IP) packets over a packet-switched network. On the receiving side, similar steps (usually in the reverse order) such as reception of the IP packets, decoding of the packets and digital-to-analog conversion reproduce the original voice stream. Even though IP Telephony and VoIP are terms that are used interchangeably, they are actually different; IP telephony has to do with digital telephony systems that use IP protocols for voice communication while VoIP is actually a subset of IP Telephony.

VoIP is a technology used by IP telephony as a means of transporting phone calls. VoIP systems employ session control protocols to control the set-up and tear-down of calls as well as audio codecs which encode speech allowing transmission over an IP network as digital audio via an audio stream. The codec used is varied between different implementations of VoIP (and often a range of codecs are used); some implementations rely on narrowband and compressed speech, while others support high fidelity stereo codecs.

There are three types of VoIP tools that are commonly used; IP Phones, Software VoIP and Mobile and Integrated VoIP. The IP Phones are the most institutionally established but still the least obvious of the VoIP tools. Of all the software VoIP tools that exist, Skype is probably the most easily identifiable. The use of software VoIP has increased during the global recession as many persons, looking for ways to cut costs have turned to these tools for free or inexpensive calling or video conferencing applications. Software VoIP can be further broken down into three classes or subcategories; Web Calling, Voice and Video Instant Messaging and Web Conferencing. Mobile and Integrated VoIP is just another example of the adaptability of VoIP. VoIP is available on many smart phones and internet devices so even the users of portable devices that are not phones can still make calls or send SMS text messages over 3G or WIFI.

CONSUMER MARKET

A major development that started in 2004 was the introduction of mass-market VoIP services that utilize existing broadband Internet access, by which subscribers place and receive telephone calls in much the same manner as they would via the public switched telephone network (PSTN). Full-service VoIP phone companies provide inbound and outbound service with Direct Inbound Dialing. Many offer unlimited domestic calling for a flat monthly subscription fee. This sometimes includes international calls to certain countries. Phone calls between subscribers of the same provider are usually free when flat-fee service is not available. A VoIP phone is necessary to connect to a VoIP service provider. This can be implemented in several ways:

- Dedicated VoIP phones connect directly to the IP network using technologies such as wired Ethernet or wireless Wi-Fi. They are typically designed in the style of traditional digital business telephones.
- An analog telephone adapter is a device that connects to the network and implements the electronics and firmware to operate a conventional analog telephone attached through a modular phone jack. Some residential Internet gateways and cable modems have this function built in.
- A soft phone is application software installed on a networked computer that is equipped with a microphone and speaker, or headset. The application typically presents a dial pad and display field to the user to operate the application by mouse clicks or keyboard input.

CORPORATE USE

Because of the bandwidth efficiency and low costs that VoIP technology can provide, businesses are gradually beginning to migrate from traditional copper-wire telephone systems to VoIP systems to reduce their monthly phone costs. VoIP solutions aimed at businesses have evolved into "unified communications" services that treat all communications—phone calls, faxes, voice mail, e-mail, Web conferences and more—as discrete units that can all be delivered via any means and to any handset, including cell phones. Two kinds of competitors are competing in this space: one set is focused on VoIP for medium to large enterprises, while another is targeting the small-to-medium business.

VoIP allows both voice and data communications to be run over a single network, which can significantly reduce infrastructure costs. The prices of extensions on VoIP are lower than for PBX and key systems. VoIP switches may run on commodity hardware, such as PCs or Linux systems. Rather than closed architectures, these devices rely on standard interfaces. VoIP devices have simple, intuitive user interfaces, so users can often make simple system configuration changes. Dual-mode cell phones enable users to continue their conversations as they move between an outside cellular service and an internal Wi-Fi network, so that it is no longer necessary to carry both a desktop phone and a cell phone. Maintenance becomes simpler as there are fewer devices to oversee.

Skype, which originally marketed itself as a service among friends, has begun to cater to businesses, providing free-of-charge connections between any users on the Skype network and connecting to and from ordinary PSTN telephones for a charge. In the United States the Social Security Administration (SSA) is converting its field offices of 63,000 workers from traditional phone installations to a VoIP infrastructure carried over its existing data network.

OPERATIONAL COST

VoIP can be a benefit for reducing communication and infrastructure costs. Examples include:

- Routing phone calls over existing data networks to avoid the need for separate voice and data networks.

- Conference calling, IVR, call forwarding, automatic redial, and caller ID features that traditional telecommunication companies (telcos) normally charge extra for, are available free of charge from open source VoIP implementations.

FLEXIBILITY

VoIP can facilitate tasks and provide services that may be more difficult to implement using the PSTN. Examples include:

- The ability to transmit more than one telephone call over a single broadband connection.
- Secure calls using standardized protocols (such as Secure Real-time Transport Protocol). Most of the difficulties of creating a secure telephone connection over traditional phone lines, such as digitizing and digital transmission, are already in place with VoIP. It is only necessary to encrypt and authenticate the existing data stream.
- Location independence. Only a sufficiently fast and stable Internet connection is needed to get a connection from anywhere to a VoIP provider.
- Integration with other services available over the Internet, including video conversation, message or data file exchange during the conversation, audio conferencing, managing address books, and passing information about whether other people are available to interested parties.
- Unified Communications, the integration of VoIP with other business systems including E-mail, Customer Relationship Management (CRM), and Web systems.

Streaming Media

Streaming media is multimedia that is constantly received by and presented to an end-user while being delivered by a streaming provider. The name refers to the delivery method of the medium rather than to the medium itself. The distinction is usually applied to media that are distributed over telecommunications networks, as most other delivery systems are either inherently streaming (e.g., radio, television) or inherently non-streaming (e.g., books, video cassettes, audio CDs). The verb 'to stream' is also derived from this term, meaning to deliver media in this manner. Internet television is a commonly streamed medium.

Live streaming also known as on-demand streaming, more specifically, means taking the media and broadcasting it live over the Internet. The process involves a camera for the media, an encoder to digitize the content, a media publisher where the streams are made available to potential end-users and a content delivery network to distribute and deliver the content. The media can then be viewed by end-users live. It can be difficult to control streaming content and prevent redistribution. Digital rights management (DRM) systems are an example of an attempt to keep this content under control of the streamer.

ONLINE GAME

An *online game* is a game played over some form of computer network. This almost always means the Internet or equivalent technology, but games have always used whatever technology was current: modems before the Internet, and hard wired terminals before modems. The expansion of online gaming has reflected the overall expansion of computer networks from small local networks to the Internet and the growth of Internet access itself. Online games can range from simple text based games to games incorporating complex graphics and virtual worlds populated by many players simultaneously. Many online games have associated online communities, making online games a form of social activity beyond single player games.

The rising popularity of Flash and Java led to an Internet revolution where websites could utilize streaming video, audio, and a whole new set of user interactivity. When Microsoft began packaging Flash as a pre-installed component of IE, the Internet began to shift from a data/information spectrum to also offer on-demand entertainment. This revolution paved the way for sites to offer games to web surfers. Some online multiplayer games like World of Warcraft, Final Fantasy XI and Lineage II charge a monthly fee to subscribe to their services, while games such as *Guild Wars* offer an alternative no monthly fee scheme. Many other sites relied on advertising revenues from on-site sponsors, while others, like *RuneScape,* or *Tibia* let people play for free while leaving the players the option of paying, unlocking new content for the members. After the dot-com bubble burst in 2001, many sites solely relying on advertising revenue dollars faced extreme adversity. Despite the decreasing profitability of online gaming websites, some sites have survived the fluctuating ad market by offsetting the advertising revenue loss by using the content as a cross-promotion tool for driving web visitors to other websites that the company owns. The term *online gaming* in many circles is being strictly defined to describe games that do not involve wagering, although many still use the term *online gaming* synonymously with *online gambling*.

This article focuses on online games that do not involve wagering, online gambling is discussed in a separate article. "Online gaming is a technology rather than a genre; a mechanism for connecting players together rather than a particular pattern of game play". Online games are played over some form of computer network, now typically on the Internet. One advantage of online games is the ability to connect to multiplayer games, although single-player online games are quite common as well.

First-person Shooter Games

During the 1990s, online games started to move from a wide variety of LAN protocols (such as IPX) and onto the Internet using the TCP/IP protocol. *Doom* popularized the concept of death match, where multiple players battle each other head-to-head, as a new form of online game. Since Doom, many first-person shooter games contain online components to allow death match or arena style play.

Real-time Strategy Games

Early real-time strategy games often allowed multiplayer

play over a modem or local network. As the Internet started to grow during the 1990s, software was developed that would allow players to tunnel the LAN protocols used by the games over the Internet.

By the late 1990s, most RTS games had native Internet support, allowing players from all over the globe to play with each other. Services were created to allow players to be automatically matched against another player wishing to play or lobbies were formed where people could meet in so called game rooms. An example was the MSN Gaming Zone where online game communities were formed by active players for games, such as *Age of Empires* and *Microsoft Ants*.

Cross-platform Online Play

As consoles are becoming more like computers, online game play is expanding. Once online games started crowding the market, open source networks, such as the Dreamcast, PlayStation 2, Nintendo GameCube and Xbox took advantage of online functionality with its PC game counterpart. Games such as *Phantasy Star Online* have private servers that function on multiple consoles. Dreamcast, PC, Macintosh and GameCube players are able to share one server. Earlier games, like 4x4 Evolution, Quake III and Need for Speed: Underground also have a similar function with consoles able to interact with PC users using the same server. Usually, a company like Electronic Arts or Sega runs the servers until it becomes inactive, in which private servers with their own DNS number can function. This form of open source networking has a small advantage over the new generation of Sony and Microsoft consoles which customize their servers to the consumer.

Browser Games

As the World Wide Web developed and browsers became more sophisticated, people started creating browser games that used a web browser as a client. Simple single player games were made that could be played using a web browser via HTML and HTML scripting technologies (most commonly JavaScript, ASP, PHP and MySQL). More complicated games such as Legend of Empires or AQ Worlds would contact a web server to allow a multiplayer gaming environment. The development of web-based graphics technologies such as Flash and Java allowed browser games to become more complex. These games, also known by their related technology as "Flash games" or "Java games", became increasingly popular. Many games originally released in the 1980s, such as Pac-Man and Frogger, were recreated as games played using the Flash plugin on a webpage. Most browser games had limited multiplayer play, often being single player games with a high score list shared amongst all players. This has changed considerably in recent years as examples like Castle of Heroes or Canaan Online show. Browser-based pet games are popular amongst the younger generation of online gamers. These games range from gigantic games with millions of users, such as Neopets, to smaller and more community-based pet games. More recent browser-based games use web technologies like Ajax to make more complicated multiplayer interactions possible and WebGL to generate hardware-accelerated 3D graphics without the need for plugins.

DATABASE SERVER

A *database server* is a computer program that provides database services to other computer programs or computers, as defined by the client–server model. The term may also refer to a computer dedicated to running such a program. Database management systems frequently provide database server functionality, and some DBMSs (e.g., MySQL) rely exclusively on the client–server model for database access.

Such a server is accessed either through a "front end" running on the user's computer which displays requested data or the "back end" which runs on the server and handles tasks such as data analysis and storage. In a master-slave model, database master servers are central and primary locations of data while database slave servers are synchronized backups of the master acting as proxies. Some examples of Database servers are Oracle, DB2, Informix, Ingres, SQL Server. Every server uses its own query logic and structure. The SQL query language is more or less the same in all the database servers.

Database Replication

Database replication can be used on many database management systems, usually with a master/slave relationship between the original and the copies. The master logs the updates, which then ripple through to the slaves. The slave outputs a message stating that it has received the update successfully, thus allowing the sending (and potentially re-sending until successfully applied) of subsequent updates.

Multi-master replication, where updates can be submitted to any database node, and then ripple through to other servers, is often desired, but introduces substantially increased costs and complexity which may make it impractical in some situations. The most common challenge that exists in multi-master replication is transactional conflict prevention or resolution. Most synchronous or eager replication solutions do conflict prevention, while asynchronous solutions have to do conflict resolution. For instance, if a record is changed on two nodes simultaneously, an eager replication system would detect the conflict before confirming the commit and abort one of the transactions. A lazy replication system would allow both transactions to commit and run a conflict resolution during resynchronization. The resolution of such a conflict may be based on a timestamp of the transaction, on the hierarchy of the origin nodes or on much more complex logic, which decides consistently on all nodes.

Database replication becomes difficult when it scales up. Usually, the scale up goes with two dimensions, horizontal and vertical: horizontal scale up has more data replicas, vertical scale up has data replicas located further away in distance. Problems raised by horizontal scale up can be alleviated by a multi-layer multi-view access protocol. Vertical scale up is running into less trouble since internet reliability and performance are improving.

INTERNET-MARKETING—IS IT DEAD?

You just finished writing another great article and look for a way to submit your piece to numerous article directories. You hope to gain a lot of SEO traffic from this article since it will be exposed in many article directories, right?

Not quite so. *You may discover too late to your dismay that so few traffic arrives at your website within a week and even within a month. What is wrong with the picture?*

You thought that by simply submitting your article would guarantee instant lots of traffic and now this does not happen to you.

You then would believe those who say that "internet article marketing is dead so don't bother" *or* "article marketing is just writing and publishing content and there's nothing else to learn".

Well I'm going to tell you that these naysayers don't know what they are talking about or are dumb enough to blindly send copies and copies of their article to thousands and thousands of directories which happen to be low quality or low traffic. These so-called article marketing experts and gurus are publishing absolute crap or @#%$*#! if you excuse my language. You need all the tricks, all the methods, all the insights and all the necessary knowledge to win this game.

Internet Article Marketing is not Dead!

The only dead things in article marketing are the methods that many internet marketers learned years ago and got stuck with. Their methods are dead, outdated or obsolete! Ten years ago, with a lot lesser article submissions on the internet, all we have to do is to just do what most people do in internet article marketing now-that is, to write and publish articles, and you'll be generating sales much easily. But, fast forward to the present and millions of article submissions later, this idea is completely USELESS and OUTDATED. Hundreds (make that thousands or even ten thousands now) of articles are being submitted to article directories every few minutes.

Well, let us first look at where those internet marketers went wrong with. We know that more and more articles are out there now. There are also copies of those articles out there. Then there are MORE copies and copies of the same articles out there. Then again, thousands and thousands COPIES of the SAME article all around! That is so insane! Imagine that you are forced to read the same newspaper everyday for the rest of your life! No one will read that same content again-and thus, that lessen the power of internet article marketing. You want them to commit and return again and again to your articles to get more traffic and then more profits.

Next is Google. Google HATES copies of content and do even blacklisting or ranking those sites to the bottom of the search results. In the contrary, they LOVE original and high quality content and will be your best friend in internet article marketing. More and more you make your article so unique and so original that no other sites have your copy of the article, Google will rank your site higher and higher against those top competitors who are still clinging to those outdated marketing ideas.

You need a different perspective about your pieces of information. Each one of your article is your "top employee", who is working for you 24/7 all week all year for free and is even accessible to everyone across the world. If you would go ahead and reuse the article in a unique and different manner every time, your presence will be certain to grow over time (and it would be faster when done properly). The reason, why there is no doubt that internet article marketing is still among the best tools for site promotions on the internet, is that it is a system that can be reused again and again and produce constant success.

Now, if you have an innovative mind into spinning the same information (again and again, but in a unique and different way) to complement your product or for itself, you should expect tons of traffic to be on the doorstep of your website, product, online store, or whatever you are promoting just from internet article marketing. This can increase link popularity and get top website ranking in Google and other search engines such as Yahoo or Bing. And *it would even be better when money starts to flow into your bank account* and the best thing about this is that it will continue to increase over time even after you stop working on your article or are taking a vacation somewhere.

FIVE THINGS ABOUT THE CHANGING WORLD OF INTERNET MARKETING

Social media may get a lot of press these days, but internet marketing is alive and well in the industrial sector as an effective channel for communicating with customers and prospects. However, the inboxes of industrial professionals are more crowded than ever. Many e-mails are deleted without being looked at; others never make it past spam filters. If you want to capture the attention of your audience, make sure you know these five new rules of e-mail marketing.

1. *General is out, specific is in*: It's not enough to send your entire industrial audience the same e-mail communications—unless your audience is completely homogenous, which is highly unlikely. To be relevant to your audience, you must send specific e-mails, personalized to their needs and interests. This takes more effort, but will deliver better results. To get more specific, segment your e-mail list. You can do this in a number of ways, from simple to complex. Here are some ways to segment your list:

    - Products owned or services used
    - Customers or prospects
    - Markets (geographic or industrial sector)
    - Behavior (based on the types of links clicked on or offers accepted)
    - Job role

    Once you segment your list, you can create e-mails with content targeted and relevant to the reader. Another way to get specific is to personalize e-mails using the name of your recipients in the subject line or in a greeting in the body of the e-mail. Also, try personalizing the 'from' line by having the e-mail sent from a person's name that your recipients will recognize, such as their account rep or a company executive.
2. *E-mail marketing service providers are affordable and dependable*: There are a multitude of e-mail marketing service providers that can provide expert services at a reasonable cost. If you are still going it alone on e-mail marketing, you might want to consider using

a service provider. E-mail marketing service providers can perform a lot of the work that will increase the effectiveness of your e-mail communications, including:

- Managing relationships with ISPs to ensure the deliverability of your e-mails
- Offering spam checking tools to improve your e-mails before sending
- Providing integrated social tools for sharing e-mail content on Facebook, Twitter and other social networking sites
- Offering a large portfolio of e-mail templates that can be easily customized to your brand
- Reporting on statistics that allow you to easily track the performance of e-mail campaigns

3. Internet must be optimized for different devices: *Users are in the habit of accessing e-mail anytime, anywhere—from home and work and on the road. From desktop computers, laptops, tablet computers, and smart phones. And there are dozens of e-mail programs in use, from Microsoft Outlook to Gmail, Yahoo and others.* Now you must optimize your e-mails for reading in different programs. A good practice is to have a link at the top of your e-mails allowing users to access a web page version of your e-mail in case the content does not render well in their program. You may also want to consider optimizing e-mail for viewing on small screen devices as well as for larger screens.
4. Testing is timeless: *E-mail testing is not new, but it is more important than ever if you want to continually improve the effectiveness of your e-mail marketing efforts. You can test various components of your e-mails and make adjustments based on what you learn to increase your results in terms of click-throughs and conversions. It's best to test one variable at a time so you can measure the impact of that specific change.*

Key variables to test in e-mails include:

- 'From' line and 'subject' line
- Day of week, time of day for sending
- Number, placement, and type of links
- Call to action
- Layout and use of graphics

5. *Implement new tactics to connect with hard-to-reach prospects*: No matter how much effort you put into growing your opt-in e-mail list, there are still a multitude of potential customers out there that you are not able to reach because they haven't heard of your company or you haven't met them yet.
   One way to connect with these potential customers is to advertise in third-party industrial e-mail newsletters that your audience reads. You can place advertisements that promote your products or brand and drive prospects to your web site for conversion purposes. Another advantage of e-newsletter advertising is that the publisher handles all the work of list management and e-mail deliverability. Look for a publisher with expertise and a respected reputation in your specific market. Check out Global Spec's industrial e-newsletters here.

CHAPTER 4

Email

Email deliverability is about ensuring requested opt-in email is delivered to the intended recipient. While no single tip will enable you to get 100% of your email delivered each one utilized as a group can go a long way to reaching that goal.

COMBINE SOCIAL MEDIA AND E-MAIL MARKETING

Right now online, your customers, clients, members and prospects are chatting up a storm. Whether they're tweeting on Twitter, posting on Facebook, forwarding YouTube videos or commenting on blogs, they're out there engaging in conversations and sharing information that's relevant to your business or cause.

Are you a Part of that Conversation?

If you're not, you may be missing out on opportunities to extend your marketing reach. Social media sites offer new ways to share your content, grow your audience and build customer relationships. In tandem with e-mail, they create a powerful marketing mix.

Social Media and e-mail Marketing Work Differently

Social media gives public conversations a forum. Anyone with an opinion, content or a link to share can join the conversation. It's fast, fluid, timely and interactive. It's also fleeting. That's where social media and e-mail communications differ. Your posts on social media websites flow downstream with all the other messages. If you tweet in the morning and your customer logs on in the afternoon, that follower may miss out on what you had to say. On the other hand, e-mail offers a more intimate level of contact with your customers. When someone opens your e-mail newsletter, you have a quiet moment of her time. You have her undivided attention. And your newsletter content has permanence, as readers can go back to it in their inboxes. And when you archive your e-mail campaigns in web page form, that content can live on forever. That adds to your business credibility and heft. In short, social media is about sharing content and engaging in conversations. E-mail marketing takes those conversations–and the relationships you're building–to the next level of engagement.

Make the most of the social media and e-mail marketing mix. E-mail and social media marketing can work together to build on what each does best. Here are five things you need to know so you can make the most of the social media and e-mail marketing mix:

1. Be where your customers are. You won't know whether your customers are on social media sites, and which ones in particular, unless you test the waters and look for them. Different people prefer different means of getting their daily info and opinion fix. Millions like the streaming feed of Twitter. Others prefer the posts on Face book. More professionally oriented people may use LinkedIn. You want to swim in the channels that are frequented by your customers and prospects.
2. Use your e-mail list to build a social media presence. The big question we get from e-mail marketers is how to get that snowball rolling down the social media mountain. Here's the good news: The secret is your e-mail list. Use it to jump-start your social

media presence by inviting your subscribers to follow you on Twitter and become your fan on Face book. They will get the ball rolling for you. How do you engage prospects on social media websites? The same way as with e-mail marketing: valuable, relevant, interesting content.

3. Repurpose content from your newsletter. Content is still king. That applies to social media, too. You don't need to create brand-new content to engage people on social networking sites. Instead, repurpose snippets of articles you've already created (or aggregated) for your e-mail newsletter. Think of these as "micro content"–one tip, one idea, one article you found interesting. A teaser and a link back to your archived newsletter or blog is all the content you need to get started posting on social media sites.
4. Invite people back to your website or blog. If your website is your online hub or headquarters, then think of social media sites as your satellites. They allow you to extend your business presence. When you post on social media, be sure to include frequent links back to your website, newsletter archive or blog, where interested people can learn more about your business. Then you can engage potential customers on a deeper level, away from the distractions of the social media world. Just be sure you're not always selling; social media is better-suited for sharing information and expertise.
5. Ask for mailing list sign-ups on multiple channels. Use your e-mail list to build a presence on social media sites, then use your presence on the sites to invite even more people to sign up for your mailing list. Put a link to your sign-up form on multiple channels, including your website and Face book fan page. Tweet about your newsletter articles on Twitter, linking readers back to your newsletter archive, where they can sign up for your mailing list.

E-mail marketing vs. social media marketing is not an either/or question. It's about doing everything possible to expand your audience and customer base. Tap into social media to engage customers in lively conversation. Then invite them back to your website, where they can learn more about your business and sign up for your newsletter. Your valuable content–and the knowledge you have about what engages your audience–is the glue that holds it all together.

INTERNET MARKETING CAN BE PROFITABLE FOR ANY BUSINESS

No matter what kind of product or service you offer. It is significantly cheaper than other advertising methods and, if done right, helps build loyalty and trust with customers. As a result, you generate more sales and more profits!

The foundation for successful *email marketing* is a targeted, permission-based email list. Marketers call contact lists their 'goldmine' because it can generate much of their sales revenue. If you've built up a list of opt-in subscribers that are qualified and interested in what you have to offer, then you've completed the first step and are on your way. Now it's time to 'mine' for gold!

Below you'll find 15 list-building and retention ideas that will help you get the best results from all your *email marketing* activities...

1. *Provide useful, relevant content*.:.Your visitors will not give you their email addresses just because they can subscribe to your newsletter free of charge. You have to provide unique and valuable information that will be of interest or use to them.
2. *Add a subscription form to every page on your website.;* Make sure it stands out so it is easy to find. If it doesn't look cluttered, you may want to include more than one on some pages. For instance, if your opt-in form always appears in the top-left corner of your site, you may want to add one at the end of your most popular articles.
3. *Add subscription forms to your social media pages*. Make sure that you don't waste this valuable source of

revenue opportunities. Integrate your sign-up forms with Face book and more!

4. *Make it easy for readers to sign up.* The more information you request, the fewer people will opt-in. In most cases, a name and an email address should suffice. If it's not necessary, don't include it here. You can always survey them once they're customers! We do recommend that you provide a link to your Privacy Policy however.
5. *Publish a Privacy Policy.* Let your readers know that they can be confident you will not share their information with others. The easiest way to do this is to set up a Privacy Policy web page and provide the link to it below your opt-in form.
6. "*Easy* This lets potential subscribers review your materials before they sign up to determine if it's something they'd be interested in.
7. *Archive past newsletters and articles.* An online library of past newsletters and articles is both appealing and useful to visitors and builds your credibility as an authority. In addition, if your articles are written with good SEO techniques in mind, they can increase traffic to your website through enhanced search engine positioning.
8. *Give gifts subscribers can actually use.* Offer an opt-in bonus for joining your subscriber list! Write an ebook or provide a PDF business report, or even hire a programmer to create downloadable or web-based software. But don't limit yourself to offering gifts to opt-ins. Give them out when your readers fill out a survey, provide a testimonial, success story, or a great product idea. Let them know when they can expect the next gift offer. Everyone likes to get something for free! And if you pass out 'goodies' throughout the year, your subscribers will feel truly appreciated-and that's good for business!
9. *Ask your subscribers to pass it on.* Word of mouth is a powerful viral technique that works great with email marketing. If your subscribers find your content interesting, amusing or informative, they'll probably

share it with their friends. This can be a great source of new customers, so make sure to remind them to 'pass it on'.

10. *Let others reprint your newsletter as long as the content is not modified.* If you're happy to share your content with the universe, then why not! Many webmasters and newsletter publishers are actively looking for high-quality content and, if they reprint your newsletter, you'll get new subscribers, and more traffic and links pointing to your site.
11. *Include a 'Sign Up' button in your newsletter.* If you're using plain text instead of HTML, be sure to provide a text link to your subscription page. You may feel that this is not required because the subscriber is already on your list, but remember that readers will forward your newsletters to others, or reprint them online. Make it easy for them to subscribe!
12. *Add a squeeze page.* A squeeze page has one goal-to acquire opt-ins and build your list. Think of it as a mini-sales letter to go along with your subscription or opt-in gift. It should feature a strong headline and a couple of powerful benefits that should make subscribers salivate to sign up! Once created, use a service such as WordTracker to find hundreds of targeted keywords, and promote your offer using pay-per-click advertising from Google, MSN and Yahoo. Now that should make a splash!
13. *Include testimonials on your squeeze page.* This is crucial. Put one or two strong testimonials from satisfied customers on your squeeze page. This can be in any format, but you may find that multimedia (audio or video) is more 'believable' and inspires more people to action.
14. *To further enhance believability,* get permission to use actual customer names, locations and/or urls (Don't use 'Bob K, FL'). Add a note inviting others to participate. After all, it's free publicity!
15. *Post on other blogs.* Post thoughtful comments and information on similar blogs with a link to your

squeeze or opt-in pages. Also comment on others' blogs through trackbacks. In most cases, your comments will be posted on their blogs with a link back to your site. This is an easy way to generate new traffic and subscribers, and get your brand out there!

DO YOUR POTENTIAL CUSTOMERS FORGET ABOUT YOU?

Your web business probably gets product inquiries from potential customers around the globe. Inquiries come via e-mail and your web site, and you try to send information to each hot prospect as quickly as you can. You know that you can drastically increase the likelihood of making a sale by satisfying each person's need for information quickly! But, after you've delivered that first bit of information to your prospect, do you send him any further information? If you are like most Internet marketers, you don't.

When you don't follow that initial message with additional information later on, you let a valuable prospect slip from your grasp! This is a potential customer who may have been very interested in your products, but who lost your contact information, or was too busy to make a purchase when your first message reached him. Often, a prospect will purposely put off making a purchase, to see if you find him important enough to follow up with later. When he doesn't receive a follow up message from you, he will take his business elsewhere.

ARE YOU LOSING PROFITS DUE TO INCONSISTENT AND INEFFECTIVE FOLLOW UP?

Following up with leads is more than just a process-it's an art. In order to be effective, you need to design a follow up system, and stick to it, EVERY DAY! If you don't follow up with your prospects consistently, INDIVIDUALLY, and in a timely fashion, then you might as well forget the whole follow up process.

Consistent Follow up gets Results!

When I first started marketing and following up with prospects, I used a follow up method that I now call the "List Technique". I had a large database containing the names and e-mail addresses of people who had specifically requested information about my products and services. These prospects had already received my first letter by the time they requested more information, so I used the company's latest news as a follow up piece. I would write follow up newsletters every now and then, and send them, in one mass mailing, to everyone who had previously requested information from me. While this probably did help me win a few additional orders, it wasn't a very good follow up method. Why isn't the "List Technique" very effective? The List Technique isn't consistent. Proponents of the List Technique tend to only send out follow up messages when their companies have "big news". List Technique messages don't give the potential customer any additional information about the product or service in question. He can't make a more informed buying decision after receiving a newsletter! If someone is wondering whether your company sells the best knick-knacks, what does he care that you've just moved your headquarters?

List Technique messages convey a "big list" mentality to your potential customers. When I used to write follow up messages using the List Technique, I was writing news bulletins to everyone I knew! I should have been sending a personal message to each individual who wanted to know more about my products.

What Follow up Method Really Works?

Following up with each lead individually, multiple times, but at set intervals, and with pre-written messages, will dramatically increase sales! Others who use this same technique confirm that they have all at least doubled the sales of various products! In order to set this system up, though, you need to do some planning. First, you'll need to develop your follow up messages. If you've been marketing on the Internet for any length of time, then you should already have a first informative letter. Your second letter marks the beginning of the follow up process, and should go into more detail than the first letter. Fill this letter with details that you didn't have the space to add to the first letter. Stress the BENEFITS of your products or services! Your next 2-3 follow up messages should be rather short. Include lists of the benefits and potential uses of your products and services. Write each letter so that your prospects can skim the contents, and still see the full force of your message.

The next couple of follow up messages should create a sense of urgency in your prospect's mind. Make a special offer, giving him a reason to order NOW instead of waiting any longer. After reading these follow up messages, your prospect should want to order immediately! Phrase each of your final 1 or 2 follow up messages in the form of a question. Ask your prospect why he hasn't yet placed an order? Try to get him to actually respond. Ask if the price is to high, the product isn't the right color or doesn't have the right features, or if he is looking for something else entirely. (By this time, it's unlikely that this person will order from you. However, his feedback can help you modify your follow up letters or products, so that other prospects *will* order from you.)

The timing of your follow up letters is just as important as their content. You don't want one prospect to receive a follow up the day after he gets your initial informative letter, while another prospect waits weeks for a follow up! Always send an initial, informative letter as soon as it is requested, and send the first follow up 24 hours afterwards. You want your hot prospects to have information quickly, so that they can make informed buying decisions! Send the next 2-3 follow up messages between 1 and 3 days apart. Your prospect is still hot, and is probably still shopping around! Tell him about the benefits of your products and services, as opposed to your competitors'. You will make the sale! Send the final follow up messages later on. You certainly don't want to annoy your prospect! Make sure that these last letters are at least 4 days apart. Following up effectively seems complicated, but it doesn't have to be! So many potential customers are lost because of poor follow up-don't you want to be one of the few to get it right?

SECTION II

Internet Marketing

CHAPTER

5

Introduction to Internet Marketing

These days internet marketing is a broad church that can be defined as the 'use of the internet to advertise and sell goods and services'. Essentially anything that is a service and which can make money on the internet is and can be interpreted as internet marketing. As a result, marketing techniques and strategies such as: cost per click advertising, banner ads, search engine marketing, e-mail marketing, affiliate marketing, interactive advertising, search engine marketing (including search engine optimization), blog marketing, article marketing, and blogging can all come under the auspices of 'internet marketing'.

Internet marketing, also known as digital marketing, web marketing, online marketing, search marketing or e-marketing, is the marketing (generally promotion) of products or services over the Internet.

Internet marketing is considered to be broad in scope because it not only refers to marketing on the Internet, but also includes marketing done via e-mail and wireless media. Digital customer data and electronic customer relationship management (ECRM) systems are also often grouped together under internet marketing.

Internet marketing ties together the creative and technical aspects of the Internet, including design, development, advertising, and sales. Internet marketing also refers to the placement of media along many different stages of the customer engagement cycle through search engine marketing (SEM), search engine optimization (SEO), banner ads on specific websites, email marketing, and Web 2.0 strategies.

In 2008, *The New York Times*, working with comScore, published an initial estimate to quantify the user data collected by large Internet-based companies. Counting four types of interactions with company websites in addition to the hits from advertisements served from advertising networks, the authors found that the potential for collecting data was up to 2,500 times per user per month.

HISTORY OF INTERNET MARKETING

With all the hype about internet marketing at the moment and the stories of 'entrepreneurs' (internet entrepreneurs) gaining million-dollar cheques every year it's often forgotten that the internet is a *very* young medium. However, I am very cogniscent of this as the internet began alongside my career as a computational scientist. The very early internet (during the late 1980s) allowed me to do things that might never have been imagined before. But the public use of the internet as a publishing and marketing medium did lag behind its scientific use as a data and information exchange tool in the early years. Indeed, it wasn't until the early 1990s that marketing first began on the internet. This was mostly based around simple text-based websites that offered little more than straight-forward product information. But during the 1990s with the advent of faster internet connections, image availability and then video availability the marketing strategies evolved into more than just selling information products, there are people now selling advertising space, software programs, business models, and many other products and services. Companies like

Google, Yahoo and MSN emerged and then evolved into providing advertising that any size of website could take advantage of and make money from. They even provided adverts targetted to the search terms and the locale of the person who havigated to a given web page. Indeed, this kind of emocratization of internet advertising has allowed return on investment for even small-scale websites to grow while the bottom line has been lowered.

Internet marketing has also grown because internet marketing is inherently computationally based. There is so much information you can gain about your users, even using farily simple software tools and if you're a marketing site you can see what products your visitors buy so that you can track them individually and can then offer them exactly the type of goods and offers that they are looking for. Which is precisely what Amazon's operating model.

Business Models. As various marketers have been experimenting with the internet and the 'latest thing' of the week has come and gone several basic business models have emerged as winners.

The main models include business-to-business (B2B) and business-to-consumer (B2C), which are effectively internet versions of the processes used by real 'bricks and mortar' companies. B2B consists of companies doing business with each other, whereas B2C involves selling directly to the end consumer. When internet businesses first came to note almost all were using B2C models, after all these were just internet versions of existing non-internet businesses. This is also the simplest model to put into operation. After all you're selling a product to a customer. The B2B strategies only evolved later as the demand for bespoke applications and systems such as autoresponders grew and systems such as Google's ads came of note. As internet marketing has matured we've also seen the growth of new strategies not seen in the 'bricks and mortar' world. A good example of these is the P2P (peer-to-peer) marketing model which is built on individuals sharing or forming communities (also sometimes known as Web 2.0). An example would be the Kazaa file sharing system and in some respects at least, it could be argued that eBay is also a kind of P2P system in that though eBay are the moderator and provid the overall system software sales are, for the most part, made between individuals. These are all proper, functioning, business models. Yet, the bread-and-butter of internet marketing remains advertising. But the truth is advertising includes direct placement of advertisements from Google or MSN or Yahoo! to affiliate marketing from internet marketing companies to affiliate marketing for the big players such as Amazon and eBay. In the end, whatever strategy you chose, it will be successful for you as long as you can make money from it. This website is designed to show you the strategies and to present you with a range of models and methods to deploy these strategies to increase your internet income.

INTERNET MARKETING FRAMEWORK

Want to use the internet to promote your business? Here's a plan.

First off: This is not a magical silver bullet that will automatically transform your business from 10% returns to overnight. If that is what your business needs right now, its a pity this information might not be useful for you. The internet marketing plan I am proposing here are a reliable set of activities you can carry out over a period of time. Do stuff, measure, tweak the plan and do some more stuff till you start to see the benefits of your efforts. At times, it can take months before the benefits become clear. Actually this is true of most marketing efforts. Act, measure, tweak, rinse and repeat. The advantage of the internet it makes these activities affordable and better measurable. So once again, this is no magic green pill for making you millions. activities affordable and better measurable. So once again, this is no magic green pill for making you millions.

Website: Build a website. It could be simple. It could be fancy. It doesn't matter much. Just make the message on the site clear concise and clean. Be clear on what you are selling and why people should buy it. Even better if you can provide a way for people to buy directly from you online, or at least place orders or show interest. It's advisable to have this website based on a CMS so you can ensure fresh and dynamic content. You can get a free enough website from Weebly.

Support sharing on your website: Add sharing and viral distribution functionality to your site. Encourage and make it easy for visitors to your site to share the content they find on your site. They could post it to their Facebook or Twitter stream, Digg or even just send your pages by email.

Blog: Get a blog for your business and make sure that the url is tied to your website's domain. Place the blog either at blog.yourdomain.com or yourdomain.com/blog. Something like that. Now make sure you always have some fresh interesting content on that blog. Put up interesting stuff every 2 weeks or so. Also make sure the sharing functionality from step 2 above applies to your blog.

Keywords: Choose a number of words or phrases you would like to dominate on the internet. This is hard, as everything is probably taken. But at least know what you want your business to be synonymous with.

On-Page search engine optimization: Now that you have chosen your keywords or phrases, sprinkle them generously all over your website in places where the search engines are looking. Page title, headings (h1,h2,h3) emphasis like bold tags around them. Do some on page search engine optimisation. Also pay attentions to the keywords and description meta tags.

Off page search engine optimization: Simply put, drop links to your website all over the internet where they are talking about things that relate to your keywords. Sign up at forums, contribute, and make your signature in all forums where you register be links to your site. Be careful not to just go around barraging forums with your marketing. Make it subtle. Contribute useful information everywhere. LinkedIn, Facebook, Twitter, StumbleUpon, Yahoogroups, Google groups, etc. But just find opportunities to link back to your site. Each link counts as a vote for your website when the search engines are ranking.

Use Google webmaster tools: Use Google webmaster tools to submit a sitemap, and see the crawl stats and suggestions for your website. Give something away free: A book, some tips, free gist, anything. Give something useful away for free on your blog and website. This has a powerful goodwill generating effect that often make people come back to your site or send links of your site to their friends.

Advertising: Advertise affordably online on Facebook, Google, AdsApart and other advertising networks online. Use these media to drive traffic to your site.

Capture leads on your website: Prompt visitors to your website to give you their contact information. Either have a feedback form or 'request more information' form or 'subscribe to our newsletter' form . . . Just take permission to get in touch with them later. Don't force it, don't annoy, just politely ask for some information or feedback.

Get a CRM to manage follow up with your leads: Get something that makes it easy to manage the leads you are getting. Salesforce, Zoho and Highrise are affordable. Integrate these directly with the lead capture mechanism of your site.

Email marketing: Once you've got people willingly subscribing for more information from you, use a very useful email marketing tool to manage most communication with them. At least, do a monthly newsletter. Campaign Monitor will do. If possible, integrate your lead capture mechanism, CRM and email marketing tool so they are all in sync.

Web monitoring: Set-up Google alerts for your keywords and product/business name (and a number of competitors if necessary). Where the links delivered to you are conversations you can join in online, please, do join in.

Get some friendly web publicity: If you have a personal website, link to your business website from there. If you have friends/associates/family with websites, cash in some favour chips and get them to link to it. The goal is to get the Google crawler to start indexing your site. You only need one decent link to get things going. Also, subscribe to a few link submission services available on the net.

Measure, measure, measure: Constantly measure how your marketing is performing. Get analytics for your site and from your advertising control panels. You will be able to see which keywords and locations are driving more traffic to you and you can adjust accordingly.

HOW INTERNET MARKETING WORKS

Internet marketing is basically a way of selling a product or a service on the internet. It is a way of advertising to potential customers to get them to visit a website and make a purchase. That is the way internet marketing works in a nutshell. To expand a little further, internet marketing is not only done by large corporations who have thousands of products to sell. There are many people who sell items online and are based from home. Many items are digital products, so they have no inventory to manage or products to ship. This kind of business is one that relies heavily on internet marketing to sell the product.

So to utilize internet marketing to its fullest, there is the need for a website that is selling a product or service. Whether it is a physical product or a digital product, there is a need to get a customer to the site and buy something so that the owner makes money. This is all carried out online and there is no need for the customer to leave their home to make the purchase. Taking internet marketing to another level is the use of email marketing. Due to email being free to send, it means that businesses have an affordable way of reaching out to their customers and potential customers to get them to visit their websites. The majority of businesses automatically add customers to a mailing list when they join their site to make a purchase. They then send out regular offers to the customers that lead to more sales and higher profits.

The way that internet marketing works has lead to some of the biggest companies making a shift from traditional offline marketing to online marketing. The cost to market online is far less than offline and the potential reach they have to find new customers is virtually unlimited. That is why online marketing is becoming so popular for large and small businesses alike.

THE NATURE OF THE INTERNET MARKETING

Since the arrival of the internet, the face of the marketing and advertising business has dramatically changed. The internet has provided an infinitely wide advertisement board where companies all over the world can post their information, product catalog and brochures. With the increasing number of products and services, internet marketing online business has become a growing industry with fair chances of good profit. Internet marketing, also called e-marketing or online marketing, is the marketing and advertising of products and services on the internet. The definition of what it is depends on because there are several jobs within the field. For example, the owners of a manufacturing company may develop a website that advertises their own products. Some advertisers can be hired to provide ways on increasing the popularity of specific products and services. There are internet marketing groups and firms that work by optimizing website content. Some websites earn by advertising other websites.

There are several forms of marketing that utilize the web. One is e-mail marketing that is the direct sending e-mails from the company to the customers. The e-mails contain new offers and products, updates and promos. However, the biggest deal of e-marketing is focused on website development. The primary tool and object of internet marketing online is the website. A good website displays the image the company wants to show to the public and the message they want to convey. Its web pages must be easy to navigate through and they must completely show the products and services offered by the company. If the site wants the viewers to be directed to other web pages, their links must be visible and placed at strategic spots. Most importantly, for a website to be effective, it needs people to see its content-the internet traffic. Internet traffic is the subject of competition among all the websites.

Search Engine Optimization (SEO) is a very popular internet marketing strategy. SEO explores the more technical aspects of web page design. It is the arrangement of website content and coding so that it will receive high rank positions when displayed by search engines. Referrals of search engines through SEO are free. To contrast, back then, companies simply pay search engines to include them in the search results but they are not guaranteed of high ranks. There are several firms that offer SEO services for other companies. Other models of e-marketing include blogging, articles and review writing, and pay per click (PPC). There are sites that host blogs for free so many online marketers, many of those just at home, make use of them to advertise products. Many also post their product reviews on blogs, including referral links. In the PPC system, a company hires several sites to host their links in forms of text or images. The hired sites are paid every time the links are visited by surfers. As a summary, all these methods work if the hosting website receives a good amount of visitors.

Internet marketing is practically a web with interdependent sectors, providing equal number of job opportunities-even to those at the comfort of their own home. That makes the internet marketing online business to continue to be a source of good income despite the tough competition. Experience, knowledge and creativity are required to succeed in this field.

SCOPE OF INTERNET MARKETING IN INDIA

The dawn of the internet era opened up amazing new possibilities. Impossible is not a word anymore! India has also joined the bandwagon and the numbers themselves do all the talking. The latest statistics* reveal that 400 million people access internet regularly in India and that is jump of 700% in last six years. And, here comes the best part; the internet users as of now comprise of only 3.6% of the population. Now you can imagine the scope of internet marketing in India!

Now that we have come to terms with the tremendous scope of internet marketing in India, we have to understand that marketing through the internet can be an entirely different ball game. In fact it is a potent combination of technology and marketing acumen. If you too want to hop into the online business bandwagon, the first aspect is developing/ hosting of your website. Then you can employ any one or all of the internet marketing techniques mentioned here.

INTERNET MARKETING TECHNIQUES

Search Engine Marketing (SEM): Search engine marketing has of late become one of the principle tools in the armory of the Sauvé internet marketer. This prominence of SEM is owing to the fact that the search engines like Google, Yahoo etc. are being used by more and more people as their principle method of searching for relevant information. And, you can hope to sell through them if your website is visible on these search engines. The principle techniques employed in SEM are:

Search Engine Optimization (SEO): A set of practices employed to get ranking for WebPages on relevant keywords (search queries). SEO does this by improving a websites structure and content.

Pay per Click (PPC): PPC takes the sponsored route to drive relevant traffic to a website. The positioning of Ads is determined by a competitive bidding structure.

Paid Inclusion: In paid inclusions, you can pay your way up on to the natural listings of search engines. As of now, Google has stopped its paid inclusion program.

E-Mail Marketing: As the name suggests, e-mail marketing is promotion through e-mails. If used effectively it can assure you maximum returns on each penny you spend. It can be used for acquiring new customers, enhance the relationship you have with your existing clientele.

Advantages: Cheap, instant, easily traceable and if used properly the return on investment can be astounding.

Disadvantages: Due to the overdoing of the e-mail campaigns by online companies, they are now being categorized as Spam mail. Thereby reducing the chances of it actually reaching the intended person.

Banner Advertising: Banner marketing involves placing your advertisement on any third party website. This Ad will link to your website, this way if the potential customer clicks on your banner, he will be directed to your website. It can be a good way of attracting relevant traffic to your website.

Interactive Advertising: It involves the use of interactive media applications to promote products online. It in fact involves the right use of text, images, Flash animations, AV clips etc. The interactive advertising platform in a way intends to send across a personalized message by giving the readers/ viewers a visual treat.

Blog/Article marketing: Articles and blogs can be used effectively to propagate a marketing campaign. By submitting in various directories like Ezine and Go articles, you can hope to generate traffic through the link you have placed on the article directing towards your website.

Moreover, in my personal opinion in a country as diverse as India, the real action in a few years of time would lie in localization. Websites which will do business in Hindi and other local language would do well. It's simply because contrary to the claims, for a major chunk of Indians English is still an alien language. That's why the scope of internet marketing in India lies in localization of websites. Talking to people in their own language does have its positive attributes. The indigenization of the web for the real Indians and the correct application of the mentioned internet marketing techniques is truly the way forward.

Internet marketing is associated with several business models:

- *E-commerce*: a model whereby goods are sold directly to consumers (B2C), businesses (B2B), or from consumer to consumer (C2C).
- *Lead-based websites*: a strategy whereby an organization generates value by acquiring sales leads from its website. Similar to walk-in customers in retail world. These prospects are often referred to as organic leads.
- *Affiliate Marketing*: a process wherein a product or service developed by one entity is sold by other active sellers for a share of profits. The entity that owns the product may provide some marketing material (e.g., sales letters, affiliate links, tracking facilities, etc.); however, the vast majority of affiliate marketing relationships come from e-commerce businesses that offer affiliate programs.
- *Local Internet marketing*: a strategy through which a small company utilizes the Internet to find and to nurture relationships that can be used for real-world advantages. Local Internet marketing uses tools such as social media marketing, local directory listing, and targeted online sales promotions.

One-to-one approach: In a one-to-one approach, marketers target a user browsing the Internet alone and so that the marketers' messages reach the user personally. This approach is used in search marketing, for which the advertisements are based on *search engine keywords* entered by the users. This approach usually works under the *pay per click* (PPC) method.

Appeal to specific interests: When appealing to specific interests, marketers place an emphasis on appealing to a specific behavior or interest, rather than reaching out to a broadly defined demographic. These marketers typically segment their markets according to age group, gender, geography, and other general factors.

Niche Marketing: Niche and hyper-niche internet marketing put further emphasis on creating destinations for web users and consumers on specific topics and products. Niche marketers differ from traditional Internet marketers as they have a more specialized topic knowledge. For example, whereas in traditional Internet marketing a website would be created and promoted on a high-level topic such as kitchen appliances, niche marketing would focus on more specific topics such as 4-slice toasters'. Niche marketing provides end users of such sites very targeted information, and allows the creators to establish themselves as authorities on the topic or product.

Geo-targeting: In Internet marketing, geo targeting and geo marketing are the methods of determining the geolocation of a website visitor with geolocation software, and delivering different content to that visitor based on his or her location, such as latitude and longitude, country, region or state, city, metro code or zip code, organization,

ADVANTAGES OF INTERNET MARKETING

Internet marketing is inexpensive when examining the ratio of cost to the reach of the target audience. Companies can reach a wide audience for a small fraction of traditional advertising budgets. The nature of the medium allows consumers to research and to purchase products and services conveniently. Therefore, businesses have the advantage of appealing to consumers in a medium that can bring results quickly. The strategy and overall effectiveness of marketing campaigns depend on business goals and cost-volume-profit (CVP) analysis.

Internet marketers also have the advantage of measuring statistics easily and inexpensively; almost all aspects of an Internet marketing campaign can be traced, measured, and tested. The advertisers can use a variety of methods, such as pay per impression, pay per click, pay per play, and pay per action. Therefore, marketers can determine which messages or offerings are more appealing to the audience. The results of campaigns can be measured and tracked immediately because online marketing initiatives usually require users to click on an advertisement, to visit a website, and to perform a targeted action.

LIMITATIONS OF INTERNET MARKETING

However, from the buyer's perspective, the inability of shoppers to touch, to smell, to taste, and "to try on" tangible goods before making an online purchase can be limiting. However, there is an industry standard for e-commerce vendors to reassure customers by having liberal return policies as well as providing in-store pick-up services.

Security concern: Information security is important both to companies and consumers that participate in online business. Many consumers are hesitant to purchase items over the Internet because they do not believe that their personal information will remain private. Some companies that purchase customer information offer the option for individuals to have their information removed from the database, also known as opting out. However, many customers are unaware if and when their information is being shared, and are unable to stop the transfer of their information between companies if such activity occurs.

Another major security concern that consumers have with e-commerce merchants is whether or not they will receive exactly what they purchase. Online merchants have attempted to address this concern by investing in and building strong consumer brands (e.g., Amazon.com, eBay, and Overstock.com), and by leveraging merchant and feedback rating systems and e-commerce bonding solutions. All these solutions attempt to assure consumers that their transactions will be free of problems because the merchants can be trusted to provide reliable products and services. Additionally, several major online payment mechanisms (credit cards, PayPal,

Google Checkout, etc.) have provided back-end buyer protection systems to address problems if they occur.

Usage trends: Technological advancements in the telecommunications industry have dramatically affected online advertising techniques. Many firms are embracing a paradigm that is shifting the focus of advertising methodology from traditional text and image advertisements to those containing more recent technologies like JavaScript and Adobe Flash. As a result, advertisers can more effectively engage and connect their audience with their campaigns that seek to shape consumer attitudes and feelings towards specific products and services.

Effects on Industries: The number of banks offering the ability to perform banking tasks over the internet has increased. Online banking appeals to customers because it is often faster and considered more convenient than visiting bank branches.

Internet auctions have become a multi-billion dollar business. Unique items that could only previously be found at flea markets are now being sold on Internet auction websites such as eBay. Specialized e-stores sell a vast amount of items like antiques, movie props, clothing, gadgets, and so on. As the premier online reselling platform, eBay is often used as a price-basis for specialized items. Buyers and sellers often look at prices on the website before going to flea markets; the price shown on eBay often becomes the item's selling price.

Advertising Industry: In addition to the major effect internet marketing has had on the technology industry, the effect on the advertising industry itself has been profound. In just a few years, online advertising has grown to be worth tens of billions of dollars annually. PricewaterhouseCoopers reported that US $ 16.9 billion was spent on Online marketing in the U.S. in 2006.

This has caused a growing impact on the United States' electoral process. In 2008, candidates for President heavily utilized Internet marketing strategies to reach constituents. During the 2007 primaries candidates added, on average, over 500 social network supporters per day to help spread their message. President Barack Obama raised over US $ 1 million in one day during his extensive Democratic candidacy campaign, largely due to online donors. Several industries have heavily invested in and benefited from internet marketing and online advertising. Some of them were originally brick and mortar businesses such as publishing, music, automotive or gambling, while others have sprung up as purely online businesses, such as digital design and media, blogging, and internet service hosting.

CHAPTER

6

E-commerce

Electronic commerce, commonly known as *e-commerce, e Commerce* or *e-comm,* consists of the buying and selling of products or services over electronic systems such as the Internet and other computer networks. It is more than just buying and selling products online. It also includes the entire online process of developing, marketing, selling, delivering, servicing and paying for products and services. The amount of trade conducted electronically has grown extraordinarily with widespread Internet usage. The use of commerce is conducted in this way, spurring and drawing on innovations in electronic funds transfer, supply chain management, Internet marketing, online transaction processing, electronic data interchange (EDI), inventory management systems, and automated data collection systems. Modern electronic commerce typically uses the World Wide Web at least at some point in the transaction's lifecycle, although it can encompass a wider range of technologies such as e-mail, mobile devices and telephones as well.

A large percentage of electronic commerce is conducted entirely electronically for virtual items such as access to premium content on a website, but most electronic commerce involves the transportation of physical items in some way. Online retailers are sometimes known as e-tailers and online retail is sometimes known as *e-tail*. Almost all big retailers have electronic commerce presence on the World Wide Web.

Electronic commerce that is conducted between businesses is referred to as business-to-business or B2B. B2B can be open to all interested parties (e.g. commodity exchange) or limited to specific, pre-qualified participants (private electronic market). Electronic commerce that is conducted between businesses and consumers, on the other hand, is referred to as business-to-consumer or B2C. This is the type of electronic commerce conducted by companies such as Amazon.com. Online shopping is a form of electronic commerce where the buyer is directly online to the seller's computer usually via the internet. There is no intermediary service. The sale and purchase transaction is completed electronically and interactively in real-time such as Amazon.com for new books. If an intermediary is present, then the sale and purchase transaction is called electronic commerce such as eBay.com.

Electronic commerce is generally considered to be the sales aspect of e-business. It also consists of the exchange of data to facilitate the financing and payment aspects of the business transactions.

COMPUTER NETWORK

A *computer network,* often simply referred to as a network, is a collection of computers and devices interconnected by communications channels that facilitate communications and allows sharing of resources and information among interconnected devices. *Computer networking* or *Data communications* (*Datacom*) is the engineering discipline concerned with the computer networks. Computer networking is sometimes considered a sub-discipline of electrical engineering, telecommunications, computer science, information technology and/or computer engineering since it relies heavily upon the theoretical and practical application of these scientific and engineering disciplines.

The three types of networks are: the Internet, the intranet, and the extranet. Examples of different network methods are:

- Local area network (LAN), which is usually a small network constrained to a small geographic area. An example of a LAN would be a computer network within a building.
- Metropolitan area network (MAN), which is used for medium size area. examples for a city or a state.
- Wide area network (WAN) that is usually a larger network that covers a large geographic area.
- Wireless LANs and WANs (WLAN and WWAN) are the wireless equivalent of the LAN and WAN.

Networks may be classified according to a wide variety of characteristics such as topology, connection method and scale.

All networks are interconnected to allow communication with a variety of different kinds of media, including twisted-pair copper wire cable, coaxial cable, optical fiber, power lines and various wireless technologies. The devices can be separated by a few meters (e.g. via Bluetooth) or nearly unlimited distances (e.g. via the interconnections of the Internet). Networking, routers, routing protocols, and networking over the public Internet have their specifications defined in documents called RFCs.

Before the advent of computer networks that were based upon some type of telecommunications system, communication between calculation machines and early computers was performed by human users by carrying instructions between them. Many of the social behaviors seen in today's Internet were demonstrably present in the nineteenth century and arguably in even earlier networks using visual signals.

- In September 1940 George Stibitz used a teletype machine to send instructions for a problem set from his Model at Dartmouth College to his Complex Number Calculator in New York and received results back by the same means. Linking output systems like teletypes to computers was an interest at the Advanced Research Projects Agency (ARPA) when, in 1962, J.C.R. Licklider was hired and developed a working group he called the "Intergalactic Network", a precursor to the ARPANET.

- Early networks of communicating computers included the military radar system Semi-Automatic Ground Environment (SAGE), started in the late 1950s.
- the commercial airline reservation system Semi-Automatic Business Research Environment (SABRE) which went online with two connected mainframes in 1960.
- In 1964, researchers at Dartmouth developed the Dartmouth Time Sharing System for distributed users of large computer systems. The same year, at Massachusetts Institute of Technology, a research group supported by General Electric and Bell Labs used a computer to route and manage telephone connections.
- Throughout the 1960s Leonard Kleinrock, Paul Baran and Donald Davies independently conceptualized and developed network systems which used packets that could be used in a network between computer systems.
- 1965 Thomas Merrill and Lawrence G. Roberts created the first wide area network (WAN).
- The first widely used telephone switch that used true computer control was introduced by Western Electric in 1965.
- *In 1969 the University of California at Los Angeles, the Stanford Research Institute, University of California at Santa Barbara, and the University of Utah were connected as the beginning of the ARPANET network using 50 kbit/s circuits.*
- Commercial services using X.25 were deployed in 1972, and later used as an underlying infrastructure for expanding TCP/IP networks.

Today, computer networks are the core of modern communication. All modern aspects of the Public Switched Telephone Network (PSTN) are computer-controlled, and telephony increasingly runs over the Internet Protocol, although not necessarily the public Internet. The scope of communication has increased significantly in the past decade, and this boom in communications would not have been possible without the progressively advancing computer network. Computer networks, and the technologies needed to connect and communicate through and between them, continue to drive computer hardware, software, and peripherals industries. This expansion is mirrored by growth in the numbers and types of users of networks from the researcher to the home user.

Purpose

Computer networks can be used for a variety of purposes:

Facilitating communications : Using a network, people can communicate efficiently and easily via email, instant messaging, chat rooms, telephone, video telephone calls, and video conferencing.

Sharing hardware : In a networked environment, each computer on a network may access and use hardware resources on the network, such as printing a document on a shared network printer; Sharing files, data, and information : In a network environment, authorized user may access data and information stored on other computers on the network. The capability of providing access to data and information on shared storage devices is an important feature of many networks. ; Sharing software : Users connected to a network may run application programs on remote computers. ==*Network classification*== The following list presents categories used for classifying networks.

Connection Method

Computer networks can be classified according to the hardware and software technology that is used to interconnect the individual devices in the network, such as optical fiber, Ethernet, wireless LAN, Home PNA, power line communication or G.hn.

Ethernet as it is defined by IEEE 802 utilizes various standards and mediums that enable communication between devices. Frequently deployed devices include hubs, switches, bridges, or routers. Wireless LAN technology is designed to connect devices without wiring. These devices use radio waves or infrared signals as a transmission medium. ITU-T G.hn technology uses existing home wiring (coaxial cable, phone lines and power lines) to create a high-speed (up to 1 Gigabit/s) local area network.

Unofficially, the Internet is the set of users, enterprises, and content providers that are interconnected by Internet Service Providers (ISP). From an engineering viewpoint, the Internet is the set of subnets, and aggregates of subnets, which share the registered IP address space and exchange information about the reachability of those IP addresses using the Border Gateway Protocol. Typically, the human-readable names of servers are translated to IP addresses, transparently to users, via the directory function of the Domain Name System (DNS).

Over the Internet, there can be business-to-business (B2B), business-to-consumer (B2C) and consumer-to-consumer (C2C) communications. Especially when money or sensitive information is exchanged, the communications are apt to be *secured* by some form of communications security mechanism. Intranets and extranets can be securely superimposed onto the Internet, without any access by general Internet users, using secure Virtual Private Network (VPN) technology.

BUSINESS-TO-CUSTOMER

Business-to-consumer (*B2C*, sometimes also called *Business-to-Customer*) describes activities of businesses serving end consumers with products and/or services.

An example of a B2C transaction would be a person buying a pair of shoes from a retailers. The transactions that led to the shoes being available for purchase, that is the purchase of the leather, laces, rubber etc. However, the sale of the shoe from the shoemaker to the retailer would be considered a B2B transaction.

Types of Business to Consumer (B2C)

While the term e-commerce refers to all online transactions, B2C stands for "business-to-consumer" and applies to any business or organization that sells its products or services to consumers over the Internet for its own use. When most people think of B2C e-commerce, they think of Amazon, the online bookseller that launched its site in 1995 and quickly took on the nation's major retailers. In addition to online retailers, B2C has grown to include services such as online banking, travel services, online auctions, health information and real estate sites. Peer-to-peer sites such as Craigslist also fall under the B2C category.

B2C e-commerce went through some tough times, particularly after the technology-heavy Nasdaq crumbled in 2000. In the ensuing dotcom carnage, hundreds of e-commerce sites shut their virtual doors and some experts predicted years of struggle for online retail ventures. Since then, however, shoppers have continued to flock to the web in increasing numbers. In fact, By 2010, consumers are expected to spend $329 billion each year online, according to Forrester Research. What's more, the percentage of U.S. households shopping online is expected to grow from 39 percent this year to 48 percent in 2010.

In October 2010, an extension of B2C, B2I was coined (sometimes referred to as B2I). While B2C includes all manners of a business marketing or selling to consumers, B2I is specifically targeted towards an individual. B2I requires specific Personalization for that individual. B2I requires Insight in order to create the personalized experience.

BUSINESS-TO-BUSINESS

Business-to-business (*B2B*) describes commerce transactions between businesses, such as between a manufacturer and a wholesaler, or between a wholesaler and a retailer. Contrasting terms are *business-to-consumer* (B2C) and *business-to-government* (B2G). The volume of B2B (Business-to-Business) transactions is much higher than the volume of B2C transactions. The primary reason for this is that in a typical supply chain there will be many B2B transactions involving sub components or raw materials, and only one B2C transaction, specifically sale of the finished product to the end customer. For example, an automobile manufacturer makes several B2B transactions such as buying tires, glass for windscreens, and rubber hoses for its vehicles. The final transaction, a finished vehicle sold to the consumer, is a single (B2C) transaction.

B2B is also used in the context of communication and collaboration. Many businesses are now using social media to connect with their consumers (B2C); however, they are now using similar tools within the business so employees can connect with one another. When communication is taking place amongst employees, this can be referred to as "B2B" communication. The term *"business-to-business"* was originally coined to describe the electronic communications between businesses or enterprises in order to distinguish it from the communications between businesses and consumers (B2C). It eventually came to be used in marketing as well, initially describing only industrial or capital goods marketing. Today it is widely used to describe all products and services used by enterprises. Many professional institutions and the trade publications focus much more on B2C than B2B, although most sales and marketing personnel are in the B2B sector.

Business-to-government (B2G) is a derivative of B2B marketing and often referred to as a market definition of "public sector marketing" which encompasses marketing products and services to various government levels-including federal, state and local-through integrated marketing communications techniques such as strategic public relations, branding, marcom, advertising, and web-based communications. Government agencies typically have pre-negotiated standing contracts vetting the vendors/suppliers and their products and services for set prices. These can be state, local or federal contracts and some may be grandfathered in by other entities. There are multiple social platforms dedicated to this vertical market and they have risen in popularity with the onset of the ARRA/Stimulus Program and increased government funds available to commercial entities for both grants and contracts.

Telecommunication is the transmission of information, over significant distances, to communicate. In earlier times, telecommunications involved the use of visual signals, such as beacons, smoke signals, semaphore telegraphs, signal flags, and optical heliographs, or audio messages via coded drumbeats, lung-blown horns, or sent by loud whistles, for example. In the modern age of electricity and electronics, telecommunications now also includes the use of electrical devices such as telegraphs, telephones, and teletypes, the use of radio and microwave communications, as well as fiber optics and their associated electronics, plus the use of the orbiting satellites and the Internet. The first breakthrough into modern electrical telecommunications came with the push to fully develop the telegraph starting in the 1830s. The use of these electrical means of communications exploded into use on all of the continents of the world during the 19th century, and these also connected the continents via cables on the floors of the ocean. The use of the first three popular systems of electrical telecommunications, the telegraph, telephone and teletype, all required the use of conducting metal wires.

Communication

Communication is the activity of conveying meaningful information. *Communication* requires a sender, a message, and an intended recipient, although the receiver need not be present or aware of the sender's intent to communicate at the time of communication; thus communication can occur across vast distances in time and space. Communication requires that the communicating parties share an area of communicative commonality. The communication process is complete once the receiver has understood the sender.

Human Communication

Human spoken and picture languages can be described as a system of symbols (sometimes known as lexemes) and the grammars (rules) by which the symbols are manipulated. The word "language" also refers to common properties of languages. Language learning normally occurs most intensively during human childhood. Most of the thousands of human languages use patterns of sound or gesture for symbols which enable communication with others around them. Languages seem to share certain properties, although many of these include exceptions. There is no defined line between a language and a dialect. Constructed languages such as Esperanto, programming languages, and various mathematical formalisms are not necessarily restricted to the properties shared by human languages. A variety of verbal and non-verbal means of communicating exists such as body language, eye contact, sign language, paralanguage, haptic communication, chronemics, and media such as pictures, graphics, sound, and writing. Convention on the Rights of Persons with Disabilities also defines the communication to include the display of text, Braille, tactile communication, large print, accessible multimedia, as well as written and plain language, human reader, and accessible information and communication technology.

Non-verbal Communication

Non-verbal communication describes the process of conveying meaning in the form of non-word messages. Research shows that the majority of our communication is non verbal, also known as body language. some of non verbal communication includes gesture, body language or posture; facial expression and eye contact, object communication such as clothing, hairstyles, architecture, symbols info-graphics, and tone of voice as well as through an aggregate of the above. Non-verbal communication is also called silent language and plays a key role in human day to day life from employment relations to romantic engagements. Speech also contains nonverbal elements known as paralanguage. These include voice quality, emotion and speaking style as well as prosodic features such as rhythm, intonation and stress. Likewise, written texts include non-verbal elements such as handwriting style, spatial arrangement of words and the use of emoticons to convey emotional expressions in pictorial form.

Visual Communication

Visual communication is the conveyance of ideas and information through creation of visual representations. Primarily associated with two dimensional images, it includes: signs, typography, drawing, graphic design, illustration, colors, and electronic resources, video and TV. Recent research in the field has focused on web design and graphically oriented usability. Graphic designers use methods of visual communication in their professional practice.

Oral Communication

Oral communication, while primarily referring to spoken

verbal communication, typically relies on both words, visual aids and non-verbal elements to support the conveyance of the meaning. Oral communication includes discussion, speeches, presentations, interpersonal communication and many other varieties. In face to face communication the body language and voice tonality plays a significant role and may have a greater impact on the listener than the intended content of the spoken words.

A great presenter must capture the attention of the audience and connect with them. For example, out of two persons telling the same joke one may greatly amuse the audience due to his body language and tone of voice while the second person, using exactly the same words, bores and irritates the audience. Visual aid can help to facilitate effective communication and is almost always used in presentations for an audience.

A widely cited and widely misinterpreted figure used to emphasize the importance of delivery states that "communication comprise 55% body language, 38% tone of voice, 7% content of words", the so-called "7%-38%-55% rule". This is not however what the cited research shows-rather, when conveying emotion, if body language, tone of voice, and words disagree, then body language and tone of voice will be believed more than words.

Written Communication and its Historical Development

Over time the forms of and ideas about communication have evolved through progression of technology. Advances include communications psychology and media psychology; an emerging field of study. Researchers divides the progression of written communication into three revolutionary stages called "Information Communication Revolutions".

During the 1st stage written communication first emerged through the use of pictographs. The pictograms were made in stone, hence written communication was not yet mobile.

During the 2nd stage writing began to appear on paper, papyrus, clay, wax, etc. Common alphabets were introduced and allowed for the uniformity of language across large distances. A leap in technology occurred when the Gutenberg printing-press was invented in the 15th century.

The 3rd stage is characterized by the transfer of information through controlled waves and electronic signals.

Communication is thus a process by which meaning is assigned and conveyed in an attempt to create shared understanding. This process, which requires a vast repertoire of skills in interpersonal processing, listening, observing, speaking, questioning, analyzing, gestures and evaluating enables collaboration and cooperation.

Barriers to successful communication include message overload (when a person receives too many messages at the same time), and message complexity.

Misunderstandings can be anticipated and solved through formulations, questions and answers, paraphrasing, examples, and stories of strategic talk. Written communication can be clear by planning follow-up talk on critical written communication as part of the normal way of doing business. Minutes spent talking now will save time later having to clear up misunderstandings later on. Then, take what was heard and reiterate in your own words, and ask them if that's what they meant.

A *capital good,* or simply *capital* in economics, is saved-up wealth or a manufactured means of production.. Individuals, organizations and governments use capital goods in the production of other goods or commodities. Capital goods include factories, machinery, tools, equipment, and various buildings which are used to produce other products for consumption. Capital goods, then, are products which are not produced for immediate consumption; rather, they are objects that are used to produce other goods and services. These types of goods are important economic factors because they are key to developing a positive return from manufacturing other products and commodities. Manufacturing companies also use capital goods. Capital goods help their company make functional goods to sell individuals valuable services. As a result, capital goods are sometimes referred to as *producers' goods* or *means of production*. An important distinction should also be made between capital goods and consumer goods, which are products directly purchased by consumers for personal or household use. For example, cars are generally considered consumer goods because they are usually bought by an individual for personal use. Dump trucks, however, are usually considered capital goods, because they are used by construction and manufacturing companies to haul various materials in order to make other products such as roads, bridges, dams, and buildings. Similarly, a chocolate candy bar is a consumer good but the machines used to produce the chocolate candy bar are considered capital goods. Capital goods are generally man-made, and do not include natural resources such as land or minerals, or human capital—the intellectual and physical skills and labor provided by human workers.

CONSUMER-TO-CONSUMER

Consumer-to-consumer (C2C) (or *citizen-to-citizen*) *electronic commerce* involves the electronically-facilitated transactions between consumers through some third party. A common example is the online auction, in which a consumer posts an item for sale and other consumers bid to purchase it; the third party generally charges a flat fee or commission. The sites are only intermediaries, just there to match consumers. They do not have to check quality of the products being offered.

Consumer-to-consumer (C2C) *marketing* is the creation of a product or service with the specific promotional strategy being for consumers to share that product or service with others as brand advocates based on the value of the product. The investment into concepting and developing a top of the line product or service that consumers are actively looking for is equatable to a Business-to-consumer (B2C) pre launch product awareness marketing spend.

C2C are becoming more popular amongst students in universities because these are large communities in the same geographical region that are low on money. So they are looking for deals very often and these kinds of websites offer this. Universities themselves set up places for students to sell textbooks and other stuff to other students, you can even advertise that you are subletting your apartment.

ONLINE AUCTION

The *online auction business model* is one in which participants bid for products and services over the Internet. The functionality of buying and selling in an auction format is made possible through auction software which regulates the various processes involved. Several types of online auctions are possible. In an English auction the initial price starts low and is bid up by successive bidders. In a Dutch auction, multiple identical items are offered in one auction, with all winning bidders paying the same price—the highest price at which all items will be sold (treasury bills, for example, are auctioned this way). Currently almost all online auctions use the English auction method.

The strategic advantages of this business model include:

1. *No time constraints*. Bids can be placed at any time (24/7). Items are listed for a number of days (usually between 1 and 10, at the discretion of the seller), giving purchasers time to search, decide, and bid. This convenience increases the number of bidders.
2. *No geographical constraints*. Sellers and bidders can participate from anywhere that has internet access. This makes them more accessible and reduces the cost of "attending" an auction. This increases the number of listed items (ie. number of sellers) and the number of bids for each item (e.g. number of bidders). The items do not need to be shipped to a central location, reducing costs, and reducing the seller's minimum acceptable price.
3. *Intensity of social interactions*. The social interactions involved in the bidding process are very similar to gambling. The bidders wait in anticipation hoping they will "win". Much like gambling addiction, some bidders may bid primarily to "play the game" rather than to obtain products or services. This creates a

highly loyal customer segment. This can also skew the prices of items/services/goods in the auction.

4. *Large number of bidders*. Because of the potential for a relatively low price, the broad scope of products and services available, the ease of access, and the social benefits of the auction process, there are a large number of bidders.
5. *Large number of sellers*. Because of the large number of bidders, the potential for a relatively high price, reduced selling costs, and ease of access, there are a large number of sellers.
6. *Network economies*. The large number of bidders will encourage more sellers, which, in turn, will encourage more bidders, which will encourage more sellers, etc., in a virtuous circle. The more the circle operates, the larger the system becomes, and the more valuable the business model becomes for all participants.
7. *Captures consumers' surplus*. Auctions are a form of first degree price discrimination. As such, they attempt to convert part of the consumers' surplus (defined as the area above the market price line but below the firm's demand curve) into producers' surplus.

Auction software is application software that can be deployed as stand-alone software for commercial and/or charity live and silent auctions, that handles all aspects of conducting an auction. This software provides users the ability to register bidders, clerk (record) sales, and cash out bidders. In addition to these key functions, auction software provides many ancillary capabilities including auction cataloging, inventory control, and consignor reconciliation. Some auction software is utilized exclusively in vertical markets such as automotive. In more recent years "auction software" has come to include software on a Web server for online auctions. This software provides the ability for users to post items for sale in an auction format as well as the ability to bid on those items

Price discrimination or price differentiation exists when sales of identical goods or services are transacted at different prices from the same provider. In a theoretical market with perfect information, perfect substitutes, and no transaction costs or prohibition on secondary exchange (or re-selling) to prevent arbitrage, price discrimination can only be a feature of monopolistic and oligopolistic markets, where market power can be exercised. Otherwise, the moment the seller tries to sell the same good at different prices, the buyer at the lower price can arbitrage by selling to the consumer buying at the higher price but with a tiny discount. However, product heterogeneity, market frictions or high fixed costs (which make marginal-cost pricing unsustainable in the long run) can allow for some degree of differential pricing to different consumers, even in fully competitive retail or industrial markets. Price discrimination also occurs when the same price is charged to customers which have different supply costs. The effects of price discrimination on social efficiency are unclear; typically such behavior leads to lower prices for some consumers and higher prices for others. Output can be expanded when price discrimination is very efficient, but output can also decline when discrimination is more effective at extracting surplus from high-valued users than expanding sales to low valued users. Even if output remains constant, price discrimination can reduce efficiency by misallocating output among consumers. Price discrimination requires market segmentation and some means to discourage discount customers from becoming resellers and, by extension, competitors. This usually entails using one or more means of preventing any resale, keeping the different price groups separate, making price comparisons difficult, or restricting pricing information. The boundary set up by the marketer to keep segments separate are referred to as a rate fence. Price discrimination is thus very common in services where resale is not possible; an example is student discounts at museums. Price discrimination in intellectual property is also enforced by law and by technology. In the market for DVDs, DVD players are designed-by law-with chips to prevent use of an inexpensive copy of the DVD (for example legally purchased in India) from being used in a higher-price market (like the US). The Digital Millennium Copyright Act has provisions to outlaw circumventing of such devices to protect the enhanced monopoly profits that copyright holders can obtain from price discrimination against higher price market segments. Price discrimination can also be seen where the requirement that goods be identical is relaxed. For example, so-called "premium products" (including relatively simple products, such as cappuccino compared to regular coffee) have a price differential that is not explained by the cost of production. Some economists have argued that this is a form of price discrimination exercised by providing a means for consumers to reveal their willingness to pay.

In game theory, *perfect information* describes the situation when a player has available the same information to determine all of the possible games (all combinations of legal moves) as would be available at the end of the game. In game theory, a game is described as a game of perfect information if perfect information is available for all moves. Chess is an example of a game with perfect information as each player can see all of the pieces on the board at all times. Other examples of perfect games include tic tac toe, irensei, and go. Games with perfect information represent a small subset of games. Card games where each player's cards are hidden from other players are examples of games of imperfect information. In microeconomics, a state of perfect information is assumed in some models of perfect competition. That is, assuming that all agents are rational and have perfect information, they will choose the best products, and the market will reward those who make the best products with higher sales. Perfect information would practically mean that all consumers know all things, about all products, at all times, and therefore always make the best decision regarding purchase. In competitive markets, unlike game-theoretic models, perfect competition does not require that agents have complete knowledge about the actions of others; all relevant information is reflected in prices.

In economics, one way we classify goods (two or more) is by examining the relationship of the demand schedules when the price of one good changes. This relationship between demand schedules leads economists to classify goods as either substitutes or complements. Substitute goods are goods which, as a result of changed conditions, may replace each other in use (or consumption). A *substitute good,* in contrast to a complementary good, is a good with a positive cross elasticity of demand. This means a good's demand is increased when the price of another good is increased. Conversely, the demand for a good is decreased when the price of another good is decreased. If goods A and B are substitutes, an increase in the price of A will result in a leftward movement along the demand curve of A and cause the demand curve for B to shift out. A decrease in the price of A will result in a rightward movement along the demand curve of A and cause the demand curve for B to shift in.

A transaction cost is a cost incurred in making an economic exchange (restated: the cost of participating in a market). For example, most people, when buying or selling a stock, must pay a commission to their broker; that commission is a transaction cost of doing the stock deal. Or consider buying a banana from a store; to purchase the banana, your costs will be not only the price of the banana itself, but also the energy and effort it requires to find out which of the various banana products you prefer, where to get them and at what price, the cost of traveling from your house to the store and back, the time waiting in line, and the effort of the paying itself; the costs above and beyond the cost of the banana are the transaction costs. When rationally evaluating a potential transaction, it is important to consider transaction costs that might prove significant. A number of kinds of transaction cost have come to be known by particular names:

- *Search and information costs* are costs such as those incurred in determining that the required good is available on the market, which has the lowest price, etc.
- *Bargaining costs* are the costs required to come to an acceptable agreement with the other party to the transaction, drawing up an appropriate contract and so on. In game theory this is analyzed for instance in the game of chicken. On asset markets and in market microstructure, the transaction cost is some function of the distance between the bid and ask.

- *Policing and enforcement costs* are the costs of making sure the other party sticks to the terms of the contract, and taking appropriate action (often through the legal system) if this turns out not to be the case.

A monopoly (monos-alone or single + polein-to sell)) exists when a specific individual or an enterprise has sufficient control over a particular product or service to determine significantly the terms on which other individuals shall have access to it. (This is in contrast to a monopsony which relates to a single entity's control over a market to purchase a good or service, and contrasted with oligopoly where a few entities exert considerable influence over an industry) Monopolies are thus characterized by a lack of economic competition to produce the good or service and a lack of viable substitute goods. The verb "monopolise" refers to the process by which a firm gains persistently greater market share than what is expected under perfect competition. A monopoly must be distinguished from monopsony, in which there is only one buyer of a product or service ; a monopoly may also have monopsony control of a sector of a market. Likewise, a monopoly should be distinguished from a cartel (a form of oligopoly), in which several providers act together to coordinate services, prices or sale of goods. Monopolies, monopsonies and oligopolies are all situations where one or a few of the entities have market power and therefore must interact with their customers (monopoly), suppliers (monopsony) and the other firms (oligopoly) in a game theoretic manner-meaning that expectations about their behavior affects other players' choice of strategy and vice versa. This is to be contrasted with the model of perfect competition where firms are price takers and do not have market power. Monopolists typically produce fewer goods and sell them at a higher price than under perfect competition, resulting in abnormal and sustained profit. (See also Bertrand, Cournot or Stackelberg equilibria, market power, market share, market concentration, Monopoly profit, industrial economics).

Monopolies can form naturally or through vertical or horizontal mergers. A monopoly is said to be coercive when the monopoly firm actively prohibits competitors from entering the field or punishes competitors who do.

A *market* is any one of a variety of systems, institutions, procedures, social relations and infrastructures whereby parties engage in exchange. While parties may exchange goods and services by barter, most markets rely on buyers offer their goods or services (including labor) in exchange for money (legal tender such as fiat money) from buyers.For a market to be competitive, there must be more than a single buyer or seller. It has been suggested that two people may trade, but it takes at least three persons to have a market, so that there is competition on at least one of its two sides. However, competitive markets rely on much larger numbers of both buyers and sellers. A market with single seller and multiple buyers is a monopoly. A market with a single buyer and multiple sellers is a monopsony. These are the extremes of imperfect competition. Markets vary in form, scale (volume and geographic reach), location, and types of participants, as well as the types of goods and services traded. Examples include:

- physical retail markets, such as local farmers' markets, which be held in town squares or parking lots on an ongoing or occasional basis, shopping centers and shopping malls.
- (non-physical) internet markets (see electronic commerce).
- ad hoc auction markets.
- markets for intermediate goods used in production of other goods and services.
- labor markets.
- international currency and commodity markets.
- stock markets, for the exchange of shares in corporations.
- artificial markets created by regulation to exchange rights for derivatives that have been designed to ameliorate externalities, such as pollution permits (see carbon trading).

- illegal markets such as the market for illicit drugs, arms or pirated products.

In mainstream economics, the concept of a *market* is any structure that allows buyers and sellers to exchange any type of goods, services and information. The exchange of goods or services for money is a transaction. Market participants consist of all the buyers and sellers of a good who influence its price. This influence is a major study of economics and has given rise to several theories and models concerning the basic market forces of supply and demand. There are two roles in markets, buyers and sellers. The market facilitates trade and enables the distribution and allocation of resources in a society. Markets allow any tradable item to be evaluated and priced. A market emerges more or less spontaneously or is constructed deliberately by human interaction in order to enable the exchange of rights (cf. ownership) of services and goods.

In economics, *market power* is the ability of a firm to alter the market price of a good or service. In perfectly competitive markets, market participants have no market power. A firm with market power can raise prices without losing its customers to competitors. Market participants that have market power are therefore sometimes referred to as "price makers," while those without are sometimes called "price takers". A firm with market power has the ability to individually affect either the total quantity or the prevailing price in the market. Price makers face a downward-sloping demand curve, such that price increases lead to a lower quantity demanded. The decrease in supply as a result of the exercise of market power creates an economic deadweight loss which is often viewed as socially undesirable. As a result, many countries have anti-trust or other legislation intended to limit the ability of firms to accrue market power. Such legislation often regulates mergers and sometimes introduces a judicial power to compel divestiture. A firm usually has market power by virtue of controlling a large portion of the market. In extreme cases-monopoly and monopsony-the firm controls the entire market. However, market size alone is not the only indicator of market power. Highly concentrated markets may be contestable if there are no barriers to entry or exit, limiting the incumbent firm's ability to raise its price above competitive levels. Market power gives firms the ability to engage in unilateral anti-competitive behavior. Some of the behaviors that firms with market power are accused of engaging in include predatory pricing, product tying, and creation of overcapacity or other barriers to entry. If no individual participant in the market has significant market power, then anti-competitive behavior can take place only through collusion, or the exercise of a group of participants' collective market power.

Market segmentation is a concept in economics and marketing. A *market segment* is a sub-set of a market made up of people or organizations with one or more characteristics that cause them to demand similar product and/or services based on qualities of those products such as price or function. A true market segment meets all of the following criteria: it is distinct from other segments (different segments have different needs), it is homogeneous within the segment (exhibits common needs); it responds similarly to a market stimulus, and it can be reached by a market intervention. The term is also used when consumers with identical product and/or service needs are divided up into groups so they can be charged different amounts. The people in a given segment are supposed to be similar in terms of criteria by which they are segmented and different from other segments in terms of these criteria. These can broadly be viewed as 'positive' and 'negative' applications of the same idea, splitting up the market into smaller groups. Examples:

- Gender
- Price
- Interests

While there may be theoretically 'ideal' market segments, in reality every organization engaged in a market will develop different ways of imagining market segments, and create Product differentiation strategies to exploit these segments. The market segmentation and corresponding product differentiation strategy can give a firm a temporary commercial advantage. Market segmenting is dividing the market into groups of individual markets with similar wants or needs that a company divides into distinct groups which have distinct needs, wants, behavior or which might want different products and services. Broadly, markets can be divided according to a number of general criteria, such as by industry or public versus private. Although industrial market segmentation is quite different from consumer market segmentation, both have similar objectives. All of these methods of segmentation are merely proxies for true segments, which don't always fit into convenient demographic boundaries. Consumer-based market segmentation can be performed on a *product specific* basis, to provide a close match between specific products and individuals. However, a number of generic market segment systems also exist, e.g. the system provides a broad segmentation of the population of the United States based on the statistical analysis of household and geo-demographic data. The process of segmentation is distinct from positioning (designing an appropriate marketing mix for each segment). The overall intent is to identify groups of similar customers and potential customers; to prioritize the groups to address; to understand their behavior; and to respond with appropriate marketing strategies that satisfy the different preferences of each chosen segment. Revenues are thus improved. Improved segmentation can lead to significantly improved marketing effectiveness. Distinct segments can have different industry structures and thus have higher or lower attractiveness

DIFFERENCE BETWEEN B2B AND B2C MARKETING

What do you think are the key difference between a B2B and B2C marketing for search? What do B2B search marketers need to do differently?

The key differences between B2B and B2C marketing are the lead time and approval layers. In B2C web site marketing, there is a normally a short lead time of anywhere from a minute to a day. Consumers may only need, at the most, to consult with a spouse or parent about a purchase before making that purchase. Sometimes they do not even need to do that. They simply can purchase on impulse. In the B2B world, the idea of an impulse buy is almost non-existent. There is normally a chain of command that needs to be followed before a purchase can be completed. This increases the lead time exponentially, depending upon how many levels the purchase must go through to be approved.

A major difference between a B2B and B2C marketing online is that the B2B websites need to keep that chain of command in mind. They need to provide information that will answer each of the questions each perspective layer in the command needs to answer.

For example, let's say that an office manager has decided that she wants to find a new place to buy pens. In the office manager's mind, she is simply thinking of the place that has a good price on pens and may offer her some perk for her for doing business with them. But she will most likely need to bring the decision to accounting on some level to see if the payment required by accounting is acceptable. While she may not need to actually get permission from accounting, this is still a layer. She will also, most likely, need to get final approval from a superior to switch pen companies. The superior may be concerned with the service the pen company will provide, the speed of delivery and the reputation of the pen company.

Making sure that B2B websites address all the questions (and desires) that all layers in the chain may have helps ensure that they will purchase your product. If the office manager sees no perk for her or that you are not the lowest price, she may never bring your company up to her superior. If payment options are not clearly marked out, the office manager may skip over it since she will not be able to answer accounting's questions. If there is no mention of the quality of the company, her superior may reject the request to switch rather than go through the hassle without knowing the level of service they will be getting.

What advice would you give to B2B websites to help them improve the ROI of their paid search marketing campaigns?

To improve the ROI of search marketing, remember the difference between a B2B and B2C marketing online is the longer lead time and multi layer approval that this process entails. Many analytic programs will, by default, track conversion on a linear level. In other words, they will only track conversions if someone clicks on an ad and goes within that visit to the conversion point. So, a B2B paid search marketer should spend time figuring out their lead time (between a first visit and a conversion) and then use an analytic program that tracks later conversions that may have begun with a click on a paid ad weeks-or even months-earlier.

As another strategy, tracking offline conversions can help you find other conversions that would not typically figure into an analytics programs calculation of your ROI. These ROI factors are not as obvious as the ones discussed above, but, especially for B2B, identifying and accounting for them helps you spend your advertising dollars more effectively. An example of tracking offline conversions would be that you might use a different phone number on the site than your usual one and would be able to track how many calls came through that number. Another offline tracking tactic would be to provide an coupon on the website for offline purchases and see how many people use that coupon.

Also, keeping in mind the layers discussed above, B2B websites should focus on micro conversion points, such as gathering contact information from a prospective client or supplying branded white papers with information that will help the visitor with his or her own decision-making process as well as the decision-making processes of others in the chain. Gathering contact info allows for other non-expensive contact points and white papers keep your company's name in front of a potential customer.

What advice would you give to B2B websites to help them improve the ROI of their search engine optimization (SEO) efforts?

Micro conversions can also help with the ROI of an SEO campaign. Also, be sure to create content for your site that focuses on all the layers for your products?' approval chain, making sure to include the appropriate language (effective keywords) for each of those different purchase points.

Another one of the similarities between B2B and B2C marketing when selling online is that you must create text that is effectively optimized with the most compelling and carefully targeted keywords possible, so that potential buyers find your site; can effectively navigate their way through your products/ services; and can arrive at a purchasing decision that satisfies their wants and needs.

With B2C web site marketing, your business sells directly to consumers and your potential customers are usually buying products/services for themselves, or for close friends and family members. Therefore, you should hone in on the benefits of the product or service for an individual or a family-money saved, comfort gained, beauty enjoyed, and convenience delivered and so forth-using keywords that a non-expert might use.

One difference between a B2B and B2C web site marketing when selling is you must contend with different entities within a business. For example, the purchasing department may be visiting your site to review products for the marketing department, the IT department or one of numerous other segments of their business.

Moreover, different departments have different expectations for products and services. So, for example, if you're selling software for marketing departments to use, the marketing staff will want to see how effective your software is to use, while the finance department wants good value for their dollar; and the IT department wants to know how easily the software can be integrated into their overall system.

The challenge for search marketers, then, is to identify who in the business is buying their products online; what level of understanding they have about the product; the jargon that they might use to find your product (which can be quite different from YOUR in-house/industry jargon); and the benefits that their business needs to receive from your products/services. Plus, the person browsing your website may not be the person who has the financial authority to okay the purchase, so you must write copy to persuade different employees/departments along the buying cycle.

When developing the overall copywriting/search marketing strategy, keep the results gleaned from your keyword research at the forefront at all times. These are your cues as to how your prospects are thinking, searching-and, ultimately, buying. Finally, another one of the similarities between B2B and B2C web site marketing is that it's important not to get so caught up in the technical details of writing for search engines that you forget to craft a uniquely compelling message written to your precise target market. Speak to the person you wish to reach (Saves your company 40%) versus extolling the virtues of your own company (We cut prices).

CHAPTER

7

Digital Marketing

Digital Marketing is the promoting of brands using all forms of digital advertising channels to reach consumers. This now includes *Television, Radio, Internet, mobile,* social media marketing and any other form of digital media.

Whilst digital marketing does include many of the techniques and practices contained within the category of Internet Marketing, it extends beyond this by including other channels with which to reach people that do not require the use of The Internet. As a result of this non-reliance on the Internet, the field of digital marketing includes a whole host of elements such as mobile phones, sms/mms, display/banner ads and digital outdoor. Previously seen as a stand-alone service in its own right, it is frequently being seen as a domain that can and does cover most, if not all, of the more traditional marketing areas such as Direct Marketing by providing the same method of communicating with an audience but in a digital fashion. Digital is now being broadened to support the "servicing" and "engagement" of customers.

DIGITAL MARKETING—PULL *VS.* PUSH

There are 2 different forms of digital marketing, each of which has its pros and cons.

Pull

Pull digital marketing technologies involve the user having to seek out and directly select (or pull) the content, often via web search. Web site/blogs and streaming media (audio and video) are good examples of this. In each of these examples, users have a specific link (URL) to view the content.

Pros: Digital Marketing and Power Users of the internet are an integral aspect to the economy. Interactive Media is a form of art and creative inspiration.

- Since requests are inherently opt-in, the size of content is generally unlimited.
- No advanced technology required to send static content, only to store/display it.

Cons

- Considerable marketing effort required for users to find the message/content.
- Some types of marketing content may be blocked in mixed content scenarios (i.e. Flash blockers)

Push

Push digital marketing technologies involve both the marketer (creator of the message) as well as the recipients (the user). Email, SMS, RSS are examples of push digital marketing. In each of these examples, the marketer has to send (push) the messages to the users (subscribers) in order for the message to be received. In the case of RSS, content is actually pulled on a periodic basis (polling), thus simulating a push.

Pros

- Faster delivery-push technologies can deliver content immediately as it becomes available.

- Consistent delivery-some push platforms have single content types, making it difficult for the user to block content by type.
- Better targeting-since push technology usually justifies subscription, more specific marketing data may be collected during registration, which allows for better targeting and more personalization.
- Better data-marketing data can be correlated to each request for content, allowing marketers to see information such as user name as well as demographic and psychographic data.

Cons

- Smaller audience-push technology not implemented on common platforms generally need client and/or server software before content can be created, distributed, and/or viewed.
- Higher cost-less popular platforms may have higher implementation costs.
- Lesser discoverability-smaller audiences mean fewer views mean less visibility in search engines.

DIGITAL MARKETING AND MULTI-CHANNEL COMMUNICATIONS

While digital marketing is effective using one message type, it is much more successful when a marketer combines multiple channels in the message campaigns. For example, if a company is trying to promote a new product release, they could send out an email message or text campaign individually. This, if properly executed, could yield positive results. However, this same campaign could be exponentially improved if multiple message types are implemented. An email could be sent to a list of potential customers with a special offer for those that also include their cell phone number. A couple of days later, a follow up campaign would be sent via text message (SMS) with the special offer.

Push and pull message technologies can also be used in conjunction with each other. For example, an email campaign can include a banner ad or link to a content download. This enables a marketer to have the best of both worlds in terms of their marketing method.

eCRM

eCRM This concept is derived from E-commerce. It also uses net environment i.e., intranet, extranet and internet. Electronic CRM concerns all forms of managing relationships with customers making use of Information Technology (IT). eCRM is enterprises using IT to integrate internal organization resources and external marketing strategies to understand and fulfill their customers needs. Comparing with traditional CRM, the integrated information for eCRM intraorganizational collaboration can be more efficient to communicate with customers.

From Relationship Marketing to Customer Relationship Marketing

The concept of relationship marketing was first coined by Leonard Berry in 1983. He considered it to consist of attracting, maintaining and enhancing customer relationships within organizations. In the years that followed, companies were engaging more and more in a meaningful dialogue with individual customers. In doing so, new organizational forms as well as technologies were used, eventually resulting in what we know as Customer Relationship Management (CRM).

The main difference between RM and CRM is that the first does not acknowledge the use of technology, where the latter uses Information Technology (IT) in implementing RM strategies.

THE ESSENCE OF CRM

The exact meaning of CRM is still subject of heavy discussions. However, the overall goal can be seen as effectively managing differentiated relationships with all customers and communicating with them on an individual basis. Underlying thought is that companies realize that they can supercharge profits by acknowledging that different groups of customers vary widely in their behavior, desires, and responsiveness to marketing. Loyal customers can not only give operational companies sustained revenue but also advertise for new marketers.

To reinforce the reliance of customers and create additional customer sources, firms utilize CRM to maintain the relationship as the general two categories B2B(Business-to-Business) and B2C(Business-to-Customer or Business-to-Consumer). Because of the needs and behaviors are different between B2B and B2C, so that the implementation of CRM should come from respective viewpoints.

DIFFERENCES BETWEEN CRM AND eCRM

Major differences between CRM and eCRM

Customer Contacts

- CRM-Contact with customer made through the retail store, phone, and fax.
- eCRM-All of the traditional methods are used in addition to Internet, email, wireless, and PDA technologies.

System Interface

- CRM-Implements the use of ERP systems, emphasis is on the back-end.
- eCRM-Geared more toward front end, which interacts with the back-end through use of ERP systems, data warehouses, and data marts.

System Overhead (Client Computers)

- CRM-The client must download various applications to view the web-enabled applications. They would have to be rewritten for different platform.

- eCRM-Does not have these requirements because the client uses the browser.

Customization and Personalization of Information

- CRM-Views differ based on the audience, and personalized views are not available. Individual personalization requires program changes.
- eCRM-Personalized individual views based on purchase history and preferences. Individual has ability to customize view.

System Focus

- CRM-System (created for internal use) designed based on job function and products. Web applications designed for a single department or business unit.
- eCRM-System (created for external use) designed based on customer needs. Web application designed for enterprise-wide use.

System Maintenance and Modification

- CRM-More time involved in implementation and maintenance is more expensive because the system exists at different locations and on various servers.
- eCRM-Reduction in time and cost. Implementation and maintenance can take place at one location and on one server.

eCRM

As the internet is becoming more and more important in business life, many companies consider it as an opportunity to reduce customer-service costs, tighten customer relationships and most important, further personalize marketing messages and enable mass customization. ECRM is being adopted by companies because it increases customer loyalty and customer retention by improving customer satisfaction, one of the objectives of eCRM. E-loyalty results in long-term profits for online retailers because they incur less costs of recruiting new customers, plus they have an increase in customer retention. Together with the creation of Sales Force Automation (SFA), where electronic methods were used to gather data and analyze customer information, the trend of the upcoming Internet can be seen as the foundation of what we know as eCRM today.

As we implement eCRM process, there are three steps life cycle:

1. Data Collection: About customers preference information for actively (answer knowledge) and passively (surfing record) ways via website, email, questionnaire.
2. Data Aggregation: Filter and analysis for firm's specific needs to fulfill their customers.
3. Customer Interaction: According to customer's need, company provide the proper feedback them.

We can define eCRM as activities to manage customer relationships by using the Internet, web browsers or other electronic touch points. The challenge hereby is to offer communication and information on the right topic, in the right amount, and at the right time that fits the customer's specific needs.

eCRM Strategy Components

When enterprises integrate their customer information, there are three eCRM strategy components.

1. *Operational*: Because of sharing information, the processes in business should make customer's need as first and seamlessly implement. This avoids multiple times to bother customers and redundant process.
2. *Analytical*: Analysis helps company maintain a long-term relationship with customers.
3. *Collaborative*: Due to improved communication technology, different departments in company

implement (intra organizational) or work with business partners (inter organizational) more efficiently by sharing information.

IMPLEMENTING AND INTEGRATING eCRM WORK

Non-electronic solution: Several CRM software packages exist that can help companies in deploying CRM activities. Besides choosing one of these packages, companies can also choose to design and build their own solutions. In order to implement CRM in an effective way, one needs to consider the following factors:

- Create a customer-focused culture in the organization.
- Adopt customer-based managers to assess satisfaction.
- Develop an end-to-end process to serve customers.
- Recommend questions to be asked to help a customer solve a problem.
- *Track all aspects of selling to customers, as well as prospects.*

Furthermore, CRM solutions are more effective once they are being implemented in other information systems used by the company. Examples are Transaction Processing System (TPS) to process data real-time, which can then be sent to the sales and finance departments in order to recalculate inventory and financial position quick and accurately. Once this information is transferred back to the CRM software and services it could prevent customers from placing an order in the belief that an item is in stock while it is not.

Electronic solution (eCRM): Contrast with traditional CRM being implemented under ERP (Enterprise Resource Planning) interface communicating in firms and with their customers, eCRM optimizes the customized environment via web browser. This provides beneficial for effective communication not only enterprises to external customers and internal departments. Business personalized each of their customer profile unified in entire organization. By "central repository", customer may communicate with different department staff in the corporate via Internet (or phone call). And firms are able to use the marketing analysis for customer more mature services. As each department integrates customers' information, they can focus on individual operational duty more efficiently, so that firm may reduce execution cost.

eCRM in B2B market: Traditional B2B customers are usually seeking ways in order to decrease the firm's expense. Customizing the specific product and reducing the repeated routine cost products for them can expense least. Due to information technology developing, websites information has been becoming an important medium to reduce collecting cost and time, and it becomes a long-term relationship eventually. At the same time, more complex collaboration can be implemented on networking platform.

eCRM in B2C market: In contrast with B2B, the attitude of B2C individually purchase is decided by the positive experience and online shopping knowledge. Previous research found B2C enjoy the shopping online is quick to transact, convenient to return, save energy to retailer, and fun to browse. Thus, the marketing investigating, customers communicating, and information obtaining are important factors to maintain customer services.

Cloud solution: Today, more and more enterprise CRM systems move to cloud computing solution, "up from 8 percent of the CRM market in 2005 to 20 percent of the market in 2008, according to Gartner". Moving managing system into cloud, companies can cost efficiently as pay-per-use on manage, maintain, and upgrade etc. system and connect with their customers streamlined in the cloud. In cloud based CRM system, transaction can be recorded via CRM database immediately.

Some enterprise CRM in cloud systems are web-based customers don't need to install an additional interface and the activities with businesses can be updated real-time. People may communication on mobile devices to get the efficient services. Furthermore, customer/case experience and the interaction feedbacks are another way of CRM collaboration and integration information in corporate organization to improve businesses' services. There are multifarious cloud CRM services for enterprise to use and here are some hints to the your right CRM system:

1. *Assess your company's needs*: some of enterprise CRM systems are featured.
2. Take advantage of free trials: comparison and familiarization each of the optional.
3. Do the math: estimate the customer strategy for company budget.
4. Consider mobile options: some system like Salesforce.com can be combined with other mobile device application.
5. Ask about security: consider whether the cloud CRM provider give enough protect as your own.
6. Make sure the sales team is on board: as the frontline of enterprise, the launched CRM system should be the help for sales.
7. Know your exit strategy: understand the exit mechanism to keep flexibility.

vCRM

Channels through which companies can communicate with its customers, are growing by the day, and as a result, getting their time and attention has turned into a major challenge. One of the reasons eCRM is so popular nowadays is that digital channels can create unique and positive experiences-not just transactions-for customers. An extreme, but ever growing in popularity, example of the creation of experiences in order to establish customer service is the use of Virtual Worlds, such as Second Life. Through this so-called vCRM, companies are able to create synergies between virtual and physical channels and reaching a very wide consumer base. However, given the newness of the technology, most companies are still struggling to identify effective entries in Virtual Worlds. Its highly interactive character, which allows companies to respond directly to any customer's requests or problems, is another feature of eCRM that helps companies establish and sustain long-term customer relationships.

Furthermore, Information Technology has helped companies to even further differentiate between customers and address a personal message or service. Some examples of tools used in eCRM:

- Personalized Web Pages where customers are recognized and their preferences are shown.
- Customized products or services.

CRM programs should be directed towards customer value that competitors cannot match. However, in a world where almost every company is connected to the Internet, eCRM has become a requirement for survival, not just a competitive advantage.

Different Levels of eCRM

In defining the scope of eCRM, three different levels can be distinguished:

- *Foundational services*: This includes the minimum necessary services such as web site effectiveness and responsiveness as well as order fulfillment.
- *Customer-centered services*: These services include order tracking, product configuration and customization as well as security/trust.
- *Value-added services: These are extra services such as online auctions and online training and education.*

Self-services are becoming increasingly important in CRM activities. The rise of the Internet and eCRM has boosted the options for self-service activities. A critical success factor is the integration of such activities into traditional channels. An example was Ford's plan to sell cars directly to customers via its Web Site, which provoked an outcry among its dealers network. CRM activities are mainly of two different types. Reactive service is where the customer has a problem and contacts the company. Proactive service is where the manager has decided not to wait for the customer to contact the firm, but to be aggressive and contact the customer himself in order to establish a dialogue and solve problems.

Steps to eCRM Success

Many factors play a part in ensuring that the implementation any level of eCRM is successful. One obvious way it could be measured is by the ability for the system to add value to the existing business. There are four suggested implementation steps that affect the viability of a project like this:

1. Developing customer-centric strategies
2. Redesigning workflow management systems
3. Re-engineering work processes
4. Supporting with the right technologies.

MOBILE CRM

One subset of Electronic CRM is Mobile CRM (mCRM). This is defined as "services that aim at nurturing customer relationships, acquiring or maintaining customers, support marketing, sales or services processes, and use wireless networks as the medium of delivery to the customers. However, since communications is the central aspect of customer relations activities, many opt for the following definition of mCRM: "communication, either one-way or interactive, which is related to sales, marketing and customer service activities conducted through mobile medium for the purpose of building and maintaining customer relationships between a company and its customer(s).

eCRM allows customers to access company services from more and more places, since the Internet access points are increasing by the day. mCRM however, takes this one step further and allows customers or managers to access the systems for instance from a mobile phone or PDA with internet access, resulting in high flexibility. Since mCRM is not able to provide a complete range of customer relationship activities it should be integrated in the complete CRM system.

There are three main reasons that mobile CRM is becoming so popular. The first is that the devices consumers use are improving in multiple ways that allow for this advancement. Displays are larger and clearer and access times on networks are improving overall. Secondly, the users are also becoming more sophisticated. The technology to them is nothing new so it is easy to adapt. Lastly, the software being developed for these applications has become worthwhile and useful to end users. There are four basic steps that a company should follow to implement a mobile CRM system. By following these and also keeping the IT department, the end users and management in agreement, the outcome can be beneficial for all.

Step 1-Needs analysis phase: This is the point to take your times and understand all the technical needs and desires for each of the users and stakeholders. It also has to be kept in mind that the mobile CRM system must be able to grow and change with the business.

Step 2-Mobile design phase: This is the next critical phase that will show all the technical concerns that need to be addressed. A few main things to consider are screen size, device storage and security.

Step 3-Mobile application testing phase: This step is mostly to ensure that the users and stakeholders all approve of the new system.

Step 4-Rollout phase: This is when the new system is implemented but also when training on the final product is done with all users.

Advantages of Mobile CRM

1. The mobile channel creates a more personal direct connection with customers.
2. It is continuously active and allows necessary individuals to take action quickly using the information.
3. Typically it is an opt-in only channel which allows for high and quality responsiveness.

4. Overall it supports loyalty between the customer and company, which improves and strengthens relationships.

Privacy

The effective and efficient employment of CRM activities cannot go without the remarks of safety and privacy. CRM systems depend on databases in which all kinds of customer data is stored. In general, the following rule applies: the more data, the better the service companies can deliver to individual customers. Some known examples of these problems are conducting credit-card transaction online of the phenomenon known as 'cookies' used on the Internet in order to track someone's information and behavior. The design and the quality of the website are two very important aspects that influences the level of trust customers experience and their willingness of reluctance to do a transaction or leave personal information.

Privacy policies can be ineffective in relaying to customers how much of their information is being used. In a recent study by The University of Pennsylvania and University of California, it was revealed that over half the respondents have an incorrect understanding of how their information is being used. They believe that, if a company has a privacy policy, they will not share the customer's information with third party companies without the customer's express consent. Therefore, if marketers want to use consumer information for advertising purposes, they must clearly illustrate the ways in which they will use the customer's information and present the benefits of this in order to acquire the customer's consent. Privacy concerns are being addressed more and more. Legislation is being proposed that regulates the use of personal data. Also, Internet policy officials are calling for more performance measures of privacy policies.

Digital Media

Another aspect of personalization is the increasing prevalence of open data on the Web. Many companies make their data available on the Web via APIs, web services, and open data standards. Ordnance Survey Open Data This data is structured to allow it to be inter-connected and re-used by third parties. Data available from a user's personal social graph can be accessed by third-party application software to be suited to fit the personalized web page or information appliance. Current open data standards on the Web include:

1. Data Portability
2. Open ID
3. Open Social
4. Attention Profiling Mark-up Language (APML)

Mobile Phones: Over time mobile phones have seen an increased emphasis placed on user personalization. Far from the black and white screens and monophonic ringtones of the past, phones now offer interactive wallpapers and MP3 TruTones. In the UK and Asia, WeeMees have become popular. WeeMees are three-dimensional characters that are used as wallpaper and respond to the tendencies of the user. Video Graphics Array (VGA) picture quality allows people to change their background with ease without sacrificing quality. All of these services are downloaded through the provider with the goal to make the user feel connected to the phone.

Television: Personalization on the TV can occur on TV apps or on the set top box user interface. Most forms of personalization occur with recommendations. For instance, a TV app may recommend certain TV shows based on user behavior or collaborative filtering.

Search Engines

When search engines employ personalization, it is referred to as personalized search. Google was the first of the major Web search engines to introduce personalized results on a massive scale. Weighing a number of factors including but not limited to user history, bookmarks, community behaviour and site click-through rate and stickiness, Google is providing results that are specific to what they believe you are searching for. Currently this service is only available to those who are logged into their Google account. Bing personalizes search results for all users based on an individual's previous searches.

Amazon.com has been the early adopter of personalization technology to recommend products to shoppers on its site, based upon their previous purchases. Amazon makes extensive use of Collaborative Filtering in its personalization technology. TV Genius has developed personalization in its television search engine for TV show searches.

Business logic, or domain logic, is a non-technical term generally used to describe the functional algorithms that handle information exchange between a database and a user interface. In a single-tier applications, business logic, presentation logic, and CRUD are often used, with each having intimate knowledge of, or being strongly coupled to, the others. This is seen as problematic, since changes to one result in changes to both of the others, requiring retesting and revalidation of the entire system for a single change. The interweaving also limits the extent to which the CRUD and the business logic can be reused. In a multilayered architecture (compared to multitier architecture) business logic is a separate module. In the common 3-tier architecture, the business logic in theory occupies the middle tier, the business-services tier or business layer. In practice, the business logic is often interwoven in the other two tiers (the user services tier and the database services tier), such as by encoding business logic in stored procedures and in decisions about input validation and display formatting. However there is not a well-defined rule.

Cluster analysis or *clustering* is the assignment of a set of observations into subsets (called clusters) so that observations in the same cluster are similar in some sense. Clustering is a method of unsupervised learning, and a common technique for statistical data analysis used in many fields, including machine learning, data mining, pattern recognition, image analysis, information retrieval, and bioinformatics.

Types

Memory-Based: This mechanism uses user rating data to compute similarity between users or items. This is used for making recommendations. This was the earlier mechanism and is used in many commercial systems. It is easy to implement and is effective. Typical examples of this mechanism are neighborhood based CF and item-based/user-based top-N recommendations.

The neighborhood-based algorithm calculates the similarity between two users or items, produces a prediction for the user taking the weighted average of all the ratings. Similarity computation between items or users is an important part of this approach. Multiple mechanisms such as Pearson correlation and vector cosine based similarity are used for this. The user based top-N recommendation algorithm identifies the k most similar users to an active user using similarity based vector model. After the k most similar users are found, their corresponding user-item matrices are aggregated to identify the set of items to be recommended. A popular method to find the similar users is the Locality sensitive hashing, which implements the nearest neighbor mechanism in linear time.

The advantages with this approach include: the explain ability of the results, which is an important aspect of recommendation systems; it is easy to create and use; new data can be added easily and incrementally; it need not consider the content of the items being recommended; and the mechanism scales well with co-rated items. There are several disadvantages with this approach. First, it depends on human ratings. Second, its performance decreases when data gets sparse, which is frequent with web related items. This prevents the scalability of this approach and has problems with large datasets. Third, it cannot handle new users or new items.

Locality Sensitive Hashing (*LSH*) is a method of performing probabilistic dimension reduction of high-dimensional data. The basic idea is to hash the input items so that similar items are mapped to the same buckets with high probability (the number of buckets being much smaller than the universe of possible input items).

Nearest neighbor search (*NNS*), also known as *proximity search, similarity search* or *closest point search,* is an optimization problem for finding closest points in metric spaces. The problem is: given a set *S* of points in a metric space *M* and a query point *q* ? *M,* find the closest point in *S* to *q*. In many cases, *M* is taken to be *d*-dimensional Euclidean space and distance is measured by Euclidean distance or Manhattan distance. Various solutions to the NNS problem have been proposed. The quality and usefulness of the algorithms are determined by the time complexity of queries as well as the space complexity of any search data structures that must be maintained. The informal observation usually referred to as the curse of dimensionality states that there is no general-purpose exact solution for NNS in high-dimensional Euclidean space using polynomial preprocessing and poly-logarithmic search time

Model-Based : Models are developed using data mining, machine learning algorithms to find patterns based on training data. These are used to make predictions for real data. There are many model based CF algorithms. These include Bayesian Networks, clustering models, latent semantic models such as singular value decomposition, probabilistic latent semantic analysis, Multiple Multiplicative Factor, Latent Dirichlet allocation and markov decision process based models.

This approach has a more holistic goal to uncover latent factors that explain observed ratings. Most of the models are based on creating a classification or clustering technique to identify the user based on the test set. The number of the parameters can be reduced based on types of principal component analysis. There are several advantages with this paradigm. It handles the sparsity better than memory based ones. This helps with scalability with large data sets. It improves the prediction performance. It gives an intuitive rationale for the recommendations. The disadvantages with this approach are in the expensive model building. One needs to have a tradeoff between prediction performance and scalability. One can lose useful information due to reduction models. A number of models have difficulty explaining the predictions.

Data mining (the analysis step of the Knowledge Discovery in Databases process, or KDD), a relatively young and interdisciplinary field of computer science, is the process of extracting patterns from large data sets by combining methods from statistics and artificial intelligence with database management. With recent tremendous technical advances in processing power, storage capacity, and inter-connectivity of computer technology, data mining is seen as an increasingly important tool by modern business to transform unprecedented quantities of digital data into business intelligence giving an informational advantage. It is currently used in a wide range of profiling practices, such as marketing, surveillance, fraud detection, and scientific discovery. The growing consensus that data mining can bring real value has led to an explosion in demand for novel data mining technologies. The related terms data dredging, data fishing and data snooping refer to the use of data mining methods to sample parts of a larger population data set that are (or may be) too small for reliable statistical inferences to be made about the validity of any patterns discovered. These methods can, however, be used in creating new hypotheses to test against the larger data populations.

In print media, ranging from magazines to promotional publications, personalization uses databases of individual recipients' information. Not only does the written document address itself by name to the reader, but the advertising is targeted to the recipient's demographics or interests using fields within the database, such as "first name", "last name", "company", etc.

The term "personalization" should not be confused with variable data, which is a much more granular method of marketing that leverages both images and text with the medium, not just fields within a database. Although personalized children's books are created by companies who are using and leveraging all the strengths of Variable Data Printing. This allows for full image and text variability within a printed book.

Promotional items industry (mugs, T-shirts, keychains, balls etc.) are regularly personalized. Personalized children's storybooks—wherein the child becomes the protagonist, with the name and image of the child personalized—are also popular. Personalized CDs for children also exist. With the advent of digital printing, personalized calendars that start in any month, Birthday Cards, cards, e-cards, posters and Photo Book can also be obtained.

Advertising mail, also known as *direct mail, junk mail,* or *admail,* is the delivery of advertising material to recipients of postal mail. The delivery of advertising mail forms a large and growing service for many postal services, and direct-mail marketing forms a significant portion of the direct marketing industry. Some organizations attempt to help people opt out of receiving advertising mail, in many cases motivated by a concern over its negative environmental impact. Advertising mail includes advertising circulars, catalogs, CDs, "pre-approved" credit card applications, and other commercial merchandising materials delivered to both homes and businesses. It may be addressed to pre-selected individuals, or unaddressed and delivered on a neighborhood-by-neighborhood basis.

Postal systems have enacted lower rates for buyers of bulk mail permits. In order to qualify for these rates, marketers must format and sort the mail in specific ways-which reduces the handling required by the postal service.

Direct mail is a common form of direct marketing, and may be employed by for-profit businesses, charities and other non-profits, political campaigns, and other organizations. Advertisers often refine direct mail practices into targeted mailing, in which mail is sent out following database analysis to select recipients considered most likely to respond positively. For example a person who has demonstrated an interest in golf may receive direct mail for golf related products or perhaps for goods and services that are appropriate for golfers. This use of database analysis is a type of database marketing. Alternatively, unaddressed direct mail may be sent on a neighborhood-by-neighborhood basis. Whether at the individual or neighborhood level, direct mail marketing allows recipients to be targeted, attempting to match the demographic profile of the recipients to one most closely matching that of likely customers. Individually targeted direct mail may be tailored based on previous transactions and gathered data. For example, all male recipients of an offer may receive a personalized package with a man's picture on the cover, while all female recipients receive a picture of a woman.

Mass personalization is defined as custom tailoring by a company in accordance with its end users tastes and preferences. The main difference between mass customization and mass personalization is that customization is the ability for a company to give its customers an opportunity to create and choose product to certain specifications, but does have limits.

ADVANTAGES OF PERSONALIZATION AND MASS CUSTOMIZATION

Sphere Sovereignty and Discretionary Control: Users like to have the sphere sovereignty and elements of discretionary control that personalization provides.

Save time: Eliminate repetitive tasks; remember transactional details; recognize habits and shorten the path to engage in such habits (example: frequently called numbers on a phone should automatically go into the phone's memory).

Save money: Prevent redundant work (example: make it easier for employees and suppliers to know someone else has already solved the problem that they are currently facing); eliminate service components unnecessary to a customer; identify lower-cost solutions that meet all other specifications.

Better information: Provide training; filter out information not relevant to a person; provide more specific information that is increasingly relevant to a person's interests; increase the reliability of information; replace "average" information with information specific to that person's environment.

Address ongoing needs, challenges, or opportunities: Provide one-stop services; allow flexibility in work hours, job responsibilities, and benefits; accommodate unique personal preferences (example: allow employees to customize their office space, within certain boundaries); recognize and reward achievement with special treatment.

Personalization allows a company to tailor a specific product in accordance with individual standards, tastes and preferences. For example, baseball jerseys can be customized based on size, colour, team and logo, however there are a finite number of choices for these variables to choose. To personalize a jersey, a name or number can be administered to it as well as custom fitting. The emergence of e-commerce has allowed for the personalization of clothing as well as the customization of audio CD's and downloading of music as well as graphic design for personal websites from the comfort of one's own home. Computer companies have been widely regarded as a market leader in made to order desktops or notebooks for high-performance and entertainment needs. Consumers are able to place orders based on product family, usage, price range, processor, and form factors. This customization ensures that each purchaser can view the merchandise available in order to make an informed decision.

DISADVANTAGES TO PERSONALIZATION

No matter how remarkable or laudable a company's efforts at personalization, there will always be some people who simply are not interested. Every firm must be prepared to recognize and instantly accommodate any of the motivating factors that would cause a person to decide he or she doesn't want any sort of personalization. Technological barriers mean that it can be difficult to accurately deploy personalization solutions. For example, the technology to easily type and enter information on a TV is limited. Most remote controllers can only interact with the TV on a basic level, which makes filling out any kind of personal profile tedious. However, this can be over come with personalization on the mobile or web applications, or by developing implicit profiles.

From an individual's perspective, there are numerous situations or attitudes that make personalization unwelcome.

Anonymity preferred. There are many reasons why people might not want to be identified, from the innocent-it's a birthday present they don't want their spouse to discover in advance on their credit card statement-to the unethical or illegal. Some people are simply private, and prefer to mind their own business and let others mind theirs. Others recognize the growing infringements on private space and choose to take the cautious route. A. Michael Froomkin, associate professor at the University of Miami School of Law, wrote, "Anonymity may be the primary tool available to citizens to combat the compilation and analysis of personal profile data, although data protection laws also may have some effect".

Lack of relevance. People do not want a relationship with companies that have no relevance to them. Computer programmers have no interest in getting to know an executive recruiter who only places sales executives. Homeowners who only buy the finest products for their home will not be interested in a cut-rate furniture store. If you've never been to Arkansas, never plan to go there, and don't know anyone there, you don't want to be on the mailing list of the Arkansas Tourism Board. On the Web, companies constantly ignore this factor and ask individuals for information before demonstrating to the person's satisfaction that their services are relevant. The prime example is companies that insist people fill out a lengthy form before they can gain access to a demo or to additional information. If a company asks people for information before it has demonstrated relevance, between 30 and 50 percent-depending on which statistics you believe-will lie to prevent revealing personal information.

Lack of credibility. If you don't trust a company, it becomes a relationship of last resort. Unless you have no choice, you don't want to deal with it. People don't need proof that a company deserves to be in this category. Often, a small suggestion that this might be the case is enough to justify caution.

Lack of security. Good intentions aren't enough. If a company fails to protect its assets, and those of its stakeholders, then people will not be willing to share anything of value with the firm. Security is like sausage making: the more you know about it, the less likely you are to be comfortable. People have real reasons to fear that today's centralized networks are not secure, because they frequently are not. Technology firms are working to solve security problems, although most admit that security is a process, not a single technological solution. There are no quick fixes.

Impossible. Sometimes, people just aren't able to take advantage of attractive offers. If a company, local government, spouse, or neighborhood forbids a person from moving forward, that's life. Likewise, if people lack the ability to accept personalization-perhaps they lack a sophisticated enough cell phone, or a fast enough Web connection-it won't happen.

Infrequent contact. People will have little interest in establishing a relationship with a cab driver in a city they rarely visit, or with the company that installs their new septic system (a once-in-twenty-five-years event.) Companies get around this limitation by broadening their services to increase the frequency of contacts. Hewlett-Packard's printer division used to focus on selling printers; now the firm realizes it can make more money selling printer cartridges, as well as paper, and in the process increase the frequency of its interactions with customers.

Little value placed on potential benefits. People may not recognize the value in offered personalization, such as when firms offer to customize product offers. Many people don't want to receive any such offers, period. Employees who are offered personalized training may not value it if they were unimpressed with their previous experiences with the training unit, and thus believe that even personalization won't make the time invested worthwhile.

As companies move towards the personal-and the number of interactions increases-it's important to gain greater objectivity about the attractiveness of a firm's offers. Today, in the early stages of our shift towards increasingly personal business relationships, most personalization is still superficial, and way too much of it is mainly personalized marketing. No matter how targeted advertising becomes, it still won't be anything more than a means to an end, and too much of it is flat-out annoying. People tolerate occasional annoyances, but when annoyances multiply, they begin to reek of harassment.

Even highly attractive offers won't make a difference to a person who doesn't value the potential benefits. Think about a new knowledge management system that theoretically delivers "better" information by filtering out "less relevant" citations. Many researchers may cringe at the thought, because they succeed by looking at raw data and thus understanding at a deeper level the background and related elements of a given situation.

Advantages

According to marketing terms "B2C businesses played a large role in the rapid development of the commercial Internet in the late 20th century. Large sums of venture capital flowed to consumers in the form of free online services and discounted shopping, spurring adoption of the new medium".

Business to Consumer e-consumer quickly developed as an alternative way for companies to sell more products to a larger market. B2C e-commerce provided not only multiple advantages to a company but also to the consumers.

The main advantages for both the business and consumer are that by opening their market up to B2C e-commerce trade they are reducing transactions costs. Businesses usually ship their products to a number of stores to make them visible to the consumer.

However, by using B2C commerce they can instead showcase all of their products on the internet which reduces the cost of transaction. B2C also allows their customers to better access information about different product and sellers which broadens the selection available to their customers. Business to consumer ecommerce is valuable to the economy because it creates a more unique way for businesses and consumers to interact.

Unique Attributes

- *Negotiation*: Selling to another business involves haggling over prices, delivery and product specifications. Not so with most consumer sales. That makes it easier for retailers to put a catalog online, and it's why the first B2C applications were for buying finished goods or commodities that are simple to describe and price.
- *Integration*: Retailers don't have to integrate with their customers' systems. Companies selling to other businesses, however, need to make sure they can communicate without human intervention.

CHAPTER

8

Sales Lead

A *sales lead,* or Sales Lead, is the identification of a person or entity that has the interest and authority to purchase a product or service. This step represents the first stage of a sales process. The lead may have a corporation or business associated (a B2B lead) with the person(s). Sales leads are generic leads-i.e a person signs up for a type of offer, instead of a particular company or brand. come from either lead generation companies processes such as trade fair | trade shows, direct marketing, advertising, Internet marketing, spam, gimmicks, or from sales person prospecting activities such as cold calling. For a sales lead to qualify as a sales prospect, or equivalently to move a lead from the process step sales lead to the process sales prospect, qualification must be performed and evaluated. Typically this involves identifying by direct interrogation the lead's product applicability, availability of funding and time frame for purchase. This is also the entry point of a sales tunnel, sales funnel or sales pipeline.

Some companies providing sales leads become the business's one source of leads by integrating outbound calling with email and postal campaigns to create a multi-touch lead.

Related to the idea of multi-touch leads is the "Seven Contact to Sale Theory", which delivers leads that start with an outbound call, followed by an email and sometimes postal piece. By the time the lead purchaser gets the lead, the customer is familiar with their brand and has an opportunity to request additional information.

When buying internet leads from a marketing company there are a wide range of different products depending on how the leads are sold and the lead companies polices. Exclusive internet leads are sold to one company, but depending on the company may be sold again the next day as a shared lead or put into a cherry picking system. Shared leads are sold to multiple companies, each lead company has a different policy on the number of times sold as the more a lead is sold the less value/quality it becomes. Many leads are sold as aged, this means the lead is anywhere from 1day to over a year old although they are usually sold based on different such as 1-7, 30-60, 60–90 days old. Once a qualified lead exists, additional operations may be performed such as background research on the lead's employer, general market of the lead, contact information beyond that provided initially or other information useful for contacting and evaluating a lead for elevation to prospect, the next sales step.

In recent years, the industry has moved away from the "shared" sales leads system, where one lead is resold to different companies. Instead advertisers are increasingly deploying marketing lead programs. As opposed to sales leads, marketing leads are not generic and are generated for a particular brand (e.g. a mom signing up for a specific brand such as HUGGIES as opposed to "diapers").

Sales leads are typically generated for closing a sale. As a result, they are information heavy-a sales lead would contain not only the basic information of a person (such as First Name, Last Name, Email, etc), but also more detailed information such as FICO Score, Household Income, etc. In complete contrast, marketing leads contain only the basic contact information of a person, such as Name, Email and Social Networking handle. Advertisers use the information contained in a marketing lead to build a long-term relationship with the consumer via email, Facebook, Twitter or a brand community site. If a sales lead eventually makes a purchase, this is called conversion and a *closed sale*. The ratio of sales leads that convert is often referred to as the conversion rate, a way to measure the effectiveness of a sales process, sales team, or sales person.

LEAD SOURCES

Leads can be generated by many different marketing campaigns or can have many different sources. Leads can be generated through mailings (fax, paper and email), fairs and trade markets, phone (call centers), database marketing and websites. Leads from websites are often called internet leads and are set apart from the other mentioned generating methods as internet applications can be submitted and send to the sales agent within minutes over the internet providing a chance to have a conversation with the lead while the sale is still fresh in their head. This is called a "real time" although each lead provider has a different definition of how long the time period.

Another lead product is called a *live transfer lead*. These leads are generated in a variety of ways by different lead generation companies. The main difference is how the leads are generated. Customer initiated live call transfers are generated when a customer calls into a call center off of advertisements, educational blogs, landing pages, etc. The call center (domestic or foreign) depending on the company may screen the lead and gather information to provide the business as well as make sure they are both motivated and qualified. Another option is to generate them by a dialer that dials a set of phone numbers, plays a message to the individuals and then those individuals have the opportunity to press 1 to be connected to a live agent. Sometimes live lead transfers are sent to a call center agent who then qualifies the individual before sending to the sales agent.

Another way to generate leads could be referring to business intelligence/information portals like Database101, Go Leads (for North America), Kompass (for Europe) or Protel Associates Ltd. The advantage of using such services is that they allow you a single point of reference to search through industries for relevant companies and find out relevant key contacts. Most of such sources are paid though but they do offer instant results with minimum amount of effort. Other channels of sales leads are Google adwords (covered under internet marketing), ads in trade publications/portals which increase website traffic. Membership in associations like Direct Marketing Association is also a viable option which advises and helps its members in generating leads. Another type of strongly sought after leads are called "organic lead". These are often confused with internet leads because the generating source is internet. While they could be considered a form of internet lead, these leads are those prospects that surf to a website through an organic channel such as search engine or inbound link and later become a lead. These are very similar to walk-in clients in retail world. Because they are not generated, they are referred to as organic. High demand for these leads is primarily because they have higher conversion rate.

SALES PROCESS

A sales process, also known as a sales tunnel or a sales funnel, is a systematic approach to selling a product or service. A growing body of published literature approaches the sales process from the point of view of an engineering discipline. Reasons for having a well thought-out sales process include seller and buyer risk management, standardized customer interaction in sales, and scalable revenue generation. A major advantage of approaching the subject of sales from a "process point of view" is that it offers a host of well-tested design and improvement tools from other successful disciplines and process-oriented industries. In turn, this offers potential for quicker progress. Quality expert Joseph Juran observed, "There should be no reason our familiar principles of quality and process engineering would not work in the sales process" A sales team's fundamental job is to move a greater number of larger deals through the sales process in less time.

Mapping a process provides a starting point for further careful analysis and continuous improvement. Diagramming a process flow is considered to be one of the seven basic quality improvement tools Elements in the list above (among many others) have been described and/or flow-charted in the published literature. Some examples have primarily focused on functions performed by a sales "department" At least one cross-functional approach depicts and integrates a variety of interdependent areas, such as sales, marketing, customer service, and information systems.

From a seller's point of view, a sales process mitigates risk by stage-gating deals based on collection of information or execution of procedures that gate movement to the next step-Of the large number of initially interested persons on the narrow end of orders only a fraction of the initially interested people remain and actually place an order. This controls seller resource expenditure on non-performing deals. Ideally this also prevents buyers from purchasing products they don't need though such a benefit requires ethical intentions by the seller. Because of the uncertainty of this assurance, buyers often have a buying or purchasing process. A formalized sales process is generally more common for companies that either have complex sales cycles, large revenue risks that require systematic assurance of revenue generation, and/or those that choose to use a more consultative sales approach (e.g. Saturn, IBM, Hewlett-Packard).

An effective sales process can be described through steps that walk a salesperson from meeting the prospect all the way through closing the sale. Often a bad sales experience can be analyzed and shown to have skipped key steps. This is where a good sales process mitigates risk for both buyer and seller. A solid sales process also has the dramatic impact of forecasting accuracy and predictability in revenue results. Many companies develop their own sales process; however, off the shelf versions are available from a number of companies in the sales performance improvement industry. A large number of these methods have been described by their promoters in books available to the public, primarily addressing tactics employed by an individual sales representative. These provide a customizable process and a set of electronic tools that can be freestanding or can be integrated if required with the company's SFA, CRM, or other opportunity management system.

In the art of selling, *Need identification* is one stage in a seven stage personal selling process. In this stage the salesperson takes a qualified prospect through a series of question and answer sessions in order to identify the requirements of the prospect. During this step, the salesperson will attempt to help the buyer identify and quantify a business need or a "gap" between where the client is today and where they would like to be in the future. Based on that gap, needs can be clarified to determine if the solution will fill all, or part of the overall gap. From this procedure the sale person is able to come up with a proposal suggesting various products/ services that will suffice the need as presented by the prospect.

Seven Stages

The full Selling Process consists of:

- 1-pre-approach
- 2-approach
- 3-need identification
- 4-presentation
- 5-handling objections
- 6-closing the sale
- 7-post-sale follow-up.

An *qualified prospect* is an organization which has expressed the need for the products or services of the seller. There is much debate in the sales profession as to what constitutes an actual "qualified" prospect. Most sales professionals apply their own unique set of variables in order to determine whether a prospect is actually "qualified". In general terms, sales professionals need to know a set of discrete data in order to determine whether or not the "prospect" will become qualified. These variables may include: business needs, authorization to transact business (financial or operational), money or budget and an "economic buyer" or in other words, who would stand to benefit the most (or lose the most) if the good or service were to be acquired (or not acquired).

Business Proposal

A *business proposal* is a written offer from a seller to a prospective buyer. Business proposals are often a key step in the complex sales process—i.e., whenever a buyer considers more than price in a purchase. There are three distinct categories of business proposals:

- formally solicited
- informally solicited
- unsolicited.

Solicited proposals are written in response to published requirements, contained in a Request for Proposal (RFP), Request for Quotation (RFQ), Request for Information (RFI) or an Invitation For Bid (IFB). RFPs provide detailed specifications of what the customers wants to buy and sometimes include directions for preparing the proposal, as well as evaluation criteria the customer will use to evaluate offers. Customers issue RFPs when their needs cannot be met with generally available products or services. RFIs are issues to qualify the vendors who are interested in providing service/products for specific requirements. Based on the response to RFI, detailed RFP is issued to qualified vendors who the organization believes can provide desired services. Proposals in response to RFPs are seldom less than 10 pages and sometimes reach 1,000's of pages, without cost data.

Customers issue RFQs when they want to buy large amounts of a commodity and price is not the only issue—for example, when availability or delivering or service are considerations. RFQs can be very detailed, so proposals written to RFQs can be lengthy but generally much shorter than an RFP-proposal. RFQ proposals consist primarily of cost data, with small narratives addressing customer issues, such as quality control.

Customers issue IFBs when they are buying some service, such as construction. The requirements are detailed, but the primary consideration is price. For example, a customer provides architectural blueprints for contractors to bid on. These proposals can be lengthy but most of the length comes from cost-estimating data and detailed schedules. Sometimes before a customer issues an RFP or RFQ or IFB, the customer will issue a Request for Information (RFI). The purpose of the

RFI is to gain "marketing intelligence" about what products, services, and vendors are available. RFIs are used to shape final RFPs, RFQs, and IFBs, so potential vendors take great care in responding to these requests, hoping to shape the eventual formal solicitation toward their products or services.

Informally solicited proposals are typically the result of conversations held between a vendor and a prospective customer. The customer is interested enough in a product or service to ask for a proposal. Typically, the customer does not ask for competing proposals from other vendors. This type of proposal is known as a sole-source proposal. There are no formal requirements to respond to, just the information gleaned from customer meetings. These proposals are typically less than 25-pages, with many less than 5 pages. Unsolicited proposals are marketing brochures. They are always generic, with no direct connection between customer needs or specified requirements. Vendors use them to introduce a product or service to a prospective customer. They are often used as "leave-behinds" at the end of initial meetings with customers or "give-aways" at trade shows or other public meetings. They are not designed to close a sale, just introduce the possibility of a sale. A proposal puts the buyer's requirements in a context that favors the sellers products and services, and educates the buyer about the capabilities of the seller in satisfying their needs. A successful proposal results in a sale, where both parties get what they want, a win-win situation.

COMPONENTS

Formally Solicited Proposal

1. Requirements Matrix, which matches customer requirements with the paragraph and page numbers of where those requirements are addressed in the proposal.
2. Executive Summary, which outlines the primary benefits of the vendors's solutions to the customer's requirements.

3. Technical Volume, which demonstrates how each requirement will be met.
4. Management Volume, which describes how the program will be managed.
5. *Cost Volume, which provides all costing data, as well as implementation plans and schedules.*

Informally Solicited Business Proposal

1. A description of the seller's capabilities or products
2. A discussion of key issues.
3. A description of the buyer's specifications and how they will be met.
4. The cost of the offering.
5. A schedule for delivery of the products or services.
6. Proof of prior experience, i.e. Testimonials from previous customers, Descriptions of previous projects.

Negotiation is a dialogue between two or more people or parties, intended to reach an understanding, resolve point of difference, or gain advantage in outcome of dialogue, to produce an agreement upon courses of action, to bargain for individual or collective advantage, to craft outcomes to satisfy various interests of two person/parties involved in negotiation process. Negotiation is a process where each party involved in negotiating tries to gain an advantage for themselves by the end of the process. Negotiation is intended to aim at compromise. Negotiation occurs in business, non-profit organizations, government branches, legal proceedings, among nations and in personal situations such as marriage, divorce, parenting, and everyday life. The study of the subject is called negotiation *theory*. Professional negotiators are often specialized, such as union negotiators, leverage buyout negotiators, peace negotiators, hostage negotiators, or may work under other titles, such as diplomats, legislators or brokers. Negotiation typically manifests itself with a trained negotiator acting on behalf of a particular organization or position. It can be compared to mediation where a neutral third party listens to each side's arguments and attempts to help craft an agreement between the parties. It is also related to arbitration which, as with a legal proceeding, both sides make an argument as to the merits of their "case" and then the arbitrator decides the outcome for both parties. There are many different ways to segment negotiation to gain a greater understanding of the essential parts. One view of negotiation involves three basic elements: *process, behavior* and *substance.* The process refers to how the parties negotiate: the context of the negotiations, the parties to the negotiations, the tactics used by the parties, and the sequence and stages in which all of these play out. Behavior refers to the relationships among these parties, the communication between them and the styles they adopt. The substance refers to what the parties negotiate over: the agenda, the issues (positions and-more helpfully-interests), the options, and the agreement(s) reached at the end.

Another view of negotiation comprises 4 elements: strategy, process and tools, and tactics. Strategy comprises the top level goals-typically including relationship and the final outcome. Processes and tools include the steps that will be followed and the roles taken in both preparing for and negotiating with the other parties. Tactics include more detailed statements and actions and responses to others' statements and actions. Some add to this persuasion and influence, asserting that these have become integral to modern day negotiation success, and so should not be omitted. Skilled negotiators may use a variety of tactics ranging from negotiation hypnosis, to a straight forward presentation of demands or setting of preconditions to more deceptive approaches such as cherry picking. Intimidation and salami tactics may also play a part in swaying the outcome of negotiations. Another negotiation tactic is bad guy/good guy. Bad guy/good guy tactic is when one negotiator acts as a bad guy by using anger and threats. The other negotiator acts as a good guy by being considerate and understanding. The good guy blames the bad guy for all the difficulties while trying to get concessions and agreement from the opponent. When a party pretends to negotiate, but secretly has no intention of compromising, the negotiator is considered to be negotiating in bad faith.

The new creative approach : Perhaps the most famous negotiation parable involves an argument over an orange. The most obvious approach was to simply cut it in half, each person getting a fair share. But, when the negotiators began talking to each other, exchanging information about their interests, a better solution to the problem became obvious. The person wanting the orange for juice for breakfast took that part and the person wanting the rind for making marmalade took that part. Both sides ended up with more. Neither agreement is particularly creative. The parable of the orange becomes a story about creativity when both parties decide to cooperate in planting an orange tree or even an orchard. In a similar way, Boeing buys composite plastic wings for its new 787 Dream liner designed and manufactured by Japanese suppliers, and then sells the completed 787s back to Japanese airlines, all with a nice subsidy from the Japanese government. This is what is meant by creativity in negotiations. At business schools these days much is being learned about creative processes. Courses are offered and dissertations offered with "innovation" as the key buzz word at academic conferences and in corporate boardrooms. And, the more heard about innovation and creative processes the greater is the appreciation that the Japanese approach to negotiations, by nature, uses many of the techniques commonly emphasized in any discussion of creative processes. Indeed, there appears to be a deeply fundamental explanation why the Japanese have been able to build such a successful society despite their lack of natural resources and relative isolation. While Japanese society does have its own obstacles to creativity-hierarchy and collectivism are two-they have developed a negotiation style that in many ways obviates such disadvantages. Indeed, the ten new rules for global negotiations advocated by Hernandez and Graham nicely coincide with an approach that comes naturally to the Japanese:

1. Accept only creative outcomes
2. Understand cultures, especially your own.
3. Don't just adjust to cultural differences, exploit them.
4. Gather intelligence and reconnoiter the terrain.

5. Design the information flow and process of meetings.
6. Invest in personal relationships.
7. Persuade with questions. Seek information and understanding.
8. Make no concessions until the end.
9. Use techniques of creativity
10. Continue creativity after negotiations.

10 Ways to Generate More Ideas.

1. Establish common goals of what this "collaboration" would create. A more workable deal? Some common long term goals? A closer partnership?
2. Establish the rules of engagement. The purpose of the exercise is to resolve differences in creative ways that work better for both parties. All ideas are possibilities, and research shows that combining ideas from different cultures can result in better outcomes than those from a single culture.
3. Trust is key, and difficult to establish in many cultures. Certain techniques might speed that process a little. Being offsite, for example. Establishing physical proximity that unconsciously signals intimacy.
4. Add diversity (gender, culture, extroverts, different work specialties, experts, outsiders) to the group. Indeed, the diversity associated with international teams and alliances is the real goldmine of creativity in negotiations.
5. Use storytelling. This both helps establish who you are and what point of view you are bringing to this collaboration.
6. Work in small groups. Add physical movement. Tell the participants to relax, play, sing, have fun, and silence is ok.
7. Work holistically and using visuals. If, for example, there are three sticking points where neither side is happy, agree to work on those points by spending a short time-10 minutes-on each point where both sides offer "crazy" suggestions. Use techniques of

improvisation. Neither side should be offended by the crazy ideas. No one should criticize. Explain that by exploring crazy ideas that better ideas are often generated.

8. Sleep on it. This enables the unconscious to work on the problems, and gives negotiators time to collect opinions before meeting again the next day. Other kinds of breaks, coffee, etc. are also helpful. The overnight part is particularly important. Anthropologist and consumer expert Clotaire Rapaille suggests that the transitions between wakefulness and sleep allow new kinds of thinking "...calming their brainwaves, getting them to that tranquil point just before sleep".
9. Doing this process over several sessions allows both sides to feel that progress is being made, and actually generates better and more polished ideas that both sides can invest in.
10. It is the process of creating something together, rather than the specific proposals, which creates bonding around a shared task and establishes new ways of working together. Each side feels honored and all can feel that something is being accomplished.

Other Negotiation Styles

Shell identified five styles/responses to negotiation. Individuals can often have strong dispositions towards numerous styles; the style used during a negotiation depends on the context and the interests of the other party, among other factors. In addition, styles can change over time.

1. *Accommodating*: Individuals who enjoy solving the other party's problems and preserving personal relationships. Accommodators are sensitive to the emotional states, body language, and verbal signals of the other parties. They can, however, feel taken advantage of in situations when the other party places little emphasis on the relationship.

2. *Avoiding*: Individuals who do not like to negotiate and don't do it unless warranted. When negotiating, avoiders tend to defer and dodge the confrontational aspects of negotiating; however, they may be perceived as tactful and diplomatic.
3. *Collaborating*: Individuals who enjoy negotiations that involve solving tough problems in creative ways. Collaborators are good at using negotiations to understand the concerns and interests of the other parties. They can, however, create problems by transforming simple situations into more complex ones.
4. *Competing*: Individuals who enjoy negotiations because they present an opportunity to win something. Competitive negotiators have strong instincts for all aspects of negotiating and are often strategic. Because their style can dominate the bargaining process, competitive negotiators often neglect the importance of relationships.
5. *Compromising*: Individuals who are eager to close the deal by doing what is fair and equal for all parties involved in the negotiation. Compromisers can be useful when there is limited time to complete the deal; however, compromisers often unnecessarily rush the negotiation process and make concessions too quickly.

ADVERSARY OR PARTNER?

Clearly, these two basically different ways of negotiating will require different approaches. To ignore this can be devastating for the result, but it all too often happens. Because in the distributive approach each negotiator is battling for the largest possible piece of the pie, it may be quite appropriate-within certain limits-to regard the other side more as an adversary than a partner and to take a somewhat harder line. This would however be less appropriate if the idea were to hammer out an arrangement that is in the best interest of both sides. If both win, it's only of secondary importance which one has the greater advantage. A good agreement is not one with maximum gain, but optimum gain. This does not by any means suggest that we should give up our own advantage for nothing. But a cooperative attitude will regularly pay dividends. What is gained is not at the expense of the other, but with him.

Bad faith negotiation: Bad faith is a concept in negotiation theory whereby parties pretend to reason to reach settlement, but have no intention to do so, for example, one political party may pretend to negotiate, with no intention to compromise, for political effect.

Emotion in negotiation: Emotions play an important part in the negotiation process, although it is only in recent years that their effect is being studied. Emotions have the potential to play either a positive or negative role in negotiation. During negotiations, the decision as to whether or not to settle, rests in part on emotional factors. Negative emotions can cause intense and even irrational behavior, and can cause conflicts to escalate and negotiations to break down, but may be instrumental in attaining concessions. On the other hand, positive emotions often facilitate reaching an agreement and help to maximize joint gains, but can also be instrumental in attaining concessions. Positive and negative discrete emotions can be strategically displayed to influence task and relational outcomes.

Affect effect: Dispositional affects affect the various stages of the negotiation process: which strategies are planned to be used, which strategies are actually chosen, the way the other party and his or her intentions are perceived, their willingness to reach an agreement and the final negotiated outcomes. Positive affectivity (PA) and negative affectivity (NA) of one or more of the negotiating sides can lead to very different outcomes.

Positive affect in negotiation: Even before the negotiation process starts, people in a positive mood have more confidence, and higher tendencies to plan to use a cooperative strategy. During the negotiation, negotiators who are in a positive mood tend to enjoy the interaction more, show less contentious behavior, use less aggressive tactics and more cooperative strategies. This in turn increases the likelihood that parties will reach their instrumental goals, and enhance the ability to find integrative gains. Indeed, compared with negotiators with negative or natural affectivity, negotiators with positive affectivity reached more agreements and tended to honor those agreements more. Those favorable outcomes are due to better decision making processes, such as flexible thinking, creative problem solving, respect for others' perspectives, willingness to take risks and higher confidence. Post negotiation positive affect has beneficial consequences as well. It increases satisfaction with achieved outcome and influences one's desire for future interactions. The PA aroused by reaching an agreement facilitates the dyadic relationship, which result in affective commitment that sets the stage for subsequent interactions. PA also has its drawbacks: it distorts perception of self performance, such that performance is judged to be relatively better than it actually is. Thus, studies involving self reports on achieved outcomes might be biased.

Negative affect has detrimental effects on various stages in the negotiation process. Although various negative emotions affect negotiation outcomes, by far the most researched is anger. Angry negotiators plan to use more competitive strategies and to cooperate less, even before the negotiation starts. These competitive strategies are related to reduced joint outcomes. During negotiations, anger disrupts the process by reducing the level of trust, clouding parties' judgment, narrowing parties' focus of attention and changing their central goal from reaching agreement to retaliating against the other side. Angry negotiators pay less attention to opponent's interests and are less accurate in judging their interests, thus achieve lower joint gains. Moreover, because anger makes negotiators more self-centered in their preferences, it increases the likelihood that they will reject profitable offers. Opponents who really get angry (or cry, or otherwise lose control) are more likely to make errors :make sure they are in your favor. Anger doesn't help in achieving negotiation goals either: it reduces joint gains and does not help to boost personal. gains, as angry negotiators don't succeed in claiming more for themselves. Moreover, negative emotions lead to acceptance of settlements that are not in the positive utility function but rather have a negative utility. However, expression of negative emotions during negotiation can sometimes be beneficial: legitimately expressed anger can be an effective way to show one's commitment, sincerity, and needs. Moreover, although NA reduces gains in integrative tasks, it is a better strategy than PA in distributive tasks (such as zero-sum). In his work on negative affect arousal and white noise, Seidner found support for the existence of a negative affect arousal mechanism through observations regarding the devaluation of speakers from other ethnic origins". Negotiation may be negatively affected, in turn, by submerged hostility toward an ethnic or gender group.

Conditions for Emotion Affect in Negotiation

Research indicates that negotiator's emotions do not necessarily affect the negotiation process. Albarracýn et al. (2003) suggested that there are two conditions for emotional affect, both related to the ability (presence of environmental or cognitive disturbances) and the motivation:

1. Identification of the affect: requires high motivation, high ability or both.
2. Determination that the affect is relevant and important for the judgment: requires that either the motivation, the ability or both are low.

According to this model, emotions are expected to affect negotiations only when one is high and the other is low. When both ability and motivation are low the affect will not be identified, and when both are high the affect will be identify but discounted as irrelevant for judgement. A possible implication of this model is, for example, that the positive effects PA has on negotiations will be seen only when either motivation or ability are low.

THE EFFECT OF THE PARTNER'S EMOTIONS

Most studies on emotion in negotiations focus on the effect of the negotiator's own emotions on the process. However, what the other party feels might be just as important, as group emotions are known to affect processes both at the group and the personal levels. When it comes to negotiations, trust in the other party is a necessary condition for its emotion to affect, and visibility enhances the effect. Emotions contribute to negotiation processes by signaling what one feels and thinks and can thus prevent the other party from engaging in destructive behaviors and to indicate what steps should be taken next: PA signals to keep in the same way, while NA points that mental or behavioral adjustments are needed. Partner's emotions can have two basic effects on negotiator's emotions and behavior: mimetic/reciprocal or complementary. For example, disappointment or sadness might lead to compassion and more cooperation. In a study by Butt *et. al.* (2005) which simulated real multi-phase negotiation, most people reacted to the partner's emotions in reciprocal, rather than complementary, manner. Specific emotions were found to have different effects on the opponent's feelings and strategies chosen:

- Anger caused the opponents to place lower demands and to concede more in a zero-sum negotiation, but also to evaluate the negotiation less favorably. It provoked both dominating and yielding behaviors of the opponent.
- Pride led to more integrative and compromise strategies by the partner.
- Guilt or regret expressed by the negotiator led to better impression of him by the opponent, however it also led the opponent to place higher demands. On the other hand, personal guilt was related to more satisfaction with what one achieved.
- Worry or disappointment left bad impression on the opponent, but led to relatively lower demands by the opponent.

Problems with Lab Negotiation Studies

Negotiation is a rather complex interaction. Capturing all its complexity is a very difficult task, let alone isolating and controlling only certain aspects of it. For this reason most negotiation studies are done under laboratory conditions, and focus only on some aspects. Although lab studies have their advantages, they do have major drawbacks when studying emotions:

- Emotions in lab studies are usually manipulated and are therefore relatively 'cold' (not intense). Although those 'cold' emotions might be enough to show effects, they are qualitatively different from the 'hot' emotions often experienced during negotiations.
- In real life there is self-selection to which negotiation one gets into, which effects the emotional commitment, motivation and interests. However this is not the case in lab studies.
- Lab studies tend to focus on relatively few well defined emotions. Real life scenarios provoke a much wider scale of emotions.
- Coding the emotions has a double catch: if done by a third side, some emotions might not be detected as the negotiator sublimates them for strategic reasons. Self report measures might overcome this, but they are usually filled only before or after the process, and if filled during the process might interfere with it.

The pervasive impact of culture on international negotiations.

The primary purpose of this section is to demonstrate the extent of cultural differences in negotiation styles and how these differences can cause problems in international business negotiations. The reader will note that national culture does not determine negotiation behavior. Rather, national culture is one of many factors that influence behavior at the negotiation table, albeit an important one. For example, gender, organizational culture, international experience, industry or regional background can all be important influences as well. Of course, stereotypes of all kinds are dangerous, and international negotiators must get to know the people they are working with, not just their culture, country, or company.

The material here is based on systematic study of international negotiation behavior over the last three decades in which the negotiation styles of more than 1,500 businesspeople in 17 countries (21 cultures) were considered. The work involved interviews with experienced executives and participant observations in the field, as well as behavioral science laboratory work including surveys and analyses of videotaped negotiations. The countries studied were Japan, S. Korea, China (Tianjin, Guangzhou, and Hong Kong), Vietnam, Taiwan, the Philippines, Russia, Israel, Norway, the Czech Republic, Germany, France, the United Kingdom, Spain, Brazil, Mexico, Canada (English-speakers and French-speakers), and the United States. The countries were chosen because they constitute America's most important present and future trading partners.

Looking broadly across the several cultures, two important lessons stand out. The first is that regional generalizations very often are not correct. For example, Japanese and Korean negotiation styles are quite similar in some ways, but in other ways they could not be more different. The second lesson learned from the research is that Japan is an exceptional place: On almost every dimension of negotiation style considered, the Japanese are on or near the end of the scale. For example, the Japanese use the lowest amount of eye contact of the cultures studied. Sometimes, Americans are on the other end. But actually, most of the time Americans are somewhere in the middle. The reader will see this evinced in the data presented in this section. The Japanese approach, however, is most distinct, even sui generis.

Cultural differences cause four kinds of problems in international business negotiations, at the levels of:

- Language
- Nonverbal behaviors
- Values
- Thinking and decision-making processes

The order is important; the problems lower on the list are more serious because they are more subtle. For example, two negotiators would notice immediately if one were speaking Japanese and the other German. The solution to the problem may be as simple as hiring an interpreter or talking in a common third language, or it may be as difficult as learning a language. Regardless of the solution, the problem is obvious. Cultural differences in nonverbal behaviors, on the other hand, are almost always hidden below our awareness. That is to say, in a face-to-face negotiation participants nonverbally—and more subtly—give off and take in a great deal of information. Some experts argue that this information is more important than verbal information. Almost all this signaling goes on below our levels of consciousness. When the nonverbal signals from foreign partners are different, negotiators are most apt to misinterpret them without even being conscious of the mistake. For example, when a French client consistently interrupts, Americans tend to feel uncomfortable without noticing exactly why. In this manner, interpersonal friction often colors business relationships, goes undetected, and, consequently, goes uncorrected. Differences in values and thinking and decision-making processes are hidden even deeper and therefore are even harder to diagnose and therefore cure. These differences are discussed below, starting with language and nonverbal behaviors.

Differences at the Level of Language

Translation problems are often substantial in international negotiations. And, when languages are linguistically distant, greater problems should be anticipated. Particularly daunting can be work in global negotiation. Often the language used is English, but it may be spoken as a second language by most executives at the table. Indeed, native speakers from England, India, and the United States often have trouble understanding one another. Exact translations in international interactions are a goal almost never attained. Moreover, language differences are sometimes exploited in interesting ways. Many senior executives in foreign countries speak and understand some English, but prefer to speak in their "stronger" native language and use an interpreter. Thus, we've see a senior Russian negotiator asking questions in Russian. The interpreter then translated the question for his American counterpart. While the interpreter spoke, the American's attention (gaze direction) was given to the interpreter. However, the Russian's gaze direction was at the American. Therefore, the Russian could carefully and unobtrusively observe the American's facial expressions and nonverbal responses. Additionally, when the American spoke, the senior Russian had twice the response time: Because he understood English, he could formulate his responses during the translation process.

But, there are problems at the level of language beyond translations and interpreters. Data from simulated negotiations are informative. In the study, the verbal behaviors of negotiators in 15 of the cultures (six negotiators in each of the 15 groups) were videotaped. The numbers in the body represent the percentages of statements that were classified into each category listed. That is, 7 percent of the statements made by Japanese negotiators were classified as promises, 4 percent as threats, 7 percent as recommendations, and so on. The verbal bargaining behaviors used by the negotiators during the simulations proved to be surprisingly similar across cultures. Negotiations in all 15 cultures were composed primarily of information-exchange tactics—questions and self-disclosures. Note that the Israelis are on the low end of the continuum of self-disclosures. Their 30 percent (near the Japanese, Spaniards, and the English-speaking Canadians at 34 percent) was the lowest across all 15 groups, suggesting that they are the most reticent about giving (that is, communicating) information. Overall, however, the patterns of verbal tactics used were surprisingly similar across the diverse cultures.

Closing is a sales term which refers to the process of making a sale. The sales sense springs from real estate, where closing is the final step of a transaction. In sales, it is used more generally to mean achievement of the desired outcome, which may be an exchange of money or acquiring a signature. Salespeople are often taught to think of targets not as strangers, but rather as prospective customers who already want or need what is being sold. Such prospects need only be "closed". "Closing" is distinguished from ordinary practices such as explaining a product's benefits or justifying an expense. It is reserved for more artful means of persuasion, which some compare with confidence tricks. For example, a salesman might mention that his product is popular with a person's neighbors, knowing that people tend to follow perceived trends. This is known as the Jones Theory. In automobile dealerships, a "closer" is often a senior salesman experienced in closing difficult deals.

The *deal transaction* is the hub of global commerce. A deal transaction is a unique event where money exchanges hands in return for a product or service. The "transaction experience" is the buying, selling, and marketing cycle defined as the pre-and post-effects of that unique sale. The transaction itself holds a key position as the hub of commerce. Each sale is identified and handled separately as a unique transaction experience. Each time a signature is provided by the buyer, and a sale is consummated by the buying organization, a single transaction has occurred, but the transaction experience may only be half way over.

BUYING CENTER

A *buying center* (also known as a *decision making unit* or *DMU*), in marketing, procurement, and organizational studies, is a group of employees, family members, or members of any type of organization responsible for finalizing major decisions, usually involving a purchase. In a business setting, major purchases typically require input from various parts of the organization, including finance, accounting, purchasing, information technology management, and senior management. Highly technical purchases, such as information systems or production equipment, also require the expertise of technical specialists. In some cases the buying center is an informal ad hoc group, but in other cases, it is a formally sanctioned group with specific mandates, criteria, and procedures. The employees that constitute the buying center will vary depending on the item being purchased.

In a generic sense, there are typically six roles within any buying center. They are:

1. Initiator who suggests purchasing a product or service.
2. Influencers who try to affect the outcome decision with their opinions.
3. Deciders who have the final decision.
4. Buyers who are responsible for the contract.

5. End users of the item being purchased.
6. Gatekeepers who control the flow of information.

Because of the specialized nature of computer and software purchases, many corporations use buying centers that are specialized for information technology acquisition. These specialized buying centers typically receive information about the technology from commercial sources, peers, publications, and experience. In this process, top management, the IT director, IT professionals, and other users participate together to find a solution. A better buying center for marketing might include:

1. Buyers
2. Deciders
3. Gatekeepers
4. Influencers
5. Users

CONVERSION RATE

In internet marketing, *conversion rate* is the ratio of visitors who convert casual content views or website visits into desired actions based on subtle or direct requests from marketers, advertisers, and content creators. If the prospect has visited a marketer's web site, examples of conversion actions might include making an online purchase or submitting a form to request additional information. The Conversion rate is defined as follows:

> Successful conversions are interpreted differently by individual marketers, advertisers, and content creators. To online retailers, for example, a successful conversion may constitute the sale of a product to a consumer whose interest in the item was initially sparked by clicking a banner advertisement. To content creators, however, a successful conversion may refer to a membership registration, newsletter subscription, software download, or other activity that occurs due to a subtle or direct

request from the content creator for the visitor to take the action.

Measures

For web sites that seek to generate offline responses, for example telephone calls or foot traffic to a store, measuring conversions can be difficult because a phone call or visitor is not automatically traced to its source, such as the Yellow Pages, website, or referral. Possible solutions include asking each caller or shopper how they heard about the business and using a toll-free number on the website that forwards to the existing line. For web sites where the response occurs on the site itself, a Conversion funnel can be setup in a site's analytics package to track user behavior.

Methods to Increase the Conversion in E-commerce

Among the many methods to increase the conversion rate, these are the most relevant:

- clear distinction of the website for a certain conversion goal (e.g. "increase sign-ins for newsletter").
- better content (e.g. text, picture, video) of the website that clearly target versus the conversion goal.
- increase usability to reduce the barriers towards the conversion goal and thus reduce the abortion rate.
- good site navigation structure to help users find and browse without thinking too much about where to click.
- show credibility signs like third-party trust logos and good site design to increase trust level of visitor.
- use AIDA (attention, interest, desire, action) to move the user through the conversion funnel.

AIDA is an acronym used in marketing that describes a common list of events that may be undergone when a person is selling a product or service. The term and approach are attributed to American advertising and sales pioneer, E. St. Elmo Lewis. In 1898 Lewis created his AIDA funnel model on customer studies in the US life insurance market to explain the mechanisms of personal selling. Lewis held that the most successful salespeople followed a hierarchical, four layer process using the four cognitive phases that buyers follow when accepting a new idea or purchasing a new product.

- A-Attention (Awareness): attract the attention of the customer.
- I-Interest: raise customer interest by focusing on and demonstrating advantages and benefits (instead of focusing on features, as in traditional advertising).
- D-Desire: convince customers that they want and desire the product or service and that it will satisfy their needs.
- A-Action: lead customers towards taking action and/ or purchasing.

Using a system like this gives one a general understanding of how to target a market effectively. Moving from step to step one loses some percent of prospects.

Conversion Optimization

In internet marketing, conversion optimization, or conversion rate optimization is the method of creating an experience for a website or landing page visitor with the goal of increasing the percentage of visitors that convert into customers. It is also commonly referred to as CRO. Conversion optimization was born out of the need of lead generation and ecommerce internet marketers to improve their website's results. As competition grew on the web during the early 2000s, Internet marketers had to become more measurable with their marketing tactics. They began experimenting with website design and content variations to determine which layouts, copy text, offers and images will improve their conversion rate.

Why conversion optimization: Frequently, when marketers target a pocket of customers that has shown spectacular lift in an ad campaign, they belatedly discover the behavior is not consistent. Online marketing response rates fluctuate widely from hour to hour, segment to segment and offer to offer. This phenomenon can be traced to the difficulty humans have separating chance events from real effects. Using the haystack process, at any given time marketers are limited to examining and drawing conclusions from small samples of data. However, psychologists (led by Kahneman and Tversky) have extensively documented tendencies which find spurious patterns in small samples, thereby explaining why poor decisions are made. Therefore, statistical methodologies can be leveraged to study large samples and mitigate the urge to see patterns where none exists.

These methodologies, or *"conversion optimization"* methods, are then taken a step further to run in a real-time environment. The real-time data collection and subsequent messaging as a result, increases the scale and effectiveness of the online campaign.

How Conversion Rate Optimization Works: Process of increasing website leads and sales without spending money on attracting more visitors by reducing your visitor "bounce rate". Some test methods enable one to monitor which headlines, images and content help one convert more visitors into customers.

There are several approaches to conversion optimization with two main schools of thought prevailing in the last few years. One school is more focused on testing as an approach to discover the best way to increase a website, a campaign or a landing page conversion rates. The other school is focused more on the pretesting stage of the optimization process. In this second approach, the optimization company will invest a considerable amount of time understanding the audience and then creating a targeted message that appeals to that particular audience. Only then willing to deploy testing mechanisms to increase conversion rates. The article "a case against multi-variant testing" outlines some of the reasons testing should not be the only component in conversion optimization work.

WIN-LOSS ANALYTICS

Win-loss analytics involves identifying and analyzing the reasons why a visitor to a website was or wasn't persuaded to engage in a desired action (conversion). This information allows web teams to improve the website's navigation and content, identify individuals that are more likely to convert, to improve marketing efforts Determining why one person engaged in a desired action and another did not has long been a topic of interest in sales, where measurement of conversion has always been possible through sales data.

In contrast, marketing has been mostly concerned with targeting with the masses, and the results of marketing have traditionally been more difficult to accurately measure. With the internet, it is much easier for marketers to collect data for analysis and evaluation in order to understand and demonstrate the effectiveness or ineffectiveness of their efforts and to make changes to improve them.

Win-loss Analytics *vs.* Web Analytics

Web analytics tools have existed since the early days of the internet and are now ubiquitous. These tools provide a bird's eye view of a website's traffic. The information that is gathered allows webmasters to make informed decisions about making changes in order to improve a website.

Win-loss analytics tools track the individual perspectives of each visitor, uncovering who the visitor was, what products they were qualified for, how well they were persuaded, and why they did or didn't convert.

Conversion Funnel

Conversion funnel is a technical term used in e-commerce operations to describe the track a consumer takes through an Internet advertising or search system, navigating an e-commerce web site and finally converting to a sale. The metaphor of a funnel is used to describe the decrease in numbers that occur at each step of the process.

Typically a large number of visitors register as page view on a referring page which is linked to the e-Commerce site either by a banner ad, ad network or conventional link. Only a small proportion of those seeing the advert or link actually click the link. The metric used to describe this ratio is the click-through-rate or CTR and represents to top level of the funnel. Typical banner and advertising click through rates are 0.02% in late 2010 and have decreased over the past three years. Click-though rates are highly sensitive to small changes such as link text, link size, link position and many others and these effects interact cumulatively. The process of understanding which creative material brings the highest click through rate is known as ad optimization.

Once the link is clicked and the visitor to the referring page enters the e-commerce site itself a only a small proportion of visitors typically proceed to the product pages creating further constriction of the metaphorical funnel. Each step the visitor takes further reduces the number of visitors-typically by 30%-80% per page. Adding the product to the shopping cart, registering or filling in contact details and of course payment all further reduce the numbers step-by-step cumulatively along the funnel. The more step, the few visitors get through to becoming paying customers. For this reason sites with similar pricing and products can have hugely different Conversion rate of visitors to customers and therefore greatly differing profits.

CHAPTER

9

Online Marketing

Online Marketing is the art and science of selling products and/or services over digital networks, such as the Internet and cellular phone networks. The art of online marketing involves finding the right online marketing mix of strategies that appeals to your target market and will actually translate into sales. The science of online marketing is the research and analysis that goes into both choosing the online marketing strategies to use and measuring the success of those online marketing strategies.

TYPES OF ONLINE MARKETING

- Ecommerce
- Online Advertising
- Search Engine Marketing
- Email Marketing
- Social Media Marketing
- Article Marketing

And that's definitely just to name a few; more online

marketing strategies are being invented all the time. Online marketing is becoming increasingly important to small businesses of all types. In the past, marketing online was something that local bricks-and-mortar businesses could justifiably ignore. It didn't make sense to waste time and money on online marketing when all your business was local. Now with increasing local search and people's new habit of searching on the Internet first, it matters. I would go so far as to say that all businesses should include some online marketing in their marketing mix.

Basic Strategies any Business Can Use

Want to get into marketing online but wondering what the options are and what online marketing strategies will best fit your business and your marketing budget? This marketing online primer presents an overview of strategies for you to choose from. I recommend choosing and implementing at least three; successful marketing online depends on diversity and persistence for most small businesses.

MARKETING ONLINE STRATEGY

Have a Blog/Website: The first step to successful marketing online is to have a home base on the Web. It doesn't really matter if you have an official website or a blog or a combination of both. Either will give you a Web address where people can find you and a convenient way of referring to you, two things that will facilitate your marketing online efforts. So even if you don't sell anything online directly, you need a website.

Online Advertising: Many small businesses in particular bother with this marketing online strategy, I suspect because they don't want to shell out for it. They only want to do free marketing online. I say, there's absolutely nothing wrong with free marketing online strategies-as long as you realize they're not. All the 'free' online marketing strategies I'm aware of take a considerable time investment, meaning they're only free if your time is worth nothing. Traditional online advertising, on the other hand, takes relatively little time and can be a very effective marketing online strategy. The first thing you need to know about it is that there are two cost models, CPM and CPC.

CPM stands for Cost Per Thousand Impressions. With this type of marketing online, you basically buy space on a web page and pay for a certain number of impressions, or the number of times your ad is going to be displayed. Many of the banner ads you see on various websites are being paid for on a CPM model. CPC stands for Cost-Per-Click advertising. In this model, you pay only for the number of times a viewer clicks on your ad, not on the number of times it's displayed.

Google AdWords is perhaps the best known Pay-per-click marketing online program. When you're marketing online with this program, you choose particular keywords that you want your ads to be associated with. When people search on Google using one of your keywords, your ad may appear next to the search results. The theory is that these people are much more likely to be interested in your products or services.

Directory Listings: Adding your business to appropriate directory listings (local directory listings, business directories, etc.) is another way of marketing online that takes little time and is relatively inexpensive. Whatever local business groups you belong to, such as your local Chamber of Commerce, probably have websites where they allow members to list their businesses online and perhaps even place ads on the site at special rates. Search out other local sites, especially those related to tourism, and make sure you're listed there, too.

Participating in Social Media: Marketing online through social media requires a much more subtle technique than marketing online through advertising or directory listings. With all social media, the trick is to participate intelligently and actually attempt to converse rather than just advertising your products or services. Comments such as "Good point. See my site www.worldsbesttamales.com for the world's best tamales" are just spam, not conversation. The downside of marketing online through social media is that it's time-consuming. If you want to do it well and see any real benefit from it, you have to work at it. The upside is that it's free and can really generate a lot of buzz about your products/services if something that you've done online (a post, a video, an article) becomes really popular.

Online Networking: LinkedIn deserves special mention in any discussion of online networking. Its stated purpose is to help the world's professionals connect with one another to accelerate their success. As of this writing, LinkedIn has over 40 million members in over 200 countries and territories around the world. It's a powerful tool for marketing online, giving you the opportunity to connect with potential customers, partners and colleagues. Besides being a great source of support and information, groups such as these also provide some marketing online opportunities. Other members may be potential customers or referral sources as they get to know you and what you do. Like social media, online networking requires taking a subtle approach to marketing online. The same basic rule applies to online networking that applies to networking face-to-face. Give, give, give and don't worry about receiving; you will, likely in bigger, more powerful ways than you ever imagined.

Email marketing is one of the best and most powerful ways of marketing online, in my opinion. For one thing, once you've developed an email list, (notice the word developed, not bought), you are, in effect, preaching to the converted, sending your marketing message directly to people who have already indicated some interest in your products or services. For another, email is an excellent tool for building a relationship with your customers, letting you build both repeat business and good word-of-mouth through your marketing online efforts. Newsletters can be sent to the email list you've built from the people who provided the necessary information on your website, for instance, providing these potential customers with news updates about your company, upcoming events and/or special offers—and, of course, reminding them that your business exists and that maybe it's time for another visit.

Marketing Online and Offline are the Same in One Way...

Just like any offline marketing, your marketing online efforts need to be planned. So don't just post something here and place something there and consider that you're marketing online. Create a marketing online campaign and plan and measure your results just as you would with any other marketing. And remember too, that targeting still matters. The more carefully you have targeted your potential customers and the more carefully you have chosen and placed your marketing advertisements or your conversations, the more successful your marketing online campaign will be. The thing that's different about marketing online, however, is its incredible reach. The Internet gives your business the chance to reach thousands and perhaps even millions of people who would never hear of your products and/or services otherwise-making marketing online a marketing opportunity you don't want to miss out on.

Simple Ways of Marketing Online

Internet marketers already know these strategies by heart. But there may be some who just entered the online business and marketing community who may not have tried some of the simple ways of marketing online. Marketing online isn't as difficult as it may sound. Internet marketers wouldn't be bragging of how much great a job it is if it was all that difficult and annoying. The downside may be that you need to put in a lot of time and effort to get a positive result in the end. Patience is also needed, and, for some, expenses are incurred. But in general marketing online is just a simple and easy task! The main point of internet marketing is to generate traffic and lead visitors and customers to your site. Your site's visibility will be the key factor for you to attract customers and make sales. Online marketing strategies have this purpose in mind.

Let us Count the Simple Ways of Marketing Online

Link Building: To achieve greater visibility in the Web, you have to have a high ranking in the search engines. To have a high ranking among the search engines, building links is vital. Search engine spiders crawl across the Web to look for the number of links you have and use it as one of the important bases on ranking your website. Build links all over the Web by reciprocal linking, creating quality content, and submitting your site to the site directories!

Keyword Search: Search for your main keyword and other terms that are related to your site. When making links, you can use your keyword and terms as an anchor text for more visibility to your site. Make use of keyword tools available online to search for the most searched for word that you can use as your keyword.

Site Directories: By submitting your site to site directories, you are also placing another link for the search engines to crawl. This adds to your number of links and can increase your rank among the search engines.

Article Submissions: One technique in leading visitors and generating traffic to your site is by submitting relevant and interesting article to article directories. Submitting articles to the directories can also help you build more links to your site, thus gaining you more links and increasing your rankings. Don't forget to make the article creative and relevant, of course. Readers won't be curious to see your website if your article doesn't get their attention.

Affiliate Marketing: The downside of this strategy is that you'll have to spend for the commissions of affiliate sales. Nevertheless, this strategy is used by many internet marketers. Affiliate marketing usually works by networking with other websites that are in the same niche as you. Now since you are both in the same niche, most usually the traffic that you can generate through affiliate marketing is targeted. This is about the best thing abut affiliate marketing (aside from generating sales). You are also building links through the links (in the ads) on the website that you are affiliated with.

Newsletters and Subscriptions: Sending newsletters to the customers and clients will not only help in building professional and friendly relationships with them, but also brings in targeted traffic to your web site. Whenever you have something new to talk about and events to promote, newsletters can be a great way to let the clients and customers in on the news.

Email Marketing: This is another popular way to generate traffic and occasionally make repeat sales. This is kind of like sending newsletters, only your are more or less not sending news but rather promoting your latest products and services. Remember that when making your emails, you should avoid making it spammy and annoying. Make your email content original, creative and interesting.

Forums: You can see the most eager visitors of the online community in forums. Participating and giving great content in the replies will help in establishing you as an expert in your niche. This will give you a boost in the eyes of the online community. You'll be able to form relationships among the community and get them to be interested in your site and business. Plus, you can place links to your website on your signature every time you make a post! This can increase your rankings and visibility in the search engines.

There really is nothing to marketing online. . . now all you need is just a lot of time and effort to make your website known across the internet.

RESALE RIGHTS FOR THE MASTER RESELLER

Imagine the situation. You just purchased resell rights to an awesome package of digital products that includes e-books, a set of PLR articles and a tool set for web masters. The sales page copy enthusiastically touted all the ways that resell rights products can be used to make income for you—from giving away free e-books on your own web site to selling the package to others. The buyers' agreement says that you have digital resell rights. Can you put your own name on it and sell the package in your eBay shop? Chances are if you do that, you'll be in violation of your buyer's agreement, at least in the situation described above. The entire issue of resell rights—and specifically what rights they grant you as a purchaser—is a complex one that is intertwined with intellectual property laws and distribution rights. Both of those fields are in a constant state of change, especially on the internet where the rights of authors, creators and copyright owners are still being defined. If you're new to the master resell rights business, the terminology and legalities can be confusing. Heck, it can be confusing if you've been doing it for years, because the definitions keep changing as content sellers keep refining and redefining the terms under which they sell content.

Master Resell Rights allow you to sell the right to sell the product along with selling the product itself. You may sell the product without including resell rights, or sell it as a package with the right to resell it. Unless specifically stated, you may not alter the product in any way, including by adding your own links or branding to the product. That means that even if there are typographical errors or errors in source code, you may not correct them before selling the product.

Private Label Rights are an entirely separate set of rights that may be included when you purchase resell rights. Private label rights give you the right to label a product with your own information. You can put your own label on PLR products and sell them as your own. In some cases, private label rights also give you the right to alter the product in any other way, but that aren't always included as part of private label rights. In some cases, the changes you may make are confined to labeling and branding, or you may be restricted to only giving the product away. Be sure to check your agreement to see exactly what you are allowed to alter when you buy private label rights.

Unrestricted private label rights When you buy unrestricted private label rights, the assumption is that you own the product and you may treat it just as you would if you had authored it yourself. That means that you may alter it, put your name on it, claim authorship of it, sell it in part or in whole, use parts of it in other projects.

What is Niche Marketing? A niche market is a focused, targetable portion (subset) of a market sector. By definition, then, a business that focuses on a niche market is addressing a need for a product or service that is not being addressed by mainstream providers. A niche market may be thought of as a narrowly defined group of potential customers. A distinct niche market usually evolves out of a market niche, where potential demand is not met by any supply. Such ventures are profitable because of disinterest on the part of large businesses and/or lack of awareness on the part of other small companies. The key to capitalizing on a niche market is to find or develop a market niche that has customers who are accessible, that is growing fast enough, and that is not owned by one established vendor already".

What is a Niche Market? Simply stated, a niche market is a fairly small group of consumers that have a very specific interest that's not currently being adequately serviced. In most cases, members of a niche market are quite passionate about the topic of their interest. If you can provide a useful product or important information to these people, you're likely to see a large number of new customers.

What is NOT a Niche? A very generalized topic, such as 'football' is definitely not a niche. If you search Google for the term 'football', you'll see about 194 million competing webpages. Just imagine how difficult it would be to get your website near the top of the search engines with so many others out there that are already firmly positioned! If you narrow down the scope a bit, let's say to 'football jersey', the competition drops to about 849,000 competing webpages. That's still a lot of competition, but it's only about 0.4% of the competition you'd see with the more generalized term of 'football'. We're definitely headed in the right direction, but we still have some distance to go. Further narrowing our search to 'custom football jersey' cuts the competition to just 10,100 web pages. Now we have a chance of getting some traffic!

Can you profit from Niches? If you put up a webpage with decent Search Engine Optimization (SEO) based upon the keyphrase 'custom football jersey', you shouldn't have too much trouble achieving a high ranking position in the search engines. Out of the 5,131 searches that are done monthly, you stand to get a fair amount of free traffic from the search engines. If you're selling custom football jerseys, that can mean money in your pocket!

Finding the Niches Although finding profitable niches isn't technically difficult, it is a boring, time consuming and tedious process. First of all, you start out with your main keyword and then try to get more specific, as in the football example above. Keep refining your keyphrase to target successively narrower groups, while comparing the amount of competition with the quantity of searches. When you find a good tight niche with low competition and a fair search volume, there's a good chance you can make money.

Niches for New Marketers A great many people succumb to the lure of internet marketing. They listen to all the guru's with their overflowing supply of ebooks that promise to make you rich, just by reading the £ 97 fountain of "secret" information. They all have the same basic sales pitch—"Give me £ 97 and I'll show you how you can become a millionaire by working less than 2 hours a week!" Don't waste your money with these scam artists, because I'm going to tell you the "secret" right here, right now, for free. The secret is that there is no secret! Contrary to what the £ 97 ebook hucksters would have you believe, there is no magic button, that when pressed brings you enormous wealth.

Selling on the internet involves the same basic concepts of selling that have been practiced for thousands of years. Although modern technology does influence the entire process, you still need to put a desirable product in front of the right audience when they're ready and able to buy. That's it-pretty simple concept, don't you think? Simple, yes-but it works!

How to select a profitable niche—This is where a lot of beginners and even experienced marketers go wrong. They find a product, then they try to develop a market for that product. In actuality, they have the process in reverse order. Instead, they should look for a hungry market that isn't being satisfied and present them with just what they're looking for. Find the eager market first, then go find a product!

How do you find niche ideas? Well, you just have to be alert. As you go thru your daily activities, be on the lookout for possible niche markets. For starters, I'm always aware of trends and current events in the real world. I read newspapers, many magazines, both general and niche-specific, I watch the news, I listen to the radio. Occasionally something that I hear or read will stick with me. I may record my thoughts on my portable voice recorder or jot down some notes, whatever happens to be convenient for me. Sometimes I'll call my office voice mail and leave myself a message.

But at some point I'll have several broad ideas to research. I want to look deeper and I want to make sure there's a good market for them before I even think about creating a product or promoting an affiliate product.

First steps in research-Once you have a list of possible niche ideas, it's time to take a cursory look and see if any of them hold promise. This can be done online for free, using these sites-google.com/trends/hottrends: This site will give you statistical charts about search trends. You'll be able to tell at a glance if interest in a particular niche is growing or declining. Obviously, you'd want to find a niche that's showing increasing interest.

buzz.yahoo.com: This site will show you the most popular search terms currently being entered. This is also a good place to build your list of more possible niche ideas.

pulse.ebay.com: This site will show you the most popular current product categories on Ebay. You can click on the categories shown and see sub-categories that will give you even more niche ideas. Ebay also provides a monthly report of their hot products at pages.ebay.com/sellercentral/ hotitems.pdf

Finding the good niches-Now that you've compiled a list of niche ideas, it's time to see which ones are worth pursuing. You can download a free tool from goodkeywords.com to see what the market looks like for these different niche ideas. This tool will take your product idea and show you the most common related terms people are searching for. It also shows how many searches were done for that term in the last month. What this does for you is to give you a very good indication of how big of a market exists in this niche. As a side benefit, you'll also see lots of closely related terms you can use for SEO on your website to get that much needed traffic. The trick here is to find keywords that are closely related to your potential niche product and have a fair number of searches every month, but they don't have a lot of competition. This is easy to do-just go to google or your favorite search engine and search for each of your potential niche key phrases. This will tell you how many web pages are competing for that particular term. You'll want to narrow your niche key phrase list down to the ones that have a fair number of searches as shown in the Good Keywords tool, but don't have a lot of competition as indicated by the search engines. When you are able to isolate the niches that have a good quantity of searches, low competition and they're showing a trend of growth, you've found a very likely winner!

It's a tedious process, but it pays off. Let's say that you investigate an idea and it looks good. You put up a website, do a little promotion to generate traffic. That niche product might only make a profit of $ 1,000 a month, which may not seem like much. But consider this-you only need to do the research one time and then you'll be making your profit month after month.

There's nothing to stop you from building upon 20 niche ideas. And even if they only make $ 1,000 each per month, that works out to $ 240,000 a year. Not too shabby!

The 5 Best Ways to Get Free Website Promotion

"How do I get free website promotion?" is a question I'm often asked. The thing to remember about free website promotion is that nothing is ever truly free. If you don't spend money promoting your website, you're going to have to spend time. So why waste time on website promotion methods that will only bring you minuscule returns, if any? If you're prepared to work on them, these five free website promotion techniques will deliver, rewarding you with increased site traffic.

1. Website Promotion through Strong SEO

SEO stands for Search Engine Optimization and it's the best thing since sliced bread in terms of free website promotion. Search Engine Optimization is the process of making website pages attractive to search engines, and the great thing is that it's not hard to learn and apply the basics to your own website(s).

Tip: If you are using non-text content on your web page(s), such as photos, image maps or JavaScript, include text for your image in the ALT tag so the search engines have something they can read.

2. Website Promotion through Reciprocal Linking

When other people put a link to your site on their site, you get free website promotion. You also get a shot at a better search engine ranking for your page. All of the big three search engines (Google, Yahoo, and MSN) use inbound links as an important part of the formula that determines a page's rank. Be aware though that this kind of free website promotion is not a numbers game; it's the quality of the links that really matters. So you want to focus your reciprocal linking efforts on relevant quality links. The standard procedure is to search for and identify relevant sites that you would like to have link to yours and then send each webmaster an email requesting a link on their site, offering a link on your site in return.

Tip: You can check a website or Web page's ranking before you try to reciprocally link with it by using SEO tools such as Page Rank Lookup and the Link Popularity Tool. Google's Toolbar also has a Page Rank Display feature. These tools are also handy for checking the status and progress of your own website and/or pages.

3. *Write Articles to Get Free Website Promotion*

The beauty of this free website promotion strategy is that once again someone else is promoting your website for you. And if you get your articles published on popular, long-lived websites or in well-known magazines, they can be sitting there giving you free website promotion for a long, long time with no further effort on your part. However, there are catches. First, you have to be able to write well on a topic or topics that other people will want to read and/or publish. Second, you have to find the quality places for your articles to be published and persuade the people making the decisions to publish them. When you find them, send an email asking if they can use a particular piece, including your article so they can look at it right away if they're interested. Be sure your email mentions that they are welcome to publish the piece for free. Also be sure that your piece ends with a resource box or 'blurb' that promotes you and your website.

Tip: Find the websites or magazines you want to be published on first, and then spend some time reading the content to see what type of material they might want and if there are any obvious holes in their content that you could cover. Then tailor your material to that particular site or magazine's needs.

4. *Website Marketing through Social Networking*

You've probably already received invitations to join one or more social networks such as Linkedin or Ryze. Among the advantages of joining that Entrepreneurs Guide Scott Allen and David Teton mention in Crossing the Social Network Chasm is high visibility at low cost. Most social networking sites, they point out, allow you to create a profile for free. There's no reason why you can't belong to several social networks at once (except time constraints), but for effective website marketing you will want to choose the network communities you join carefully. Some seem to be more personal chat centers than business networking groups and will be useless in terms of business and/or website promotion.

Tip: Scott Allen and David Teton recommend having your profile prepared before you join a social network. A 'master copy' of your profile information makes it easy to copy and paste and create a new profile when you join a social networking group.

5. *Website Marketing through Blogging*

Creating a blog of your own is another great free website marketing strategy because it lets you apply several free website marketing strategies at once. By blogging about your subject, you'll get the chance to become an active member of the blogging community, building a web of relationships and links. And of course, your blog will be keyword rich, increasing your Search Engine Optimization. You can set up a blog as part of an existing website, or give your new blog a site of its own. These Business Blogs FAQs include a blog definition as well as information on how to create a blog of your own.

Tip: Most blogs include the facility to make comments on posts. When you're reading another blog that's relevant to your topic, take the time to comment on a post (making sure that your comment says something that's equally relevant). It's another opportunity to do some free website marketing while getting known in the blogging community.

These are not the only free website marketing strategies that you can use of course. But these are the best, and if you select several of these and concentrate on them, they'll yield the return in increased site traffic that you're looking for.

Checklist When Working with a Web Design Services Company So you've chosen your small business web site developer. Now what? After agreeing on your contract and conferring with your business partners or colleagues on the direction you want your website to take, go through the following points to smooth your interaction and eliminate any potential headaches.

1. *Send all your marketing materials and company info.* Very often, small business owners have composed their

own marketing campaigns on the fly and are surprised to have to supply artfully-written copy and carefully selected photos to their web design partners. Compile all your company slogans, vision-mission, and photos in a CD, flash drive, or zip file-or better yet, compile Basic Info Checklist: What Information Every Small Business Website Should Have ?

2. *Check your spelling and copyrights*. Did everything pass through the spell check? You should either use royalty-free, buy stock images, or have your designer design or buy for you the right to use original photographs and images. Just because it's online does not mean it's free for you to use-unless you want an infringement lawsuit.
3. *Identify your market* and which products or services you want to highlight. An honest web design firm who has your best interest will not just copy and paste your marketing collateral. With so much competition on the web, he should highlight the products most valuable both to you and site visitors.
4. *Be clear about your purpose for your homepage*, and every page. Will your potential customers be looking for a way to contact you after hearing about you? Are they looking for schedules of your seminars or pricelists? Specify these to your designer to make sure they prioritize what you think are most important for your customers.
5. *List possible reasons why people would contact you*. Different people have different needs from you. Some may want to ask for a quote if you're a service provider. Are you an industry expert who's invited to speaking engagements? Knowing this will help your designer craft a contact form that's truly easy for your users to tell you what they need from you.
6. *Integrate with your social network profiles*. Are you already active on Facebook, LinkedIn or Twitter ? Bring your social network to your website and back by having your designer display your latest tweets or

letting your customers find you on Facebook. Speakers, personal coaches, and individual professionals are recommended to maximize this capability.

7. *Is your website a part of a bigger offline marketing campaign?* If so, you may want your web development partner firm to design separate landing pages for any promo codes you might give out. You'll also want to be able to monitor how effective your flyers are in bringing visitors to your website using analytics software that your provider can set up for you.
8. *Communicate!* You and your website developer should have a system in place for giving updates or approvals. Whether it's just through email exchanges, instant messaging, phone calls, or an online project collaboration tool like Our Email Marketing Client Site or Basecamp-keep in constant contact but give ample time and space for them to do their work.

Freelance web designers, professional web site development firms, and big web shops are not created equal. Some work fast, some are pricey, some just use templates while others come up with truly unique designs. Keeping these 8 points in mind will help you keep your sanity and let you stay focused on your core operations while awaiting the Internet creation of your 24/7 salesperson.

PROMOTION

Generally, promotion is communicating with the public in an attempt to influence them toward buying your products and/or services. How does promotion differ from advertising? Promotion is the broader, all inclusive term. Advertising is just one specific action you could take to promote your product or service. Promotion, as a general term, includes all the ways available to make a product and/or service known to and purchased by customers and clients.

The word promotion is also used specifically to refer to a particular activity that is intended to promote the business, product or service. A store might advertise that it's having a big promotion on certain items, for instance, or a business person may refer to an ad as a promotion. Contests and advertising are two examples of popular promotion activities.

Advertising

Advertising is attempting to influence the buying behavior of your customers or clients by providing a persuasive selling message about your products and/or services.

There are many different types of advertising that are effective for small businesses, from traditional forms of advertising such as signage, yellow pages listings and newspaper advertising through newer forms such as pay per click advertising on the Internet.

Technically, advertising is only one way of promoting your business, and you will want to be sure that whatever form of advertising you choose fits in with your marketing plan and overall marketing strategy.

Directed Advertising Gets Results. If you're the only product/service provider in a consumer's time of need, you may get a sale based on that even if you haven't established firm trust. How can you set this up this kind of advertising? It depends on your business. But I'll give some examples of advertising based on benefits.

An appliance dealer can give/send magnetic advertising specialties for people to put on their appliances. To supplement this, the dealer can establish a program of getting information about the specifications people will want/need in a replacement appliance, such as measurements, capacity, gas/ electric, color, etc. Then when an appliance breaks down, the customer can call for a price quote without having to supply the necessary information. (During a stressful time, people aren't apt to want to hassle with this information; they just want a solution NOW!)

Entertainment is a benefit; it may not induce anybody to buy the advertised product but it may get them to pay attention to the ad. Since people are more cure oriented than prevention oriented, it's necessary to fully describe the undesirable effect.

EIGHT WAYS TO BOOST YOUR ONLINE PRESENCE

When engineers and technical professionals are searching for components, suppliers, and services, they turn to online resources first. That means the stronger, broader, and deeper your online presence, the more opportunity you will have to be found by and connect with potential customers. Here are eight ways to boost your online presence. You can do all of them in 2011.

1. Exhibit at an Online Event

Online events are gaining popularity among the industrial audience. According to Market Research Media, the virtual conference and trade show market is predicted to experience a 56% compound annual growth rate between 2010-2015. With an online event, you gain a powerful forum for branding, exposure, relationship building and thought leadership. Attendees experience the same essential benefits of a face-to-face event, all from the convenience of their desktop.

Tip: Seek out exhibitor opportunities at online events that specifically target your audience.

2. Implement a Searchable Online Catalog

When your potential customers need a product or component, they often start by searching online catalogs. A searchable online catalog is great way to attract highly-motivated buyers ready to make a purchasing decision. Users want flexible search options: by specification, part number, keyword, and category.

Tip: Look for a partner with experience and expertise in developing and maintaining robust online catalogs.

3. Expand Your Visibility through an and Network

Online banner ads are a great way to increase brand visibility and drive qualified traffic to your site—often at very attractive rates. The key is to make sure your ads appear only on relevant industrial Web sites so you don't waste any impressions on the wrong audience.

Tip: Ask your media partner if they offer an ad program that will display your ads on a broad yet highly-targeted network of industrial Web sites.

4. Put more offers and calls-to-action on your Web site

Your Web site should not only be an information resource for your audience, it should also be a lead-generating machine. You can boost your capability here by putting relevant offers on almost every page: white papers, Webinars, product samples, and more.

Tip: Ask your visitors to fill out a short form with their name, company, and e-mail address in exchange for taking advantage of your offer.

5. Advertise in Third-party E-newsletters

Third-party e-newsletter advertisements are a great way to expand your online reach and maintain a consistent presence in front of your target audience. You can promote new products, make special offers, connect with hard to reach decision makers not on your e-mail lists, and leave behind the costs and hassles of managing the e-mail list and producing the content for the e-newsletter.

Tip: Look for e-newsletters that are published on a regular basis, reach your target audience, and have an opt-in subscriber base.

6. Get featured in online industrial directories

Online directories are a good way to gain exposure and build relevant links back to your Web site. The best directories for suppliers are those that give you the option of adding your logo or other image, and including multiple links.

Tip: Look for an online directory that can give you a robust presence beyond just your name and Web site being listed.

7. Pitch story ideas to online publications

Editors and reporters are always looking for industry experts they can interview when they're working on stories. Get to know the relevant editors and reporters in your space and pitch them story ideas that will be of interest to their readers. Having your company name showing up in the media and on those Web sites your customers frequent will help improve the reputation of your brand and can help position your company as a thought leader.

Tip: Reach out to editors and reporters in multiple ways, including e-mail, phone, and even postal mail.

8. Create compelling landing pages on your Web site

You invest time and resources in online marketing programs and in developing offers to drive prospects to your Web site. Don't just send them to your home page. Create targeted, focused landing pages that promote your offer and compel visitors to accept it—generating a lead for your sales team. Keep the landing pages short and sweet. Avoid too much clutter or extraneous information that will distract visitors from your offer.

Tip: Keep landing page forms simple and ask only for the minimum amount of information that will enable you to communicate with prospects.

Bonus tip: Update your online content. Search engines and customers will appreciate it if the content on your Web site is up-to-date. Newer content ranks better in search results and potential customers are always looking for the most recent product information. Conversely, stale or out-of-date content reflects poorly on your company.

THE ONLINE ADVERTISING INDUSTRY : ECONOMICS, EVOLUTION, AND PRIVACY

Advertising delivered over the internet—"online advertising"—has become a significant source of revenue for web-based businesses. Fifty-six of the top 100 websites based on page views in February 2008 presented advertising; these 56 accounted for 86 percent of the total page views for these 100 sites.1 Twenty-six of these 56 sites, accounting for 77 percent of all page views for the top 100 sites, likely earn most of their revenue from selling advertising.

Internet-based advertising is the source of a "gale of creative destruction" (in the words of Schumpeter, 1942) that is sweeping across the advertising and media landscape, especially in the United States. Newspapers, particularly, are losing readers and advertisers to web media supported by online advertising. That has lead to a downward spiral as indirect network effects work in reverse. The market caps of the major publicly traded newspaper businesses in the United States declined by 42 percent between January 2004 and August 2008, compared to a 15.6 percent increase for the Dow Jones Industrial average over that same time period (Blodget, 2008). With the additional pressure of the financial crisis, newspapers in several major cities including Denver and Seattle have closed down and others including the *New York Times* are in distress. More generally, online advertising is disrupting all aspects of the global advertising industry, which had estimated revenues of $ 625 billion in 2007 (Minton, 2007), from how creative work is done, to how advertising campaigns are run, and to how advertising is bought and sold.

Online advertising methods are, arguably, leading to significant reductions in transactions costs between merchants and consumers. The methods enable merchants to deliver information that is targeted to those consumers who value the information the most and are most likely to act on it. An oft-quoted line in the advertising business states ruefully: "Half the money I spend on advertising is wasted. The only trouble is I don't know which half". The new techniques replace a sledgehammer with a scalpel. In doing so, they collect and analyze detailed information about how people use their computers-raising difficult issues concerning the expectation of privacy and the regulation of the online advertising industry. No research has yet examined the value of the productivity improvements created by online advertising technology but they appear significant. Consider a business that sells 4 saltwater fishing rods to people who enjoy fly fishing. The traditional approach to matching this buyer and seller involved the creation of a magazine, such as *FlyFisherman*, with content that attracts the relevant people. In contrast, the online approach relies on a variety of techniques to match an advertising message to a consumer. A search engine indexes web results that are relevant to a consumer who types in the phrase "saltwater fishing rod", and with this information, the search engine can sell ads to sellers of saltwater fishing rods. Contextual advertising on web pages could do the same thing. A consumer who visits a blog for fly fishermen could be presented with an advertisement. Developing behavioral targeting techniques, discussed below, can also identify individuals who are interested in fly fishing and determine whether they are looking around the web for information that would suggest they might be in the market for a saltwater rod.

This presents the evolution of the online advertising business. It examines the supply of online advertising "inventory", which equals the space times the views of that space; the demand for that inventory; and intermediaries that operate between the sell and buy sides. It also explores some of the key developments such as behavioral targeting for matching advertising messages to consumers and considers some economic aspects of the privacy issues that these technologies raise. Aside from providing a survey of an important new segment of advertising this essay suggests, at various points, that many of the interesting questions, and economic puzzles, about the advertising industry—offline and online—remain to be addressed.

For example, online advertising is a "two-sided market" (Rochet and Tirole, 2003; Anderson et al., 2005), as is advertising generally. Intermediaries operate platforms that facilitate advertisers and consumers connecting with each other. Innovative intermediaries operate exchanges and face the critical liquidity issues discussed in the market microstructure literature (O'Hara, 1998; also see Evans and Schmalensee, 2009).

Evolution of Online Advertising

Online advertising started in 1994 when HotWired, a web magazine, sold a banner ad to ATandT and displayed it on their web page (Kaye and Medoff, 2001). The ad was sold based on the number of "impressions"—individuals who saw the ad—which was the model followed by most traditional media for this sort of brand advertising. Many web ads were subsequently sold based on "cost per mille", which is advertising terminology for cost per 1000 viewers of the advertisement and often referred to as CPM. Paying by number of viewers remained the norm until Procter and Gamble negotiated a deal with Yahoo! in 1996 which compensated the web portal for ads based on the "cost-per-click" (commonly known as CPC). Yahoo! was paid only when a user clicked on the ad; this was the web-version of the direct response method commonly used by advertisers for things such as mail and telephone solicitations. However, we will see that most "display ads" on websites—the ads that look like those in newspapers and magazines—were still sold based on thousands of views as of 2008.

The exploding supply of web pages led to the birth, in 1994, of several search engines that also sold advertising to make money. At first, they sold banner ads on a cost-per-mille basis—that is, based on how many people saw the ad. However, that approach led to a conflict for the search engine between helping people find things quickly and keeping eyeballs trained on the site to make money. The search engines later moved to the cost-per-click model. GoTo.com—which is now owned by Yahoo!—introduced many of the key technological and business model innovations in the next three years ("GoTo to Overture", 2005; "History of Pay Per Click, 2007). These included adopting the cost-per-click approach to pricing and the use of auctions to allocate the advertising spots on the page showing results of the search. During this same period, fairly traditional methods of advertising were mimicked on the web. These included web versions of business directories similar to the yellow pages such as yellowpages.com; web versions of newspaper classified ads such as Craigslist; and web versions of direct mail and telephone marketing such as CheetahMail. These web-based vehicles were charged for in ways that were similar to their traditional counterparts with the exception of Craigslist, which provided a significant amount of free advertising to consumers. The remainder of this essay does not discuss web-based directories or email advertising because they do not raise particularly novel issues.

Online advertising revenue has increased steadily over time in absolute terms and as a fraction of all advertising revenue. Consistent figures are available since 2000. They show that U.S. online advertising has increased from $ 8.1 billion in 2000 to $ 21.2 billion in 2007 and from 3.2 percent of all advertising to 8.8 per cent over that time period (based on Interactive Advertising Bureau Press Releases 2000-07). The relative mix of online advertising has also changed. The evolution of various online advertising formats from 2000 until the first half of 2008. In 2008, search and display-related ads were the leading advertising formats with 44 per cent and 21 per cent share of the total revenue, respectively. However, ads that are linked to the results of a keyword search have grown explosively from 1 percent of online advertising revenue in 2000 to 44 percent in 2008, while display ads dropped from 48 percent of total revenue in 2000 to 21 percent of total revenue by the first half of 2008. In 2009, fifteen years after its birth, the online advertising industry remains in considerable flux. The delivery of online advertising exhibits rapid technological change. At the same time, new economic structures are emerging and business relationships among the key players are changing. For example, in 2008, Google completed its acquisition of DoubleClick, which was a major technology provider, and Microsoft entered into negotiations, ultimately aborted, to buy Yahoo! On one side of the business are advertisers that want to reach consumers and consider online advertising as a possible way to do that. On the other side are consumers who may or may not be receptive to receiving advertising messages. In between are various intermediaries.

The fully integrated intermediaries touch consumers and advertisers directly. The search-based advertising platforms (Evans, 2008) are examples: they bring consumers to their search results pages and sell access to these consumers directly to advertisers; their platforms integrate all the necessary technology for doing this. Many intermediaries are partly integrated. Publishers such as reuters.com bring consumers to their sites and have direct sales forces that sell advertising inventory directly to advertisers. But these publishers also typically rely on technology providers ("ad servers") that handle passing ads from the advertisers to the publishers' advertising spaces as well as advertising networks which aggregate online advertising inventory and sell it to advertisers. Finally, some publishers are highly specialized and contract most tasks out. That is true of blogs—even large ones—which rely on ad networks such as Google's Content Network to sell ads for them and to provide the relevant technology. Figure 1 shows the relationship between the various agents. Almost all of the participants in intermediation between advertisers and consumers operate multi-sided platforms, sometimes working with agents for the advertiser or consumer. For example, media-buying firms work for advertisers and advertising agencies on the "buy side" and with publishers on the "sell side". This results in an industry of interlocking multisided platforms. Some of these platforms have more "sides" than just buy and sell. Facebook, for example, operates a software platform (Evans, 2009) that encourages developers to write applications that also enlist advertisers and consumers. As with advertising generally, a key feature of online advertising is that consumers are paid with content and services to receive advertising messages and advertisers pay to send these messages. A fundamental question, not addressed here, is why this particular pricing and reward structure has held over long periods of time and across many different types of advertising. Among other things, the answer would help to illuminate the extent to which advertising is a method for reducing transactions costs between buyers and sellers or a source of imperfection that distorts decision making (Bagwell, 2002).

ONLINE *VERSUS* OFFLINE ADVERTISING

The fundamental differences between online and traditional advertising result from a combination of internet technologies and the nature of the web. The structure of online communications makes it easy for publishers and ad networks to learn considerably more about online users than has been possible with traditional media such as print, radio, and television. Online media or their ad networks typically know for certain from the internet technologies for linking people to sites that an individual is viewing their site. That is very different from a radio station, or a newspaper, which have limited ability to determine whether a particular individual is listening or reading. Online media can often learn valuable details about the individual that has signed on to the site. Each user has an IP (Internet protocol) address which typically identifies the location of the individual down to at least the zip code level in the United States. People who browse from home and from smaller companies typically have a unique IP address that remains the same over time. Using this address it is possible for online media and advertising networks to track other sites that users with that IP address have visited and to match up other details about the individual or household. (Some large companies change the IP addresses of individual users frequently so that the address cannot identify the user uniquely nor provide a precise geographic location. As a result online media cannot determine much about people who browse from these companies.)In addition, individual websites, such as wsj.com and myspace.com, may have detailed information on registered users which they can also use for advertising. Print, radio and television media generally do not know this level of information for individual users; cable systems with set-top boxes also have specific information on viewers (Lafayette, 2008) but do not have ready access to the browsing behavior of those individuals.

Traditional media usually have static scheduled content. Television and radio shows are broadcast at a particular time, newspapers are published daily, and magazines weekly or monthly. Advertisers and their intermediaries have no way of knowing whether an individual can hear or see their advertisements. Television viewers may leave the room and radio listeners may switch the channel when the ads come on. Readers may not necessarily look at particular newspaper and magazine pages with advertising. Consumers have much greater control over the content they view on websites. Advertisers and their intermediaries know with great confidence what content a consumer is viewing at a particular point in time. These facts have two implications. First, advertisements can be targeted to the particular view that is taking place. The platform can determine the time of day and location of the view and may also be able to determine various other characteristics of the viewer. Most on-line advertising inventory is selected in "almost" real time and customized for the particular viewer. The technology makes decisions on the ad to insert in a particular space so quickly that when you look at web page you cannot detect that it has been designed in less than the blink of an eye. Thus, advertisers have the ability to customize their advertising purchases in a way that is not cost-effective offline. Second, the advertising platform can often discern the context of why the viewer has come to the publisher's web page. For example, search engines know the keywords a user requested, and publishers know the content of the page the user is looking at. Both may know recent search or browsing behavior. Ads can be customized based on this information.

These features can make online advertising a more efficient matchmaking vehicle for advertisers and viewers than offline advertising. Advertisers can target their messages to those consumers for whom the messages are most relevant and who are most likely to buy as a result of receiving this message. Viewers are more likely to receive messages that are relevant and valuable to them. An implication of this observation is that there are economic incentives for advertising and viewing to move online.

Supply of Advertising Space and its Market Structure

Any website that attracts viewers is a potential supplier of advertising inventory. Some websites choose to make money mainly in other ways: for example, e-commerce, gaming, adult sites, and a few others are largely free of advertising. But, as noted earlier, websites that account for a preponderance of page views among the top 100 sites earn most of their revenue from advertising. The 20 largest advertising-supported sites in terms of page views, as of February 2008, and describes the content they use to attract eyeballs. Notable sites include Google, which primarily uses search results as well as user-uploaded video for its YouTube site; Yahoo!, which owns properties ranging from entertainment to automotive to email on which it presents ads; and Facebook, which operates a social networking site in which users see advertising on their own pages, the pages of their friends, and on other pages specifically designed for advertisers. The Table also reports 2008 advertising revenue for sites where this is publicly available—that ranges from a low of $ 130 million for Facebook to a high of $ 7.4 billion for Google.

The supply of advertising inventory is highly skewed. Thousands of web sites supply some advertising inventory in addition to the top one hundred. While comprehensive data on sites that supply advertising is not available, which is likely a good approximation of the distribution. As of February 2008, the top 10 sites accounted for 36 percent of page views, the top 300 accounted for 54 percent of page views, and top 10,000 websites attracted 67 percent of the total page views. There are four large fully integrated suppliers of advertising inventory in the United States: AOL, Google, MSN, and Yahoo! Each of these sites is a "publisher" in the sense that it presents content which is used to attract viewers to their pages. Each also acts as a "distributor" of ad space by directly selling inventory to either advertisers or "brokers" that act as middlemen and match publishers with advertisers. Finally, these four sites supply most of their own technology. To be more specific, they operate the software and communication technology that takes copy from an advertiser and inserts it into space at the appropriate time for a viewer. In addition, MSN and Yahoo! are horizontally integrated into search; both of these entities have their search query tool incorporated in their portals.

Most of the other large suppliers are partly integrated. They usually rely on providers of publisher-serving technology for the software and communications system that receives copy from advertisers and then make decisions on where and when to insert that copy into inventory. They typically have their own sales forces that distribute their inventory to advertisers. But they also rely on advertising networks to sell space that they cannot or do not want to sell themselves (see the discussion below on price discrimination). Smaller websites ordinarily do not have enough volume to support a sales force. They often rely on an advertising network which may also provide the necessary technology. For example, a publisher can paste html code supplied by the advertising network into the part of the webpage the publisher wants to sell; that code will retrieve and insert an advertisement. There are at least three main sources of supply of online advertising inventory, each of which results in different methods for selling advertising. First, search engines generate search-results pages. Search engines need to enable users to find what they are looking for quickly and to move from the search results page to the desired webpage. In the late 1990s, search engines struggled to find the right balance between providing valuable search results to attract eyeballs and selling advertisers access to these eyeballs. Most ended up dividing the search results page into the "organic search results" that are based on the relevance of the web page to the keywords entered by the user; and the "paid search results" which are clearly demarcated text advertisements that also look like search results. Although organic search results are valuable to advertisers,3 search engine providers do not charge advertisers for these listings. Instead, advertisers often hire "search engine optimization" companies, such as Performics, to increase their rankings in the search results. Each page typically has around ten slots available for a paid search advertisement. Advertisers bid on a cost-per-click for these slots and the search provider allocates the slots, roughly speaking, on the basis of expected revenue it will receive—that is, cost-per-click times expected clicks) (Evans, 2008; Varian, 2007). To maximize revenues from the scarce space, the search engines can use the cost-per-click bids and the expected number of clicks that the ads will receive to allocate the spots. Projecting the number of clicks and the effects of different allocation mechanisms is a difficult problem; the various search engine providers have solved that problem to varying degrees and their relative success in doing so explains in part differences in the revenue they receive for each search conducted (Evans, 2008).

Online media sites provide content that is broadly similar to what consumers get from traditional media. In fact, many traditional media companies have established web sites which use some material that is also provided through offline channels. Prominent examples include cnn.com, nytimes.com, mtv.com, and cosmopolitan.com. Other sites such as Yahoo! Redeploy content from a variety of sources such as newswire services. Finally, some sites, such as youtube.com and drudgereport.com, provide content only online and often do so innovatively. With the exception of the video sites, these sites allocate portions of their pages to advertisements much like newspaper pages do. They generally sell the ads on a cost-per-mille basis—that is, based on how many eyeballs see their pages—through their own sales team and through advertising networks. provides a sample layout: as with newspapers ads, different spots are perceived as more valuable because they are likely to receive more attention from consumers. Conversations with knowledgeable industry participants indicate that ads in the top half of the page garner a cost-per-mille of around $ 12.50 while ads in the bottom half of the page realize about half of that. Banners and skyscraper ads typically go for more than $ 12.50 cost-per-mille.

The more desirable space tends to be sold directly, while the less desirable space tends to be sold through advertising networks. These ad networks pay between 15 and 45 percent of the cost-permille for a display ad on the top half of the page depending on the quality of the space.

People go to social networking sites to obtain updates on what their friends are doing, to update their own pages, and through these and other activities to communicate with their friends. These sites have allocated some space for advertising and have sold this inventory to advertisers. This space is sometime known as the "dead zone" because of the lack of attention that social networking users pay to it. The average cost-per-mille payments to social networking sites are often less than $ 0.50. The social networking sites, and on-line advertising businesses, are working on advertising methods that work more effectively with social networking communities.

Google, for example, has developed a technology that makes it possible for advertisers to identify and target "influencers" in social networking communities to distribute messages (Helft, 2008). Whether social networking sites can achieve cost-per-mille payments for their viewers that are comparable to other types of on-line advertising remains to be seen. The promise of advertising on social networking websites is that word-of-mouth referrals are the primary influence on purchase decisions (BIGresearch, Simultaneous Media Usage Study (SIMM12), June 2008), and perhaps online communities can be used to create a source for such referrals.

The supply of advertising inventory is highly heterogeneous. It differs in size, the likelihood that consumers will pay attention to it, and the characteristics of the viewers. Not surprisingly, the price that advertisers pay per thousand views varies from a few cents to several hundred dollars in the case of high-income professionals. (This heterogeneity and price distribution is also true for traditional advertising.) Controlling for quality, however, suppliers of advertising engage in extensive "value-based pricing"—which economists call price discrimination.

The search-based advertising platforms, in principle, use second-price auctions to allocate slots and in this way seek to extract higher payments from those willing to pay more. Indeed, we might expect that the rents earned from the advertiser side would be bid away, at least partly, on the viewer side through competition among platforms (Rochet and Tirole, 2003; Armstrong, 2006), including through explicit subsidies to viewers to join the platform. That has happened to a degree. Microsoft adopted some mechanisms for providing incentives to viewers in 2008; for instance, the Windows Live search site has a button labeled "Search a lot, Earn a lot" which describes incentives for searching that include free Xbox, Microsoft software, frequent flier miles, cash back and more visited on November 28, 2008). Yahoo! has also entered into incentive arrangements for people to download toolbars that rely on its search engine. For example, Yahoo shares revenue with companies that get people to search with Yahoo and those companies in turn provide benefits—such as donations to charity—to individuals who download a toolbar that contains the Yahoo search feature. A different kind of competition for attention does take place. Google, Microsoft and Yahoo! compete to become the default search engine on the browser, on various tool bars that are distributed, and in publisher web sites. Although consumers can readily change these default settings the search engine providers presumably pay for these because enough consumers stick with the default. These deals provide incentives to entities that can provide search engine defaults for their users to compete harder to these users by providing greater quality. Online publishers engage in price discrimination as well. This practice is similar to other business-to-business transactions which are often characterized by individual negotiations, and the online practices are similar to the offline practices. In both cases, heterogeneous supply is being matched up with heterogeneous demand through bilateral exchanges and with limited public information. Media companies can take space they do not choose to sell directly and make it available to intermediaries that sell it indirectly. Larger online publishers typically have contracts with several advertising networks and have technology that selects the highest price for inventory in more or less real time. Online advertising networks are discussed in more detail below.

Demand for Online Advertising Space

Businesses spend money on advertising because it helps them sell products to consumers. Economists have developed a variety of models concerning the role of advertising, but most of that work focuses on how advertising might affect demand. There is little empirical work that assesses the extent to which advertising spending reduces transactions costs by providing valuable information (including quality signals) to consumers and matching buyers and sellers; provides disinformation that harms consumers; or is designed to alter preferences. In addition, few studies have examined the demand for advertising from the vantage-point of how the advertisers decide how much to spend or how to allocate that spending across different forms of advertising (Silk *et. al.*, 2002). Existing work together with anecdotal information suggest that advertisers—and their agents—determine an overall advertising budget, allocate that budget among different methods (such as brand advertising on national television) for achieving the objectives of an advertising campaign, and select various alternative advertising outlets for spending their dollars. Traditional methods have included placing ads on different media such as television, radio, newspapers, magazines, billboards, and directories and engaging in sales as mail and telemarketing. Each method draws upon many suppliers of advertising inventory, which vary in their coverage of the population as well as the characteristics of those covered. Advertisers typically develop "campaigns", which utilize a mixture of these methods and suppliers, to achieve objectives which may range from increasing sales of an existing product, to introducing a new one, to affecting the image of the company or brand. They base their decisions on the level and allocation of their budgets on formal or informal analyses of the rate of return on investment (Duboff, 2007). For these ad campaigns, the different advertising methods can be substitutes to the extent they provide alternative ways of delivering messages to an audience and complements to the extent they can reinforce each other find that 57 percent of the 28 pairs of the cross-elasticities they estimated indicated the methods were, on net, substitutes and the remainder were complements—although typically weak ones. Advertisers typically hire firms to design and execute advertising campaigns. Although these firms often have relationships through a conglomerate, such as WPP, they have become more specialized over time (Berndt *et. al.*, 2008). Increasingly one firm does the creative work and plans the campaign while another firm engages in buying and placing media. While some firms have arisen that specialize in online advertising, most creative work and media buying is performed by advertising firms that manage both offline and online work for advertisers. Within the online part of the business, advertisers or their agents also purchase various technologies for distributing online advertisements to suppliers of advertising inventory and measuring the success of online campaigns.

INTERMEDIATION BETWEEN THE ADVERTISING BUY AND SELL SIDES

The advertising industry has to solve a massive matching problem between businesses and consumers. A large number of advertisers want to deliver multiple messages to a large number of consumers. Indeed, advertising agencies were formed in the mid-nineteenth century to deal with the coordination of supply and demand among businesses that wanted to advertise outside their locality and the daily and weekly newspapers (Pope, 1983). The online advertising industry has developed a variety of technologies and business methods for solving this matching problem. The most innovative and best-known involve "search-based advertising", in which advertisers and consumers are matched based on the "keywords" that people enter into search engines. Consumers are attracted to the search engine because they are interested in content on the web. Advertisers use these keywords as proxies for the likelihood that consumers would be interested receiving a message that might lead to a sale.

Auction methods are then used to allocate the advertising inventory to the businesses that are willing to pay most for most clicks, which in turn depends on the amount they are willing to pay and the number of clicks their ads will receive (Evans, 2008). Other innovations are occurring in the buying and selling of display advertising on publisher websites. As of 2008, the preponderance of display advertising (measured by revenues) was bought and sold the old-fashioned way. Large online publishers have salespeople who sell their inventory to media buyers for large advertisers. That method of selling advertising space is only viable when there are enough people viewing that space—and thus enough expected revenue—to warrant the cost of salespeople calling on individual advertisers. Computer-based methods for matching the supply of advertising inventory and the demand for advertising inventory have made it possible for smaller sites to sell their inventory profitably. These methods also enable larger publishers to sell inventory that their salespeople have not sold. A number of advertising networks have arisen which broker multilateral exchanges between publishers and advertisers. These advertising networks enter into agreements with publishers to sell available advertising and with advertisers to deliver viewers with specified characteristics in return for a fee. Some of these networks provide behaviorally targeted ads discussed below although many place ads based on crude demographic information. Google has developed a computerized solution that has proved economic for many small web sites such as blogs.

Google's Content Network supplies advertising inventory from "hundreds of thousands" of web sites that have joined its network. In what is known as "contextual advertising", Google's advertising network auctions keywords that appear on the web page of participating publishers and inserts ads from participating advertisers based on the appearance of those keywords and possibly some other characteristics of the website. The publisher pastes html code into its webpage to receive and display the ad, while the advertiser typically uses an auction and advertising campaign management tool that is bundled into the software package it uses for search campaigns. (Sears, 2005). Many larger websites also use Google's contextual advertising for some of their less desirable space.

It appears likely that online advertising provides two potentially significant economic efficiencies. First, a promising conjecture is that online advertising allows the economy to reduce the amount of resources devoted to creating content for aggregating and sorting potential buyers. Society may not need to invest as much in magazines, newspapers, and other media whose main purpose is aggregating the right eyeballs for advertisers. Although consumers value that content they have not had to pay for its cost of production. Second, online advertising likely increases the accuracy of the match between the buyer and the seller. The seller has greater ability to target consumers that are likely to buy and the consumer is more likely to receive useful messages and less likely to receive time-consuming but irrelevant messages. In both cases one can argue that there are some losses that also need to be considered. The news media gathers and reports news through professional journalists in some cases scattered through the world including war zones. One can argue that the news media provides an important public service in a democratic society and that its value exceeds what individuals or advertisers may pay for it. Moreover, as with any technological change some people gain and others lose. Those who strongly prefer the touch and feel of newspapers will lose if not enough people are willing to support the costs of these newspapers. In addition, online advertising may provide more efficient matching and delivery of ads but that begs the longstanding question of whether advertising is providing people with valuable information that helps them make better buying decisions, or whether it is getting people to buy based on deceptive information or by persuading them to do things that they will soon regret.

Issues in Industry Evolution

Online advertising is one of those "gales of creative destruction" that will reshape several industries and radically change traditional ways of delivering advertising messages from sellers to prospective buyers.

Behavioral Targeting and Data Analytics

As noted earlier it is possible for online entities to gather data on what people have done online including what they have searched for, what web sites they have browsed, and perhaps even what they have purchased online. Those data together with other information on these people can be used to target advertisements to people based on their behavior.

For example, an advertising intermediary could help an automobile insurer target individuals who probably have good risk profiles, who may be buying an expensive new car, and who are therefore likely to in the market for automobile insurance. The intermediary could infer that the individual may have bought new expensive car from the fact that the individual has been browsing particular websites that people go to when they are going to purchase a luxury automobile. The intermediary might also be able to infer from online behavior that the individual falls into a low-risk insurance category. It could infer from a user's IP address and browsing behavior that the user is probably a woman (from browsing behavior) who lives in a well-off suburb (from the IP address), in a region with low accident and theft rates (from the IP address), and is over the age of 25 (from browsing behavior). The intermediary might identify potential sales targets by just using simple screening methods such as these or may use more sophisticated statistical methods to predict the sort of the prospects the insurance company is looking for.

Either way the advertising intermediary can use these methods to determine whether a particular individual who is browsing a website at a particular moment has exhibited the web browsing behaviors and personal characteristics that make that person a good target for an ad. It can make that decision almost instantaneously and then insert an ad into advertising space on the page that the target is viewing. The advertiser would typically pay a premium over standard online advertising rates for views by these targeted individuals because the likelihood that they will "convert" the view by this "qualified prospect" into a sale and thus their expected profits is higher.

Although behavioral targeting is an area of intense innovation, as of 2009 only a small portion of the advertising revenue earned by publishers results from selling these sorts of behaviorally targeted advertisements. Two factors limit the current deployment of this seemingly efficient method of advertising. First, since behavioral targeting narrows the group of people that see an advertisement the likelihood that these individuals will ultimately purchase the product has to be high enough to offset the reduction in the number of people that view that advertisement. On average only about 1 out of 400 viewers click on a given ad (Marketing Sherpa, 2008) and only a fraction of those viewers purchase the product. Unless behavioral targeting is sufficiently precise advertisers may prefer to reach a larger group of individuals all else equal. Reaching 10,000 people of whom 1/1000 (or 10) will ultimately purchase a product is better than reaching 2,000 people of whom 1/500 (4) will ultimately purchase the product. There is a tradeoff between precision and reach. In this example, all else equal, a behavioral screen that targeted a fifth of the potential population would have to identify people that were more than five times as likely to buy to be better than targeting everyone. Precision is limited by the amount and quality of data that are available. (In addition, behavioral targeting is not relevant for brand advertising that is generally aimed at a broad audience to influence their views on a company or a product rather than to make a direct sale.)

Second, the advertising platform that implements a behavioral targeting campaign must have access to a large enough universe of viewers to find enough candidates to make the campaign worthwhile to the advertiser. There are fixed costs of designing and executing advertising campaigns; the advertiser needs to make enough sales to recover these costs and make a return. Suppose that it costs £ 10,000 to design a campaign and the expected incremental profit from each sale that results from this campaign is £ 10. Then the campaign would have to generate an expected 1000 conversions to recover the fixed costs. If only 1 out of 1000 consumers that are exposed to an ad is converted to a sale, the campaign would need to reach at least 1,000,000 individuals for it to break even. Consider a behavioral targeting campaign that converts 1 out of 500 consumers by targeting the 20 percent of the potential universe of people that are the most likely buyers. To yield 1000 conversions that campaign would need to reach 2,500,000 people. The total sample needed depends generally on the conversion rate and the targeting rates which depend on each other. Many advertising networks are not large enough to engage in highly refined behavioral targeting while some of the largest advertising platforms have not yet deployed highly refined targeting.

Several developments may increase the use of behavioral targeting methods. With improvements in predictive techniques and the availability of data on viewers behavioral targeting would become more precise and advertisers would increasingly prefer targeting to reach. If advertising networks that use behavioral targeting methods increase their scale, or if larger advertising platforms increasingly deploy behavioral targeting and data collection methods, they will obtain enough viewers to make behavioral campaigns economically efficient. Privacy concerns discussed below could limit the development of behavioral targeting. Consumers may resist having advertising platforms collect detailed information about their browsing behavior and government regulations may limit the ability of advertising intermediaries to collect these data.

Creative Destruction and the Migration of Offline to Online

Traditional advertising sustains a complex ecosystem of businesses. A wide range of media entities earn significant portions—sometimes all—of their revenues from the sale of advertising inventory. These include newspapers, magazines, free television, free radio, billboards, and yellow pages. In turn, these businesses support a variety of content generation businesses, including television production companies and musicians. Diverse other businesses work with advertisers including advertising agencies, media buyers, and audience measurement firms. Every business in this ecosystem felt a breeze as on-line advertising arrived in the mid 27 1990s, and then felt a stiff wind by the early 2000s as the online advertising industry came together.

Online advertising methods pose a serious threat to traditional methods for several reasons. First, they increase the efficiency of matching buyers and sellers and delivering advertising messages to the buyers. In the long run one would expect that this will reduce the economic importance of traditional intermediaries such as advertising agencies, media buyers and sellers, and direct sales forces.

Second, they increase the supply of advertising inventory significantly. By providing a method for earning revenue from attracting viewers, online advertising attracts the entry of content providers that supply advertising inventory. During the 2000s that has included of user generated video sites such as YouTube, social networking sites such as Face book. There are low financial barriers to the formation of these sites as a result of web technologies. This increased supply of advertising inventory puts downward pressure on advertising rates, promises to reduce the returns that traditional media can get from advertising, and therefore potentially reduces the quality-adjusted supply of content by traditional media.

Third, online advertising increases the supply of online content which provides a substitute for traditional content. The potential returns from online advertising encourage entities such as Yahoo! and MSN, as well as traditional media, to present various kinds of content online that consumers used to consume mainly offline. In addition, of course, viewers are moving from offline to online media because, as with the move from radio to television, they simply like the content better along certain dimension, which can include the ease, flexibility, and interactive dimensions of access. Thus far the evidence shows that as a result of online content consumers have substituted away from radio and newspaper content but not television content.

The production and programming sides of the business could operate much like they do today although many of the business methods, and assorted institutions, for selling and delivering advertising would change. The same is true for radio which is already being delivered over the internet. One cannot consume internet radio on the morning drive to work at the moment but that may change once there is more extensive wireless internet coverage and cars become equipped with internet-enabled electronics. The forces of creative destruction have hit the newspaper industry the hardest and the earliest. The industry is in free fall as a result of the self-reinforcing migration of readers and advertisers online.. Although many newspapers have developed web versions that attract significant number of viewers, their increased online advertising revenues have only partly compensated for their loss of traditional advertising revenues. As radio and television move to internet-enabled platforms they could find the same decline in advertising revenues with the same impact on the economics of providing traditional content.

The industrial structure of the online advertising industry could evolve in a variety of ways. One possibility is that the industry will have a highly concentrated set of intermediaries at its center, with many content providers around this core. Some of the intermediaries will focus on mass advertising while others will focus on niches. The ultimate structure depends on the relative importance of several factors: the strength of indirect network effects and scale economies on one side, and the possible benefits of specialization of knowledge in certain areas.

ONLINE BANKING

Online banking (or *Internet banking*) allows customers to conduct financial transactions on a secure website operated by their retail or virtual bank, credit union or building society. Online banking solutions have many features and capabilities in common, but traditionally also have some that are application specific.

The common features fall broadly into several categories

- Transactional (e.g., performing a financial transaction such as an account to account transfer, paying a bill, wire transfer, apply for a loan, new account, etc.)
  - Payments to third parties, including bill payments and telegraphic/wire transfers
  - Funds transfers between a customer's own transactional account and savings accounts
  - Investment purchase or sale
  - Loan applications and transactions, such as repayments of enrollments
- Non-transactional (e.g., online statements, cheque links, cobrowsing, chat)
  - Viewing recent transactions

  - o Downloading bank statements, for example in PDF format
  - o Viewing images of paid cheques
- Financial Institution Administration
- Management of multiple users having varying levels of authority
- Transaction approval process.

Features commonly unique to Internet banking include :

- Personal financial management support, such as importing data into personal accounting software. Some online banking platforms support account aggregation to allow the customers to monitor all of their accounts in one place whether they are with their main bank or with other institutions.

The UK's first home online banking services was set-up by Bank of Scotland for customers of the Nottingham Building Society (NBS) in 1983. The system used was based on the UK's Prestel system and used a computer, such as the BBC Micro, or keyboard connected to the telephone system and television set. The system (known as 'Homelink') allowed on-line viewing of statements, bank transfers and bill payments. In order to make bank transfers and bill payments, a written instruction giving details of the intended recipient had to be sent to the NBS who set the details up on the Homelink system. Typical recipients were gas, electricity and telephone companies and accounts with other banks. Details of payments to be made were input into the NBS system by the account holder via Prestel. A cheque was then sent by NBS to the payee and an advice giving details of the payment was sent to the account holder. BACS was later used to transfer the payment directly.

Stanford Federal Credit Union was the first financial institution to offer online internet banking services to all of its members in October 1994 Today, many banks are internet only banks. Unlike their predecessors, these internet only banks do not maintain brick and mortar bank branches. Instead, they typically differentiate themselves by offering better interest rates and online banking features.

Security

Protection through single password authentication, as is the case in most secure Internet shopping sites, is not considered secure enough for personal online banking applications in some countries. Basically there exist two different security methods for online banking.

- The PIN/TAN system where the PIN represents a password, used for the login and TANs representing one-time passwords to authenticate transactions. TANs can be distributed in different ways, the most popular one is to send a list of TANs to the online banking user by postal letter. The most secure way of using TANs is to generate them by need using a security token. These token generated TANs depend on the time and a unique secret, stored in the security token (this is called two-factor authentication or 2FA). Usually online banking with PIN/TAN is done via a web browser using SSL secured connections, so that there is no additional encryption needed.

Another way to provide TANs to an online banking user is to send the TAN of the current bank transaction to the user's (GSM) mobile phone via SMS. The SMS text usually quotes the transaction amount and details, the TAN is only valid for a short period of time. Especially in Germany and Austria, many banks have adopted this "SMS TAN" service as it is considered very secure.

- Signature based online banking where all transactions are signed and encrypted digitally. The Keys for the signature generation and encryption can be stored on smartcards or any memory medium, depending on the concrete implementation.

Internet Advertising and its Effects on the Industry

Internet Advertising and marketing has had a huge effect on the industries world wide for that matter. Internet advertisements offering music downloads of songs and music, has had an impact on the music industry as well as the video sales due to the fact that people just don't go out and buy CD's as often as they used too. Flea markets and roadside markets or second hand shops have felt the plunge as well, now that Internet advertising shows items being sold by online auctions or individual websites. Book sales are down and the production or publishing companies are suffering because of obtaining them through Internet advertisements of e-books of novels as well as new releases. Sometimes the e-books have a fee but nothing like that of actually buying a real book.

Banking and financial institutions were suffering until the idea of online banking came into the scheme of things. But even with this being said, the banks and financial institutions have felt the effects of Internet advertising online banking forcing the loss of employment for those who would originally be employed to do the services the online banking now provides. There are other companies who provide their services on the internet and the internet advertising used to let people know about these services only seem to make the idea of everything going to the computer simply harder for the industry. Many people look for Internet advertisements on televisions, or wholesale furniture even, this has an impact on different companies who would normally sell these things.

It used to be a concern as far as security on the Internet, when Internet advertisements would show a product you could purchase online, but this issue was resolved with the introduction of encryption of sites that deal with personal information. There are more security features that are now in places over the Internet to protect data. Also, with the higher speed of Internet connections, many that look up internet advertisements can find what they are looking for a lot faster than having to get into a vehicle and drive across town to find the same item. Currently 150 million people use the online banking system, partly for convenience, and partly for the convenience of when they see an Internet advertisement that shows an item they need or want, it is much easier to obtain.

The effects the Internet advertising has on industry continues to surge, while in the meantime the industry suffers more. Online Internet advertising has grown to at least tens of billions of dollars annually. Last year the total spent by people by using Internet advertising, auctions, or department stores by the use of being on the Internet was approximately $ 16.9 billion dollars. The industry is truly being affected by the Internet advertising and the impact that the internet itself is having on the world. It is expected to continue to climb, and if this is what is going to be what effect will all this have on industry in the future?

Web Page

A *web page* or *webpage* is a document or information resource that is suitable for the World Wide Web and can be accessed through a web browser and displayed on a monitor or mobile device. This information is usually in HTML or XHTML format, and may provide navigation to other web pages via hypertext links. Web pages frequently subsume other resources such as style sheets, scripts and images into their final presentation. Web pages may be retrieved from a local computer or from a remote web server. The web server may restrict access only to a private network, e.g. a corporate intranet, or it may publish pages on the World Wide Web. Web pages are requested and served from web servers using Hypertext Transfer Protocol (HTTP). Web pages may consist of files of static text and other content stored within the web server's file system (static web pages), or may be constructed by server-side software when they are requested (dynamic web pages). Client-side scripting can make web pages more responsive to user input once on the client browser. Web pages will often require more screen space than is available for a particular display resolution. Most modern browsers will place a scrollbar (a sliding tool at the side of the screen that allows the user to move the page up or down, or side-to-side) in the window to allow the user to see all content. Scrolling horizontally is less prevalent than vertical scrolling, not only because such pages often do not print properly, but because it inconveniences the user more so than vertical scrolling would (because lines are horizontal; scrolling back and forth for every line is much more inconvenient than scrolling after reading a whole screen; also most computer keyboards have page up and down keys, and many computer mice have vertical scroll wheels, but the horizontal scrolling equivalents are rare).

When web pages are stored in a common directory of a web server, they become a website. A website will typically contain a group of web pages that are linked together, or have some other coherent method of navigation. The most important web page to have on a website is the index page. Depending on the web server settings, this index page can have many different names, but the most common is index.html. When a browser visits the homepage for a website, or any URL pointing to a directory rather than a specific file, the web server will serve the index page to the requesting browser. If no index page is defined in the configuration, or no such file exists on the server, either an error or directory listing will be served to the browser. A web page can either be a single HTML file, or made up of several HTML files using frames or Server Side Includes (SSIs). Frames have been known to cause problems with web accessibility, copyright, navigation, printing and search engine rankings and are now less often used than they were in the 1990s. Both frames and SSIs allow certain content which appears on many pages, such as page navigation or page headers, to be repeated without duplicating the HTML in many files. Frames and the W3C recommended alternative of 2000, the <object> tag also allow some content to remain in one place while other content can be scrolled using conventional scrollbars. Modern CSS and JavaScript client-side techniques can also achieve all of these goals and more. When creating a web page, it is important to ensure it conforms to the World Wide Web Consortium (W3C) standards for HTML, CSS, XML and other standards. The W3C standards are in place to ensure all browsers which conform to their standards can display identical content without any special consideration for proprietary rendering techniques. A properly coded web page is going to be accessible to many different browsers old and new alike, display resolutions, as well as those users with audio or visual impairments.

Personalization involves using technology to accommodate the differences between individuals. Once confined mainly to the Web, it is increasingly becoming a factor in education, health care (i.e. personalized medicine), television, and in both "business to business" and (B2B) "business to consumer" (B2C) settings. Web pages are personalized based on the characteristics (interests, social category, context,...) of an individual. Personalization implies that the changes are based on implicit data, such as items purchased or pages viewed. The term customization is used instead when the site only uses explicit data such as ratings or preferences. On an intranet or B2E Enterprise Web portals, *personalization* is often based on user attributes such as department, functional area, or role. The term *customization* in this context refers to the ability of users to modify the page layout or specify what content should be displayed. There are three categories of personalization:

1. Profile/Group based
2. Behaviour based (also known as Wisdom of the Crowds)
3. Collaboration based

Web personalization models include rules-based filtering, based on "if this, then that" rules processing, and collaborative filtering, which serves relevant material to customers by combining their own personal preferences with the preferences of like-minded others. Collaborative filtering works well for books, music, video, etc. However, it does not work well for a number of categories such as apparel, jewelry, cosmetics, etc. Recently, another method, "Prediction Based on Benefit", has been proposed for products with complex attributes such as apparel.

There are three broad methods of personalization:

1. Implicit
2. Explicit
3. Hybrid

With implicit personalization the personalization is performed by the web page (or information system) based on the different categories mentioned above. With explicit personalization, the web page (or information system) is changed by the user using the features provided by the system. Hybrid personalization combines the above two approaches to leverage the best of both worlds. Many companies offer services for web recommendation and email recommendation that are based on personalization or anonymously collected user behaviors. Following the example of Amazon.com, the online retailing industry has been early adopters of 3rd party personalization tools offered by companies like PredictiveIntent, MyBuys, Barilliance, iGoDigital, 4-Tell and Certona. Other 3rd party vendors like Choice Stream or Vignette bring personalization to content and display advertising.

Personalization is also being considered for use in less overtly commercial applications to improve the user experience online. Remote control manufacturer Ruwido developed an interactive IPTV platform in 2010 called Voco Media, which controls digital media in the living room using web personalization. It uses personalization as a tool that supports modern forms of TV usage, by allowing users to create different profiles for each family member, personalized menu structures and fingerprint recognition.

Personalized search refers to search experiences that are tailored specifically to an individual's interests by incorporating information about the individual beyond specific query provided. Pitkow et al. describe two general approaches to personalizing search results, one involving modifying the user's query and the other re-ranking search results. While many search engines take advantage of information about people in general, or about specific groups of people, personalized search depends on a user profile that is unique to the individual. Research systems that personalize search results model their users in different ways. Some rely on users explicitly specifying their interests or on demographic/ cognitive characteristics But user supplied information can be hard to collect and keep up to date. Others have built implicit user models based on content the user has read or their history of interaction with Web pages.

CHAPTER

10

Affiliate Marketing

Affiliate marketing is a marketing practice in which a business rewards one or more affiliates for each visitor or customer brought about by the affiliate's own marketing efforts. Examples include rewards sites, where users are rewarded with cash or gifts, for the completion of an offer, and the referral of others to the site. The industry has four core players: the merchant (also known as 'retailer' or 'brand'), the network, the publisher (also known as 'the affiliate'), and the customer. The market has grown in complexity to warrant a secondary tier of players, including affiliate management agencies, super-affiliates and specialized third party vendors.

Affiliate marketing overlaps with other Internet marketing methods to some degree, because affiliates often use regular advertising methods. Those methods include organic search engine optimization, paid search engine marketing, e-mail marketing, and in some sense display advertising. On the other hand, affiliates sometimes use less orthodox techniques, such as publishing reviews of products or services offered by a partner.

Affiliate marketing—using one website to drive traffic to another—is a form of online marketing, which is frequently overlooked by advertisers. While search engines, e-mail, and website syndication capture much of the attention of online retailers, affiliate marketing carries a much lower profile. Still, affiliates continue to play a significant role in e-retailers' marketing strategies.

ADVERTISING

Advertising is a form of communication used to persuade an audience (viewers, readers or listeners) to take some action with respect to products, ideas, or services. Most commonly, the desired result is to drive consumer behavior with respect to a commercial offering, although political and ideological advertising is also common. Advertising messages are usually paid for by sponsors and viewed via various media; including traditional media such as newspapers, magazines, television, radio, outdoor or direct mail; or new media such as websites and text messages.

Commercial advertisers often seek to generate increased consumption of their products or services through "branding," which involves the repetition of an image or product name in an effort to associate certain qualities with the brand in the minds of consumers. Non-commercial advertisers who spend money to advertise items other than a consumer product or service include political parties, interest groups, religious organizations and governmental agencies. Nonprofit organizations may rely on free modes of persuasion, such as a public service announcement.

Display advertising is a type of advertising that typically contains text (i.e., copy), logos, photographs or other images, location maps, and similar items. In periodicals, display advertising can appear on the same page as, or on the page adjacent to, general editorial content. In contrast, classified advertising generally appears in a distinct section, was traditionally text-only, and was available in a limited selection of typefaces.

Display advertisements are not required to contain images, audio, or video: Textual advertisements are also used where text may be more appropriate or more effective. An example of textual advertisements is commercial messages sent to mobile device users, emails, etc. Display advertising also appears on the Internet, as a form of internet marketing. Display advertising appears on web pages in many forms, including web banners. These banners can consist of static or animated images, as well as interactive media that may include audio and video elements. Adobe Systems Flash or.gif are the preferred presentation formats for such interactive advertisements. The Interactive Advertising Bureau, an industry trade group, sets some standards for online shapes and sizes. Yahoo currently has the largest share of the U.S. market in online display advertising. As of February 28th, 2011 display advertising is a $ 17 billion business globally.

Display advertising on the Internet is widely used for branding. This is why metrics like interaction time are becoming more relevant. However, this may change in the future as display advertising is becoming much more targeted to users, much like how search engine ads can be extremely relevant users based on what they are searching for. Display advertisers use cookie and browser history to determine demographics and interests of users and target appropriate ads to those browsers. Banner ad standards have changed over the years to larger sizes, in part due to increased resolution of standard monitors and browsers, in part to provide advertisers with more impact for their investment. The standards continue to evolve. Posters, fliers, transit cards, tents, scale models are examples of display advertising. Banner ads can be targeted to internet browsers in many different ways in order to reach the advertiser's most relevant audience. Behavioral retargeting, demographic targeting, geographic targeting, and site based targeting are all common ways in which advertisers choose to target their banner ads.

ONLINE MARKETING

Online Marketing is the art and science of selling products and/or services over digital networks, such as the Internet and cellular phone networks. The art of online marketing involves finding the right online marketing mix of strategies that appeals to your target market and will actually translate into sales. The science of online marketing is the research and analysis that goes into both choosing the online marketing strategies to use and measuring the success of those online marketing strategies.

Customers: In recent years, online shopping has become popular; however, it still caters to the middle and upper class. In order to shop online, one must be able to have access to a computer, a bank account and a debit card. Shopping has evolved with the growth of technology. According to research found in the Journal of Electronic Commerce, if one focuses on the demographic characteristics of the in-home shopper, in general, the higher the level of education, income, and occupation of the head of the household, the more favourable the perception of non-store shopping., Enrique.(2005) The Impact of Internet User Shopping Patterns and Demographics on Consumer Mobile Buying

The advantages of online marketing are myriad. Chief among them is that it is relatively inexpensive compared to other types of *marketing,* especially when you compare cost with the scope of the target audience. For a comparatively reduced advertising budget, companies can now reach a far larger demographic.

Customers can shop at their own convenience, and are able to research products and prices from the comfort of their own home, rather than having to traipse around brick-and-mortar stores. Owing to the very nature of the internet, marketers can measure all sorts of statistics pertaining to the success of their *online marketing* campaigns. For example, they can track the number, length and frequency of website visits, and which pages were visited and for how long. Information such as this is incredibly useful in designing a marketing website and for implementing and testing strategies to encourage customer base growth.

Disadvantages: Although dialup connection services appear to be on the way out, mobile devices have taken over as broad band's weaker cousin. The more limited connectivity and reduced hardware performance require businesses to similarly temper their online multimedia marketing extravaganzas to cater to this massively pervasive medium. A balance must be struck between catering to the PC based platforms and mobile devices. Many companies, as a way of dealing with this dichotomy, release their own stripped-down applications for mobile devices so the user can experience a similar level of presentation without the problems that occur when a limited capacity device struggles to cope with broadband-focused material.

Another disadvantage of *online marketing* is the consumer cannot gain first hand experience of a physical product before he or she buys it. For example, you cannot try on a sweater you buy online. Many companies combat this shortfall by employing rigorous return policies and in-store pickups.

Security issues are also a concern for many online consumers. The transfer of personal information over the internet is ripe for exploitation by unscrupulous merchants who can sell or give your information to other companies. Generally, the bigger and more well-known the company, the lesser the security risk.

Online marketing has become the storefront process for many of the world's largest companies. In this current climate of connectivity, any company without an online presence may as well not exist. To many, it is by far the most important part of their marketing strategy.

ONLINE MARKETING STRATEGIES

Regardless of the type of business you run, whether it is a home business selling products online, a single local retailer, or a chain of shops in multiple cities, having an online presence can be a very valuable thing. That said, different types of businesses will benefit more from different types of online marketing, and finding an internet marketing strategy that works for your business is an effective way to get the most bang for your buck. Here, we will address several different types of web marketing strategies, each of which is more appropriate for a particular business model.

The internet marketing strategy for a home business will ideally be quite different than that for other business models. Because home businesses typically do not stock their own inventory, or have a real-world retail location, it is often in your best interest to provide a high volume of content on your website. Having a larger amount of content on your business site will provide your customers with a place to get information on your business, and to learn more about the products and services you provide. This will also increase the proportion of customers you attract through search engines, as rich content is the best way to optimize a website for search engines.

Local businesses that have a real world retail location for products, or who offer services within a limited local area, will likely see the best results from a localized internet marketing strategy. Local businesses can take advantage of a type of online marketing known as geo location or geo targeting, which allows them to have their online advertisements seen only by users who are accessing the internet from a particular area. For example, a plumbing company that operates within a single city can make sure that only users browsing the web from within that city see their ads, thus ensuring that they do not waste advertising money on people who will not access their services.

Lastly, franchises that cover a wider area can use a broader internet marketing strategy that will promote their corporate brand, and offer tools to help users find store locations in various cities. Promoting your business through related websites and on commonly accessed sites such as Google and Facebook are both good ways to market a business that covers a large area, particularly if you offer well known products or services that can be accessed in various locations.

Developing a successful internet marketing strategy is an essential part of your online success. In order to succeed, you must develop and implement a strategic plan that includes all of the following:

- A great product
- A web site specifically designed to sell
- A killer marketing strategy

Each step plays an important role in your overall strategy and must be developed to its fullest potential. If even one step fails, your chances of success will be minimal.

Developing Your Product

Your first step will be to develop a great product. You're probably thinking that's easier said than done, but it's really not. The absolute best product is one that you can develop yourself and deliver over the Internet. With today's technology, there is absolutely no reason why you can't create your own product. The knowledge you have within your own mind is extremely valuable. Everybody is good at something, has a special talent or some specialized knowledge. Use this knowledge to create a product.

The key to developing a great product is exclusiveness. Your product should be unique and not be in competition with hundreds of other similar products. You must give your potential customers exactly what they want. Develop a high-quality product that fills a void to increase your chance of success.

Another consideration of great importance is your target market. Keep in mind, the Internet is a global marketplace. Develop a product with a large geographic target and a wide appeal. A great product will fulfill a need or desire and provide instant gratification.

Here are a few of the top sellers:

- Software
- Information
- Private sites
- Internet services

Before you develop your product, do some research—find out exactly what people want and develop your product accordingly. The most important consideration when developing your product is quality. Your product should not only deliver what you promise, but should go above and beyond the expected and overdeliver. Your customers satisfaction is of the utmost importance.

Developing Your Web Site

Once you've developed a great product, your next step will be to develop a great web site. Your web site must be specifically designed to sell your product. Everything within your web site should have one purpose—getting your visitor to take action. Words are the most powerful marketing tool you have. The right words will turn your visitors into customers. The wrong words will cause them to click away and never return. Your words are the entire foundation of your business. Your product, your web site and your marketing strategies all depend upon your words. Fancy graphics don't make sales—words do. Every word, sentence and headline should have one specific purpose—to lead your potential customer to your order page. Write your web site copy as if you are talking to just one person. Identify a problem and validate that one visitor's need for a solution. Continue to write and explain why your product is the solution to their problem. Tell them exactly what your product will do for them—why it will solve their problems and how. Pack your copy with benefits and more benefits. Write to persuade—that's the bottom line.

Developing Your Marketing Strategies

Your marketing strategy is the final process of your plan. Your plan must include both short-term and long-term strategies in order to succeed.

Short term marketing strategies are those that bring you a temporary boost in traffic. Although these techniques are very important to your over-all plan, they are only a temporary traffic source and must not be solely relied upon.

Long-term marketing strategies are those that bring you a steady stream of targeted traffic over time. These strategies will continue to produce results even years down the road. By creating and implementing a balanced marketing strategy, using both short-term and long-term strategies, you will drive a steady stream of targeted traffic to your web site.If you use this simple formula when creating your Internet marketing strategy and excel at all three, you can literally guarantee your success.

Origin

The concept of revenue sharing—paying commission for

referred business—predates affiliate marketing and the Internet. The translation of the revenue share principles to mainstream e-commerce happened in November 1994 almost four years after the origination of the World Wide Web. The concepts of affiliate marketing on the Internet was conceived of, put into practice and patented by William J. Tobin, the founder of PC Flowers and Gifts.

In business, revenue sharing refers to the sharing of profits and losses among different groups. One form shares between the general partner(s) and limited partners in a limited partnership. Another form shares with a company's employees, and another between companies in a business alliance. On the Internet, revenue sharing is also known as cost per sale, and accounts for about 80% of affiliate compensation programs. E-commerce web site operators using revenue sharing pay affiliates a certain percentage of sales revenues (usually excluding tax, shipping and other 3rd party cost that the customer pays) generated by customers whom the affiliate refer via various advertising methods. Another form of online revenue sharing consists in people working together and registering online in a way similar to that of a corporation, and sharing the proceeds. A third form of revenue sharing on the internet consists of enticing internet users to sign up and create content by offering a share of advertising revenue.

Amazon.com (Amazon) launched its associate program in July 1996: Amazon associates could place banner or text links on their site for individual books, or link directly to the Amazon home page. When visitors clicked from the associate's website through to Amazon and purchased a book, the associate received a commission. Amazon was not the first merchant to offer an affiliate program, but its program was the first to become widely known and serve as a model for subsequent programs.

In February 2000, Amazon announced that it had been granted a patent on components of an affiliate program. The patent application was submitted in June 1997, which predates most affiliate programs, but not PC Flowers and Gifts.com (October 1994), AutoWeb.com (October 1995), Kbkids.com/BrainPlay.com (January 1996), EPage (April 1996), and several others.

COMPENSATION METHODS

Predominant compensation methods: Eighty percent of affiliate programs today use revenue sharing or cost per sale (CPS) as a compensation method, nineteen percent use cost per action (CPA), and the remaining programs use other methods such as cost per click (CPC) or cost per mille (CPM).

Diminished compensation methods: Within more mature markets, less than one percent of traditional affiliate marketing programs today use cost per click and cost per mille. However, these compensation methods are used heavily in display advertising and paid search.

Cost per mille requires only that the publisher make the advertising available on his website and display it to his visitors in order to receive a commission. Pay per click requires one additional step in the conversion process to generate revenue for the publisher: A visitor must not only be made aware of the advertisement, but must also click on the advertisement to visit the advertiser's website.

Cost per click was more common in the early days of affiliate marketing, but has diminished in use over time due to click fraud issues very similar to the click fraud issues modern search engines are facing today. Contextual advertising programs are not considered in the statistic pertaining to diminished use of cost per click, as it is uncertain if contextual advertising can be considered affiliate marketing.

While these models have diminished in mature e-commerce and online advertising markets they are still prevalent in some more nascent industries. China is one example where Affiliate Marketing does not overtly resemble the same model in the West. With many affiliates being paid a flat "Cost Per Day" with some networks offering Cost Per Click or CPM.

PERFORMANCE MARKETING

Affiliate marketing is also called "performance marketing", in reference to how sales employees are typically being compensated. Such employees are typically paid a commission for each sale they close, and sometimes are paid performance incentives for exceeding targeted baselines. Affiliates are not employed by the advertiser whose products or services they promote, but the compensation models applied to affiliate marketing are very similar to the ones used for people in the advertisers' internal sales department.

The phrase, "Affiliates are an extended sales force for your business", which is often used to explain affiliate marketing, is not completely accurate. The primary difference between the two is that affiliate marketers provide little if any influence on a possible prospect in the conversion process once that prospect is directed to the advertiser's website. The sales team of the advertiser, however, does have the control and influence up to the point where the prospect signs the contract or completes the purchase.

Cost per mille (CPM), also called *cost ‰* and *cost per thousand* (CPT) (in Latin *mille* means thousand), is a commonly used measurement in advertising. Radio, television, newspaper, magazine, out-of-home advertising, and online advertising can be purchased on the basis of what it costs to show the ad to one thousand viewers (CPM). It is used in marketing as a benchmark to calculate the relative cost of an advertising campaign or an ad message in a given medium. Rather than an absolute cost, CPM estimates the cost per 1000 views of the ad. This traditional form of measuring advertising success can also be used in tandem with performance based models such as percentage of sale, or cost per conversion (CPA).

Multi-tier programs: Some advertisers offer multi-tier programs that distribute commission into a hierarchical referral network of sign-ups and sub-partners. In practical terms, publisher "A" signs up to the program with an advertiser and gets rewarded for the agreed activity conducted by a referred visitor. If publisher "A" attracts publishers "B" and "C" to sign up for the same program using his sign-up code, all future activities performed by publishers "B" and "C" will result in additional commission (at a lower rate) for publisher "A".

Two-tier programs exist in the minority of affiliate programs; most are simply one-tier. Referral programs beyond two-tier resemble multi-level marketing (MLM) or network marketing but are different: Multi-level marketing (MLM) or network marketing associations tend to have more complex commission requirements/qualifications than standard affiliate programs.

From the Advertiser Perspective

Pros and cons: Merchants favor affiliate marketing because in most cases it uses a "pay for performance" model, meaning that the merchant does not incur a marketing expense unless results are accrued (excluding any initial setup cost). Some businesses owe much of their success to this marketing technique, a notable example being Amazon.com. Unlike display advertising, however, affiliate marketing is not easily scalable.

Implementation options: Some merchants run their own (i.e., in-house) affiliate programs using popular software while others use third-party services provided by intermediaries to track traffic or sales that are referred from affiliates (*see* outsourced program management). Merchants can choose from two different types of affiliate management solutions: standalone software or hosted services, typically called affiliate networks. Payouts to affiliates or publishers are either made by the networks on behalf of the merchant, by the network, consolidated across all merchants where the publisher has a relationship with and earned commissions or directly by the merchant itself.

Affiliate Management and Program Management Outsourcing

Successful affiliate programs require significant work and maintenance. Having a successful affiliate program is more difficult than when such programs were just emerging. With the exception of some vertical markets, it is rare for an affiliate program to generate considerable revenue with poor management or no management (i.e., "auto-drive").

Uncontrolled affiliate programs did—and continue to do so today—aid rogue affiliates, who use spamming, trademark infringement, false advertising, "cookie cutting" typo squatting and other unethical methods that have given affiliate marketing a negative reputation.

The increased number of Internet businesses and the increased number of people that trust the current technology enough to shop and do business online allows further maturation of affiliate marketing. The opportunity to generate a considerable amount of profit combined with a crowded marketplace filled with competitors of equal quality and size makes it more difficult for merchants to be noticed. In this environment, however, being noticed can yield greater rewards.

Recently, the Internet marketing industry has become more advanced. In some areas online media has been rising to the sophistication of offline media, in which advertising has been largely professional and competitive. There are significantly more requirements that merchants must meet to be successful, and those requirements are becoming too burdensome for the merchant to manage successfully in-house. An increasing number of merchants are seeking alternative options found in relatively new outsourced (affiliate) program management (OPM) companies, which are often founded by veteran affiliate managers and network program managers. OPM companies perform affiliate program management for the merchants as a service, similar to advertising agencies promoting a brand or product as done in offline marketing.

Locating Affiliate Programs

There are three primary ways to locate affiliate programs for a target website:

1. Affiliate program directories,
2. Large affiliate networks that provide the platform for dozens or even hundreds of advertisers, and
3. The target website itself. (Websites that offer an affiliate program often have a link titled "affiliate program", "affiliates", "referral program", or "webmasters"—usually in the footer or "About" section of the website.)

If the above locations do not yield information pertaining to affiliates, it may be the case that there exists a non-public affiliate program. Utilizing one of the common website correlation methods may provide clues about the affiliate network. The most definitive method for finding this information is to contact the website owner directly, if a contact method can be located.

Past and current issues : Since the emergence of affiliate marketing, there has been little control over affiliate activity. Unscrupulous affiliates have used spam, false advertising, forced clicks (to get tracking cookies set on users' computers), adware, and other methods to drive traffic to their sponsors. Although many affiliate programs have terms of service that contain rules against spam, this marketing method has historically proven to attract abuse from spammers.

E-mail spam: In the infancy of affiliate marketing, many Internet users held negative opinions due to the tendency of affiliates to use spam to promote the programs in which they were enrolled. As affiliate marketing matured, many affiliate merchants have refined their terms and conditions to prohibit affiliates from spamming.

Search engine spam : As search engines have become more prominent, some affiliate marketers have shifted from sending e-mail spam to creating automatically generated web pages that often contain product data feeds provided by merchants. The goal of such web pages is to manipulate the relevancy or prominence of resources indexed by a search engine, also known as spamdexing. Each page can be targeted to a different niche market through the use of specific keywords, with the result being a skewed form of search engine optimization. Spam is the biggest threat to organic search engines, whose goal is to provide quality search results for keywords or phrases entered by their users. Google's PageRank algorithm update ("BigDaddy") in February 2006—the final stage of Google's major update ("Jagger") that began in mid-summer 2005—specifically targeted spamdexing with great success. This update thus enabled Google to remove a large amount of mostly computer-generated duplicate content from its index.

Websites consisting mostly of affiliate links have previously held a negative reputation for under delivering quality content. In 2005 there were active changes made by Google, where certain websites were labeled as "thin affiliates". Such websites were either removed from Google's index or were relocated within the results page (i.e., moved from the top-most results to a lower position). To avoid this categorization, affiliate marketer webmasters must create quality content on their websites that distinguishes their work from the work of spammers or banner farms, which only contain links leading to merchant sites.

Some commentators originally suggested that Affiliate links work best in the context of the information contained within the website itself. For instance, if a website contains information pertaining to publishing a website, an affiliate link leading to a merchant's Internet service provider (ISP) within that website's content would be appropriate. If a website contains information pertaining to sports, an affiliate link leading to a sporting goods website may work well within the context of the articles and information about sports. The goal in this case is to publish quality information within the website and provide context-oriented links to related merchant's websites. However, more recent examples exist of "thin" affiliate sites that are using the Affiliate Marketing model to create value for Consumers by offering them a service. These thin content service Affiliate fall into three categories:

- Price comparison
- Cause related marketing
- Time saving

Consumer Countermeasures: The implementation of affiliate marketing on the internet relies heavily on various techniques built into the design of many web-pages and web-sites, and the use of calls to external domains to track user actions (click tracking, Ad Sense) and to serve up content (advertising) to the user. Most of this activity adds time and is generally a nuisance to the casual web-surfer and is seen as visual clutter. Various countermeasures have evolved over time to prevent or eliminate the appearance of advertising when a web-page is rendered. Third party programs (Ad Aware, Spy Bot, pop-up blockers, etc.) and particularly, the use of a comprehensive HOSTS file can effectively eliminate the visual clutter and the extra time and bandwidth needed to render many web pages.

Adware: Although it differs from spyware, adware often uses the same methods and technologies. Merchants initially were uninformed about adware, what impact it had, and how it could damage their brands. Affiliate marketers became aware of the issue much more quickly, especially because they noticed that adware often overwrites tracking cookies, thus resulting in a decline of commissions. Affiliates not employing adware felt that it was stealing commission from them. Adware often has no valuable purpose and rarely provides any useful content to the user, who is typically unaware that such software is installed on his/her computer.

Trademark bidding: Affiliates were among the earliest adopters of pay per click advertising when the first pay-per-click search engines emerged during the end of the 1990s. Later in 2000 Google launched its pay per click service, Google Ad Words, which is responsible for the widespread use and acceptance of pay per click as an advertising channel. An increasing number of merchants engaged in pay per click advertising, either directly or via a search marketing agency, and realized that this space was already well-occupied by their affiliates. Although this situation alone created advertising channel conflicts and debates between advertisers and affiliates, the largest issue concerned affiliates bidding on advertisers names, brands, and trademarks. Several advertisers began to adjust their affiliate program terms to prohibit their affiliates from bidding on those type of keywords. Some advertisers, however, did and still do embrace this behavior, going so far as to allow, or even encourage, affiliates to bid on any term, including the advertiser's trademarks.

LACK OF SELF-REGULATION AND COLLABORATION

Affiliate marketing is driven by entrepreneurs who are working at the edge of Internet marketing. Affiliates are often the first to take advantage of emerging trends and technologies. The "trial and error" approach is probably the best way to describe the operation methods for affiliate marketers. This risky approach is one of the reasons why most affiliates fail or give up before they become successful "super affiliates", capable of generating £ 10,000 or more per month in commission. This "frontier" life combined with the attitude found in such communities is likely the main reason why the affiliate marketing industry is unable to self-regulate beyond individual contracts between advertisers and affiliates. Affiliate marketing has experienced numerous failed attempts to create an industry organization or association of some kind that could be the initiator of regulations, standards, and guidelines for the industry.

Online forums and industry trade shows are the only means for the different members from the industry—affiliates/publishers, merchants/advertisers, affiliate networks, third-party vendors, and service providers such as outsourced program managers—to congregate at one location. Online forums are free, enable small affiliates to have a larger say, and provide anonymity. Trade shows are cost-prohibitive to small affiliates because of the high price for event passes. Larger affiliates may even be sponsored by an advertiser they promote.

Lack of Industry Standards

Certification and training: Affiliate marketing currently lacks industry standards for training and certification. There are some training courses and seminars that result in certifications; however, the acceptance of such certifications is mostly due to the reputation of the individual or company issuing the certification. Affiliate marketing is not commonly taught in universities, and only a few college instructors work with Internet marketers to introduce the subject to students majoring in marketing.

Education occurs most often in "real life" by becoming involved and learning the details as time progresses. Although there are several books on the topic, some so-called "how-to" or "silver bullet" books instruct readers to manipulate holes in the Google algorithm, which can quickly become out of date or suggest strategies no longer endorsed or permitted by advertisers.

Outsourced Program Management companies typically combine formal and informal training, providing much of their training through group collaboration and brainstorming. Such companies also try to send each marketing employee to the industry conference of their choice. Other training resources used include online forums, weblogs, podcasts, video seminars, and specialty websites. Affiliate Summit is the largest conference in the industry, and many other affiliate networks host their own annual events.

Code of conduct: A code of conduct was released by affiliate networks Commission Junction/be Free and Performics in December 2002 to guide practices and adherence to ethical standards for online advertising.

Marketing term: Members of the marketing industry are recommending that "affiliate marketing" be substituted with an alternative name. Affiliate marketing is often confused with either network marketing or multi-level marketing. Performance marketing is a common alternative, but other recommendations have been made as well.

Cookie stuffing: Cookie stuffing involves placing an affiliate tracking cookie on a website visitor's computer without their knowledge, which will then generate revenue for the person doing the cookie stuffing. This not only generates fraudulent affiliate sales, but also has the potential to overwrite other affiliates' cookies, essentially stealing their legitimately earned commissions.

Click to Reveal: Many voucher code web sites use a click to reveal format, which required the web site user to click to reveal the voucher code. The action of clicking places the cookie on the website visitor's computer. The IAB have stated that "Affiliates must not use a mechanism whereby users are encouraged to click to interact with content where it is unclear or confusing what the outcome will be".

Affiliate Services

- Affiliate tracking software
- Affiliate programs directories
- Affiliate networks (see also Category: Internet advertising services and affiliate networks)
- Affiliate manager and Outsourced Program Management (OPM or APM) (manages affiliates)
- Category: Internet marketing trade shows.

CHAPTER

11

Search Engine Marketing

Search Engine Marketing, (SEM), is a form of Internet marketing that seeks to promote websites by increasing their visibility in search engine result pages (SERPs) through the use of, paid placement, contextual advertising, and paid inclusion Search engine optimization (SEO) is "optimizing" website pages to achieve higher ranking in search results via the process of selecting specific keyword expressions associated to the website SEM is utilizing various means of "marketing" a website in order for it to become more relevant in regard to search engine searches and their rankings. It should be asserted that SEM is NOT SEO and vice versa. SEM constitutes Ad words; which comprises of pay per call (particularly beneficial for local providers as it enables potential consumers to get in touch directly to a company with one click), article submissions, advertising and making sure SEO has been done. Also, key word analysis needs to be done for both SEO and SEM; but not necessarily at the same time. SEM is a constant and tedious task. It frequently needs to be updated and monitored continually. Another part of SEM is Social Media Marketing (SMM). SMM is a type of marketing that involves exploiting social media to influence consumers that one company's products and/or services are valuable. You can do SEM without doing SMM but you can't do SMM without doing SEM because SMM is a higher level of SEM.

BEST PRACTICES

SEM is more art than science. SEM = PR+ Advertising. Each search engine has its own formula for ranking search results. These algorithms change often, primarily to make results more relevant to the searcher. However, there are a few general best practices in search engine marketing.

1. Use unique and descriptive titles on all pages and provide unique descriptions and keyword metatags on every page;
2. Use plain ASCII text on your Web pages and use alt text for images and non-text elements;
3. Include a keyword-rich text description at the tops of pages and use text links with keyword-rich descriptions in your navigation and content;
4. Use keywords in URLs and ensure your dynamic pages are search engine friendly;
5. Adhere to Web standards of interoperability, accessibility and usability and add relevant, high-quality links from other sites to your site.

Don'ts

1. Avoid using redirects or refreshes or doorway pages.
2. Do not duplicate pages, sites, or content. Alternatively, choose one for the search engines and exclude the search engines from the others.
3. Do not cloak and restrict the use of splash.

MAJOR SEM TOOLS

There are four categories of tools to help you optimize Web sites. 1. Keyword research and analysis: (a) Make sure the site can be indexed in the search engines; (b) find the most relevant and popular key terms and phrases for the site and its products; and (c) use those key phrases on the site in a way that will generate and convert traffic.

1. Web site saturation and popularity: show how much presence a Web site has on search engines through the number of pages of the site that are indexed on each search engine (saturation) and how many times the site is linked to by other sites (popularity). Generally, the more Web presence you have, the easier it is for people to find your site. It requires your pages containing those keywords people are looking for and ensure that they rank high enough in search engine rankings. Most search engines include some form of link popularity in their ranking algorithms. The followings are major tools measuring various aspects of saturation and link popularity: Link Popularity, Top 10 Google Analysis, and Market leap's Link Popularity and Search Engine Saturation.
2. Back end tools (including Web analytic tools and HTML validators): Web analytic tools can help you to understand what is happening to your website and measure your Web site's success. They range from simple traffic counters to tools that work with log files and to more sophisticated tools that are based on page tagging (putting JavaScript or an image on a page to track actions). These tools can deliver conversion-related information. There are three major tools used by EBSCO: (a) log file analyzing tool: Web Trends by NetiQ; (b) tag-based analytic programs Web Side Story's Hitbox; (c) transaction-based tool: Tea Leaf Reali Tea.

SEM PLAN

Through trial and error you will be able to see how SEM drives highly targeted visitors to your online exhibitions. The following are the steps to a successful SEM plan:

1. Research on your target audience.

2. Set your online goals and key performance indicators.
3. Build an initial list of important keywords that represent your current and most relevant content and potential content.
4. Validate your keywords by testing and refining them your with keyword selector tools such as Yahoo Keyword Selector, Google Keyword Selector, Google Trends and Keyword Discovery.
5. Check your current ranking.
6. Optimize the website by improving your web design and architecture and web page content.
7. Pursue link building and partnerships.
8. Colonize the Web by publishing and circulating it in wiki, blogs, and video and picture sites(e.g. Flickr and Youtube).
9. Get in the news such as Google News with RSS feeds.
10. Install good tracking software, track and analyze your performance for better results.

SEARCH ENGINE OPTIMIZATION

Search Engine Optimization (*SEO*) is the process of improving the visibility of a website or a web page in search engines via the "natural" or un-paid ("organic" or "algorithmic") search results. Other forms of search engine marketing (SEM) target paid listings. In general, the earlier (or higher on the page), and more frequently a site appears in the search results list, the more visitors it will receive from the search engine's users. SEO may target different kinds of search, including image search, local search, video search, academic search, news search and industry-specific vertical search engines. This gives a website web presence.

As an Internet marketing strategy, SEO considers how search engines work, what people search for, the actual search terms typed into search engines and which search engines are preferred by their targeted audience. Optimizing a website may involve editing its content and HTML and associated coding to both increase its relevance to specific keywords and to remove barriers to the indexing activities of search engines. Promoting a site to increase the number of backlinks, or inbound links, is another SEO tactic.

The initialism "SEO" can refer to "search engine optimizers," a term adopted by an industry of consultants who carry out optimization projects on behalf of clients, and by employees who perform SEO services in-house. Search engine optimizers may offer SEO as a stand-alone service or as a part of a broader marketing campaign. Because effective SEO may require changes to the HTML source code of a site and site content, SEO tactics may be incorporated into website development and design. The term "search engine friendly" may be used to describe website designs, menus, content management systems, images, videos, shopping carts, and other elements that have been optimized for the purpose of search engine exposure.

Another class of techniques, known as black hat SEO or spamdexing, uses methods such as link farms, keyword stuffing and article spinning that degrade both the relevance of search results and the quality of user-experience with search engines. Search engines look for sites that employ these techniques in order to remove them from their indices.

RELATIONSHIP WITH SEARCH ENGINES

By 1997 search engines recognized that webmasters were making efforts to rank well in their search engines, and that some webmasters were even manipulating their rankings in search results by stuffing pages with excessive or irrelevant keywords. Early search engines, such as Infoseek, adjusted their algorithms in an effort to prevent webmasters from manipulating rankings.

Due to the high marketing value of targeted search results, there is potential for an adversarial relationship between search engines and SEO service providers. In 2005, an annual conference, AIRWeb, Adversarial Information Retrieval on the Web was created to discuss and minimize the damaging effects of aggressive web content providers.

Companies that employ overly aggressive techniques can get their client websites banned from the search results. In

2005, the Wall Street Journal reported on a company, Traffic Power, which allegedly used high-risk techniques and failed to disclose those risks to its clients. Wired magazine reported that the same company sued blogger and SEO Aaron Wall for writing about the ban. Google's Matt Cutts later confirmed that Google did in fact ban Traffic Power and some of its clients.

Some search engines have also reached out to the SEO industry, and are frequent sponsors and guests at SEO conferences, chats, and seminars. In fact, with the advent of paid inclusion, some search engines now have a vested interest in the health of the optimization community. Major search engines provide information and guidelines to help with site optimization. Google has a Sitemaps program to help webmasters learn if Google is having any problems indexing their website and also provides data on Google traffic to the website. Google guidelines are a list of suggested practices Google has provided as guidance to webmasters. Yahoo! Site Explorer provides a way for webmasters to submit URLs, determine how many pages are in the Yahoo! index and view link information. Bing Toolbox provides a way from webmasters to submit a sitemap and web feeds, allowing users to determine the crawl rate, and how many pages have been indexed by their search engine.

Search Engine Reputation Management (or SERM) tactics are often employed by companies and increasingly by individuals who seek to proactively shield their brands or reputations from damaging content brought to light through search engine queries. Some use these same tactics reactively, in attempts to minimize damage inflicted by inflammatory (or "flame") websites (and weblogs) launched by consumers and, as some believe, competitors.

Given the increasing popularity and development of search engines, these tactics have become more important than ever. Consumer generated media (like blogs) has amplified the public's voice, making points of view-good or bad-easily expressed. This is further explained in this front page article in the Washington Post.

Search Engine Reputation Management strategies include Search engine optimization (SEO) and Online Content Management. Because search engines are dynamic and in constant states of change and revision, it is essential that results are constantly monitored.

Social networking giant Facebook has been known to practice this form of reputation management. When they released their Polls service in Spring 2007, the popular blog TechCrunch found that it could not use competitors' names in Polls. Due largely to TechCrunch's authority in Google's algorithms, its post ranked for Facebook polls. A Facebook rep joined the comments, explained the situation and that the bugs in the old code had been updated so that it was now possible. Also until social sites like Facebook allow Google to fully spider their site then they won't really have a massive effect on reputation management results in the search engine. The only way to take advantage of such site is to make sure you make your pages public. It is suggested that if a company website has a negative result directly below it then up to 70% of surfers will click on the negative result first rather than the company website.

Search Engine Reputation Management (or SERM) tactics are often employed by companies and increasingly by individuals who seek to proactively shield their brands or reputations from damaging content brought to light through search engine queries. Some use these same tactics reactively, in attempts to minimize damage inflicted by inflammatory (or "flame") websites (and weblogs) launched by consumers and, as some believe, competitors. Given the increasing popularity and development of search engines, these tactics have become more important than ever. Consumer generated media (like blogs) has amplified the public's voice, making points of view-good or bad-easily expressed. This is further explained in this front page article in the Washington Post.

Search Engine Reputation Management strategies include Search engine optimization (SEO) and Online Content Management. Because search engines are dynamic and in constant states of change and revision, it is essential that results are constantly monitored. Social networking giant Facebook has been known to practice this form of reputation management. When they released their Polls service in Spring 2007, the popular blog TechCrunch found that it could not use competitors' names in Polls. Due largely to TechCrunch's authority in Google's algorithms, its post ranked for Facebook polls. A Facebook rep joined the comments, explained the situation and that the bugs in the old code had been updated so that it was now possible.

Also until social sites like Facebook allow Google to fully spider their site then they won't really have a massive effect on reputation management results in the search engine. The only way to take advantage of such site is to make sure you make your pages public. It is suggested that if a company website has a negative result directly below it then up to 70% of surfers will click on the negative result first rather than the company website.

CHAPTER

12

Social Media Marketing

Social media marketing is a recent addition to organizations' integrated marketing communications plans. Integrated marketing communications is a practice organizations follow to connect with their target markets. Integrated marketing communications coordinates promotional elements: advertising, personal selling, public relations, publicity, direct marketing and sales promotion Increasingly, viral marketing campaigns are also grouped into integrated marketing communications. In the traditional marketing communications model, the content, frequency, timing, and medium of communications by the organization is in collaboration with an external agent, i.e. advertising agencies, marketing research firms and public relations firms. However, the growth of social media has impacted the way organizations communicate. With the emergence of Web 2.0, the internet provides a set of tools that allow people to build social and business connections, share information and collaborate on projects online.

Social media marketing programs usually center on efforts to create content that attracts attention and encourages readers to share it with their social networks. A corporate message spreads from user to user and presumably resonates because it is coming from a trusted, third-party source, as opposed to the brand or company itself. Social media has become a platform that is easily accessible to anyone with internet access. Increased communication for organizations fosters brand awareness and often, improved customer service. Additionally, social media serves as a relatively inexpensive platform for organizations to implement marketing campaigns. With emergence of channels like Twitter, the barrier to entry in social media is greatly reduced.

PLATFORMS

Social media marketing is known as *SMO* or Social Media Optimization and benefits organizations and individuals by providing an additional channel for customer support, a means to gain customer and competitive insight, recruitment and retention of new customers/business partners, and a method of managing reputation online. Key factors that ensure its success are its relevance to the customer, the value it provides them with and the strength of the foundation on which it is built. A strong foundation serves as a platform in which the organization can centralize its information and direct customers on its recent developments via other social media channels, such as article and press release publications. Oftentimes, corporate social media platforms are used to offer unique incentives to customers who are willing to engage.

SOFTWARE TOOLS

Several companies are now providing specialized tools and platform for social media marketing. Tools can be used for a variety of different things such as:

- Social Media Monitoring
- Social Aggregation
- Social Book Marking and Tagging
- Social Analytics and Reporting

- Automation
- Social Media
- Blog Marketing
- Validation

Some popular tools include:

- Sysomos-Social media monitoring and analytics provider
- Hubspot-Inbound social media marketing
- Klout-Monitoring and analytics

SOCIAL MEDIA OUTLETS

Twitter, Facebook, YouTube, Blogs: Social networking websites allow individuals to interact with one another and build relationships. When products or companies join those sites, people can interact with the product or company. That interaction feels personal to users because of their previous experiences with social networking site interactions. Social networking sites like Twitter, Facebook, YouTube and blogs allow individual followers to "retweet" or "repost" comments made by the product being promoted. By repeating the message, all of the users connections are able to see the message, therefore reaching more people. Social networking sites act as word of mouth. Because the information about the product is being put out there and is getting repeated, more traffic is brought to the product/company. Through social networking sites, products/companies can have conversations and interactions with individual followers. This personal interaction can instill a feeling of loyalty into followers and potential customers. Also, by choosing whom to follow on these sites, products can reach a very narrow target audience.

Cell phone usage has also become a benefit for social media marketing. Today, many cell phones have social networking capabilities: individuals are notified of any happenings on social networking sites through their cell phones, in real-time. This constant connection to social networking sites means products and companies can constantly remind and update followers about their capabilities, uses, importance, etc.

Because cell phones are connected to social networking sites, advertisements are always in sight.

CAMPAIGNS

Betty White: Social networking sites can have a large impact on the outcome of events. In 2010, a Facebook campaign surfaced in the form of a petition. Users virtually signed a petition asking NBC Universal to have actress Betty White host Saturday Night Live. Once signing, users forwarded the petition to all of their followers. The petition went viral and on May 8th, 2010, Betty White hosted SNL.

The 2008 presidential campaign had a huge presence on social networking sites. Democratic candidate, Barack Obama, was very visible on Twitter and Facebook. His social networking site profile pages were constantly being updated and interacting with followers. The use of social networking sites gave Barak Obama's campaign access to e-mail addresses, as posted on social networking site profile pages. This allowed the Democratic Party to launch e-mail campaigns asking for votes and campaign donations.

Local Businesses: Small businesses also use social networking sites as a promotional technique. Businesses can follow individuals social networking site uses in the local area and advertise specials and deals. These can be exclusive and in the form of "get a free drink with a copy of this tweet". This type of message encourages other locals to follow the business on the sites in order to obtain the promotional deal. In the process, the business is getting seen and promoting itself.

TACTICS

Twitter allows companies to promote products on an individual level. The use of a product can be explained in short messages that followers are more likely to read. These messages appear on followers' home pages. Messages can link to the product's website, Facebook profile, photos, videos, etc. This link provides followers the opportunity to spend more time interacting with the product online. This interaction can create a loyal connection between product and individual and can also lead to larger advertising opportunities. Twitter promotes a product in real-time and brings customers in.

Facebook profiles are more detailed than Twitter. They allow a product to provide videos, photos, and longer descriptions. Videos can show when a product can be used as well as how to use it. It can include testimonials as other followers can comment on the product pages for others to see. Facebook can link back to the product's Twitter page as well as send out event reminders. Facebook promotes a product in real-time and brings customers in.

Blogs allow a product or company to provide longer descriptions of products or services. The longer description can include reasoning and uses. It can include testimonials and can link to and from Facebook and Twitter pages. Blogs can be updated frequently and are promotional techniques for keeping customers.

IMPLICATIONS OF TRADITIONAL ADVERTISING

Minimizing Use: Traditional advertising techniques include print and television advertising. The Internet had already overtaken television as the largest advertising market. Websites often include banner or pop-up ads. Social networking sites don't always have ads. In exchange, products have entire pages and are able to interact with users. Television commercials often end with a spokesperson asking viewers to check out the product website for more information. Print ads are also starting to include barcodes on them. These barcodes can be scanned by cell phones and computers, sending viewers to the product website. Advertising is beginning to move viewers from the traditional outlets to the electronic ones.

Leaks: Internet and social networking leaks are one of the issues facing traditional advertising. Video and print ads are often leaked to the world via the Internet earlier than they are scheduled to premiere. Social networking sites allow those leaks to go viral, and be seen by many users more quickly. Time difference is also a problem facing traditional advertisers. When social events occur and are broadcast on television, there is often a time delay between airings on the east coast and west coast of the United States. Social networking sites have become a hub of comment and interaction concerning the event. This allows individuals watching the event on the west coast (time-delayed) to know the outcome before it airs. The 2011 Grammy Awards highlighted this problem. Viewers on the west coast learned who won different awards based on comments made on social networking sites by individuals watching live on the east coast. Since viewers knew who won already, many tuned out and ratings were lower. All the advertisement and promotion put into the event was lost because viewers didn't have a reason to watch.

Integrated marketing communications (IMC) is a process for managing customer relationships that drive brand value primarily through communication efforts. Such efforts often include cross-functional processes that create and nourish profitable relationships with customers and other stakeholders by strategically controlling or influencing all messages sent to these groups and encouraging data-driven, purposeful dialog with them. IMC includes the coordination and integration of all marketing communication tools, avenues, and sources within a company into a seamless program in order to maximize the impact on end users at a minimal cost. This integration affects all firm's business-to-business, marketing channel, customer-focused, and internally directed communications.

IMC Components

- *The Foundation*-corporate image and brand management; buyer behavior; promotions opportunity analysis.
- Advertising Tools-advertising management, advertising design: theoretical frameworks and types of appeals; advertising design: message strategies and executional frameworks; advertising media selection. Advertising also reinforces brand and firm image.
- *Promotional Tools*-trade promotions; consumer promotions; personal selling, database marketing, and customer relations management; public relations and sponsorship programs.

- Integration Tools-Internet Marketing; IMC for small business and entrepreneurial ventures; evaluating and integrated marketing program.

Marketing Mix Component

The Internet has changed the way business is done in the current world. The variables of segmentation, targeting and positioning are addressed differently. The way new products and services are marketed have changed even though the aim of business in bringing economic and social values remain unchanged. Indeed, the bottom line of increasing revenue and profit are still the same. Marketing has evolved to more of connectedness, due to the new characteristics brought in by the Internet. Marketing was once seen as a one way, with firms broadcasting their offerings and value proposition. Now it is seen more and more as a conversation between marketers and customers. Marketing efforts incorporate the "marketing mix". Promotion is one element of marketing mix. Promotional activities include advertising (by using different media), sales promotion (sales and trades promotion), and personal selling activities. It also includes Internet marketing, sponsorship marketing, direct marketing, database marketing and public relations. Integration of all these promotional tools, along with other components of marketing mix, is a way to gain an edge over a competitor. The starting point of the IMC process is the marketing mix that includes different types of marketing, advertising, and sales efforts. Without a complete IMC plan there is no integration or harmony between client and customers. The goal of an organization is to create and maintain communication throughout its own employees and throughout its customers. Integrated marketing is based on a master marketing plan. This plan should coordinate efforts in all components of the marketing mix. A marketing plan consists on the following steps.

1. Situation analysis
2. Marketing objectives
3. Marketing budget

Integrated marketing communications aims to ensure consistency of message and the complementary use of media. The concept includes online and offline marketing channels. Online marketing channels include any e-marketing campaigns or programs, from search engine optimization (SEO), pay-per-click, affiliate, email, banner to latest web related channels for webinar, blog, micro-blogging, RSS, podcast, Internet Radio, and Internet TV. Offline marketing channels are traditional print (newspaper, magazine), mail order, public relations, industry relations, billboard, traditional radio, and television. A company develops its integrated marketing communication program using all the elements of the marketing mix (product, price, place, and promotion). Integrated marketing communications plans are vital to achieving success. The reasons for their importance begin with the explosion of information technologies. Channel power has shifted from manufacturers to retailers to consumers.

Using outside-in thinking, Integrated Marketing Communications is a data-driven approach that focuses on identifying consumer insights and developing a strategy with the right (online and offline combination) channels to forge a stronger brand-consumer relationship. This involves knowing the right touch points to use to reach consumers and understanding how and where they consume different types of media. Regression analysis and customer lifetime value are key data elements in this approach.

Importance of IMC

Several shifts in the advertising and media industry have caused IMC to develop into a primary strategy for marketers:

1. From media advertising to multiple forms of communication.
2. From mass media to more specialized (niche) media, which are centered on specific target audiences.
3. From a manufacturer-dominated market to a retailer-dominated, consumer-controlled market.
4. From general-focus advertising and marketing to data-based marketing.

5. From low agency accountability to greater agency accountability, particularly in advertising.
6. From traditional compensation to performance-based compensation (increased sales or benefits to the company).
7. From limited Internet access to 24/7 Internet availability and access to goods and services.

4 P'S *v.* 4 C'S

- *Not Product, but Consumer:* You have to understand what the consumer's wants and needs are. Times have changed and you can no longer sell whatever you can make. The product characteristics have to match the specifics of what someone wants to buy. And part of what the consumer is buying is the personal "buying experience".
- *Not Price, but Cost*: Understand the consumer's cost to satisfy the want or need. The product price may be only one part of the consumer's cost structure. Often it is the cost of time to drive somewhere, the cost of conscience of what you buy, the cost of guilt for not treating the kids, the investment a consumer is willing to make to avoid risk, etc.
- *Not Place, but Convenience*: As above, turn the standard logic around. Think convenience of the buying experience and then relate that to a delivery mechanism. Consider all possible definitions of "convenience" as it relates to satisfying the consumer's wants and needs. Convenience may include aspects of the physical or virtual location, access ease, transaction service time, and hours of availability.
- *Not Promotion, but Communication:* Communicate, many mediums working together to present a unified message with a feedback mechanism to make the communication two-way. And be sure to include an understanding of non-traditional mediums, such as word of mouth and how it can influence your position in the consumer's mind. How many ways

can a customer hear (or see) the same message through the course of the day, each message reinforcing the earlier images?

EFFECTIVE COMMUNICATIONS ELEMENTS

The goal of selecting the elements of proposed integrated marketing communications is to create a campaign that is effective and consistent across media platforms. Some marketers may want only ads with greatest breadth of appeal: the executions that, when combined, provide the greatest number of attention-getting, branded, and motivational moments. Others may only want ads with the greatest depth of appeal: the ads with the greatest number of attention-getting, branded, and motivational points within each.

Although integrated marketing communications is more than just an advertising campaign, the bulk of marketing dollars is spent on the creation and distribution of advertisements. Hence, the bulk of the research budget is also spent on these elements of the campaign. Once the key marketing pieces have been tested, the researched elements can then be applied to other contact points: letterhead, packaging, logistics, customer service training, and more, to complete the IMC cycle.

One common type of integrated marketing communication is personal selling. Personal selling can be defined as "face to face selling in which a seller attempts to persuade a buyer to make a purchase".

CHAPTER

13

Internet Marketing Strategy

Developing a successful internet *marketing strategy* is an essential part of your online success. In order to succeed, you must develop and implement a strategic plan that includes all of the following:

- A great product
- A web site specifically designed to sell
- A killer marketing strategy

Each step plays an important role in your overall strategy and must be developed to its fullest potential. If even one step fails, your chances of success will be minimal.

DEVELOPING YOUR PRODUCT

Your first step will be to develop a great product. You're probably thinking that's easier said than done, but it's really not. The absolute best product is one that you can develop yourself and deliver over the Internet. With today's technology, there is absolutely no reason why you can't create your own product. The knowledge you have within your own mind is extremely valuable. Everybody is good at something, has a special talent or some specialized knowledge. Use this knowledge to create a product.

The key to developing a great product is exclusiveness. Your product should be unique and not be in competition with hundreds of other similar products. You must give your potential customers exactly what they want. Develop a high-quality product that fills a void to increase your chance of success.

Another consideration of great importance is your target market. Keep in mind, the Internet is a global marketplace. Develop a product with a large geographic target and a wide appeal. A great product will fulfill a need or desire and provide instant gratification. Here are a few of the top sellers:

- Software
- Information
- Private sites
- Internet services

Before you develop your product, do some research—find out exactly what people want and develop your product accordingly. The most important consideration when developing your product is quality. Your product should not only deliver what you promise, but should go above and beyond the expected and overdeliver. Your customers satisfaction is of the utmost importance.

DEVELOPING YOUR WEB SITE

Once you've developed a great product, your next step will be to develop a great web site. Your web site must be specifically designed to sell your product. Everything within your web site should have one purpose—getting your visitor to take action. Words are the most *powerful marketing tool* you have. The right words will turn your visitors into customers. The wrong words will cause them to click away and never return.

Your words are the entire foundation of your business. Your product, your web site and your marketing strategies all depend upon your words. Fancy graphics don't make sales—words do.

Every word, sentence and headline should have one specific purpose—to lead your potential customer to your order page. Write your web site copy as if you are talking to just one person. Identify a problem and validate that one visitor's need for a solution. Continue to write and explain why your product is the solution to their problem. Tell them exactly what your product will do for them—why it will solve their problems and how. Pack your copy with benefits and more benefits. Write to persuade—that's the bottom line.

DEVELOPING YOUR MARKETING STRATEGIES

Your marketing strategy is the final process of your plan. Your plan must include both short-term and long-term strategies in order to succeed. Short term marketing strategies are those that bring you a temporary boost in traffic. Although these techniques are very important to your over-all plan, they are only a temporary *traffic source* and must not be solely relied upon. Short term marketing strategies include:

- Purchasing Advertising
- Participating in Forums
- Search Engines

Long term marketing strategies are those that bring you a steady stream of targeted traffic over time. These strategies will continue to produce results even years down the road. Long term marketing strategies include:

- Opt-in Lists
- Blogging
- Social Networking Sites
- Social Bookmarking Sites
- Giving Away Freebies
- Article Marketing

By creating and implementing a balanced marketing strategy, using both short-term and long-term strategies, you will drive a steady stream of targeted *traffic to your web site*. If you use this simple formula when creating your *Internet marketing strategy* and excel at all three, you can literally guarantee your success.

WHAT IS AN EFFECTIVE INTERNET MARKETING STRATEGY?

If you're still struggling to finally reach your financial independence & make a nice living from your home, then listen... The only reason why you're failing is because *you don't have a good website marketing strategy*. If you ask any successful offline world entrepreneur how it's possible to build a great business without a proper strategy, he'll start laughing. But many *internet marketing* experts are trying to make money without even realizing what on earth they're doing online...

If you believe that you can jump in, create a website, submit it to a few directories or blogs, sit down, relax and watch those thousands of dollars (that you've seen in many marketers' checks) to come, then you need to stop right there. It ain't gonna happen. You need to think: who you are and where do you want to be in the future. Whether offline or online, there are only two things that matter: "Buying" and "Selling". Basically, to simplify, it all comes down to this:

Who is Your Customer?

What is he or she specifically looking for? You must know their problems or desires. You must be in their shoes and find out what is that would make them feel better (an offer).

What is Your Offer?

Why should they buy from you? How come you're better than the rest? Why should they trust you? Are you offering your own or someone else's product? How will you create an irresistible offer so they beg you to sell it to them?

Think about it. . . . There are millions of people buying online every single day. If they're not buying from you then whose fault is that—theirs or yours? Before you even start creating internet marketing strategy for your website(s), you need to do a research. That's where it all begins actually. Just like in any business, you have to understand where you are and what can you do.

#1 Phase—Online Research

In this phase, you must research your market. *Who are your main competitors*? What are they doing online? PPC, SEO, press releases, develop their own products, do affiliate marketing or Adsense? What are their weaknesses? Do they offer a guarantee? Is their product really good? Do they build links constantly or not? *Who is your favourite customer*? Where do they hangout: MySpace or YouTube? Are they freebie seekers or desperate buyers? What forces them to buy one or another product? Read reviews, forums, testimonials to find out as much as you can about your target market.

#2 Phase—Data Analysis

If you've performed a thorough online market research, it's time to systematize the data you have. Write down *what are the main strengths and weaknesses of your competitors*. Maybe you have more time than your competitors? Or maybe you know some targeted traffic source that others don't. How might this affect your business? Which are the places your target market usually visits? What are their main concerns? Maybe they're not satisfied with the products in the market. Can offer something better, maybe in a form of a bonus? After that, you come to the next step, which is developing your internet marketing strategy.

#3 Phase—Strategy Development

When you already know your target market and your competitors, you are able to start creating your internet marketing strategy (or strategies). Just sit down and think about: who you are and what you can offer to the target market. It involves a little bit of planning. What marketing methods you'll use and which ones you can afford? PPC, SEO, email, blogging, podcasting, video blogging, webinars, viral traffic generation, link building, banner exchange or others...?

You must prioritize your web marketing tactics. Find out what's going to bring you positive ROI in the shortest time possible.

Do you have enough time to perform search engine optimization? If so, then sit and do everything you can, day in day out, to rank at the top in search engines. Don't have time? Then buy PPC traffic and start testing your landing pages effectively. Or buy resell rights to products and sell them on ClickBank with the help of JV partners.

Don't have time AND money? Then you better get one or another, otherwise you're dead. Seriously, you must find ways to get time or money. You need to think about how you can exploit other people's time and money to build your own web business. That's what rich people do and that's what you must do if you want to survive in this competitive world.

#4 Phase—Monitoring Performance

When you have an internet marketing plan, you can start implementing it right away. The last step is to start monitoring your internet marketing campaigns. Which keywords people typed into search engines to find your site? Which keywords brought you the most money in *PPC marketing*? Are you satisfied with your *SEO rankings* or not? Do majority of your visitors leave your site without even spending 30 seconds? And so on. . . . Only with the help of close monitoring you can discover what works and what doesn't. Testing landing pages, testing Adwords ads against each other (A/B split testing) can show you some amazing results. *And remember—you never know for sure until you TEST it*!

YOUR PROMOTIONAL STRATEGY

Creating a successful Internet presence involves much more than designing a great web site or having the "perfect" product. Listing your web site with the Search Engines is your first step. However, you must not solely depend upon the Search Engines to bring you traffic. You must design a complete promotional strategy and work it every day.

Search Engines

Your first step will be to submit your site to the Search

Engines. Although there are many Internet marketers who are constantly trying to maintain a top listing in the Search Engines, in my humble opinion, it's simply a waste of time. Each Search Engine is different and has different guidelines in regard to how they rank a web page. In addition, their guidelines change very frequently and it is literally impossible to keep up with them. Your best option will be to optimize your web site to the best of your ability, submit your pages to the Search Engines and forget it. (Resubmit your main pages any time you make any significant changes.) Your time can be better spent using other marketing techniques other than fighting the Search Engine wars.

Your first step will be to optimize your web pages to the best of your ability. Visit http://www·searchenginewatch·com for a complete overview of the Search Engines and optimization.

Opt-in List

As soon as your web site is up and running, you should *immediately* begin building an opt-in list. Above all else, you MUST remember *the money is in the list*. An opt-in list is a list or database containing email addresses of individuals who have chosen to receive your email messages. They provide you with a direct line of communication with potential customers and *enable you to promote your products or services*. Developing your own list of targeted potential customers is the absolute most important marketing strategy you can use. No matter what strategies you're currently using, if you're not collecting the email addresses of your potential customers, you're literally guaranteeing your failure.

Opt-in lists provide you with the ability to create a targeted list of potential customers in which you can advertise on a continual basis. You will have a direct line of communication, which will increase your sales considerably.

The key to creating an effective opt-in list is to provide your subscribers with quality information. The best way to do this is to provide them with a weekly, bi-weekly, or monthly ezine. An ezine is a newsletter or publication that is sent to subscribers who have chosen to receive your publication.

In order to build a database of potential customers and start collecting email addresses, you'll first need to set up a mailing list. This mailing list must enable your visitor's to submit their information and subscribe them to your list. There are many free list services that will enable you to set up a mailing list. However, they are not recommended. They will not allow you to personalize your messages with your subscriber's names, which if very important.

Building Your Subscriber Base

There are many powerful ways to build your subscriber base. However, for this article, we will only focus on the "best" ways.

Your Web site

Place a subscription box on every page of your web site. Make sure you don't overlook this powerful means of gaining new subscribers. Your visitors will enter your web site from many other pages other than your main page. They may never even visit your main page, so make sure your subscription box is visible on every page of your web site.

Incentive Subscriptions

This powerful means of obtaining subscribers entails offering your visitors a free gift in return for their subscription. This free gift may be a free ebook, software, or report. This method of obtaining new subscribers will increase your subscription rate immensely.

Writing Articles

Write informative articles and allow them to be freely published. By writing articles, you can significantly increase your subscriptions. The key to using this method effectively is to include your subscription information within your bylines.

Free Ebooks

Create a powerful free ebook and allow it to be freely distributed. Place your subscription box within your ebook to enable your readers to subscribe. Your ebook will have the potential to be viewed by millions of Internet users. Creating and developing an opt-in list is an absolute must. You must take every opportunity to promote your publication and gain new subscribers. The more subscribers you have, the more sales you'll make. Make sure you don't overlook this powerful method of making sales. If you're not collecting your visitors' email addresses, don't wait another day to start. Opt-in lists are one of the most powerful marketing tools on the Internet.

There is no formula for an effective Internet marketing strategy. It depends on your individual situation. When you realize your strengths and weaknesses, you'll be able to come up with a great *marketing plan*. No matter if you're thinking about Adsense site, affiliate site or your own product. When you find out what you're able to accomplish with your resurces at the moment, you can create a great web marketing strategy for your online business and finally breakthrough on the internet.

B2B INTERNET MARKETING STRATEGIES

- Educate Your Prospects
- Create a New Framework
- Create Oppor tunities to Communicate
- Speak Their Language
- Email Training Series
- Product Discussion List
- Additional Information by Email
- Web Meetings and Presentations
- Teach the Gatekeeper, Too!
- Sequenced Communications

Educate Your Prospects

If you can help your prospect feel like an expert, claim authors Margaret Mark and Carol S. Pearson, they are more likely to buy than if they feel confused. Mark and Pearson's book, The Hero and the Outlaw: Harnessing the Power of Archetypes to Create a Winning Brand, discusses how successful brands correspond to fundamental patterns in the unconscious mind known as archetypes. Many business prospects fit the role of an archetype that uses intelligence and analysis to understand the world.

A strategy based on fear, uncertainty and doubt is at odds with what motivates this prospect. Instead, Mark and Pearson suggest never talking down to clients or using a hard sell. Business professionals want to feel smart, competent and in charge of the transaction. They like to collect all the data to make informed decisions, and enjoy complicated products (like PCs) that demand a learning curve and are difficult to master. And if the prospect feels like they are being pushed, they are likely to walk away, because they view a purchase as a rational decision based on information.

One of the most precious commodities for the business professional is their time. So embrace time-saving technologies like email or web meetings (instead of trying to set up golf outings).

Create a New Framework

Good marketing doesn't merely attempt to influence what people think about a particular company's product or service—good marketing instead focuses on creating a favorable framework through which people can evaluate your product or service. The traditional approach to selling a product or service is to focus on the particular features and benefits of the solution, and why it is better/faster/cheaper than the competition. Instead, create a new framework for business professionals to apply their specific industry experience, customer feedback and financial analysis to your solution. Rather than focus on price, your conceptual framework allows prospective clients to better understand the forces that shape their business and how your solution is an integral part of their success.

Create Opportunities to Communicate

But how do you both educate your prospects and envelop them in a framework that places your business in a favorable light? The answer is to balance persistence against communication overload. When you first meet a potential customer, you typically ask for a business card and try to learn more about their company. Implied in the exchange of business cards is the opportunity to follow-up with more information. But once you have sent more information, and politely asked if they have further questions, how do you stay top-ofmind without coming across as nagging? Create reasons to communicate high-value ideas and information to your business prospects, and balance persistence against overload. Create industry-specific email distribution lists and forward relevant articles and upcoming events to both your clients and sales prospects. Forward the latest whitepaper or research study that may help them do their job more effectively. Reinforce through this communication that part of the 'value-add' of purchasing from your company is the added attention you will bring to the relationship.

Speak Their Language

When it comes to communicating to prospects that have different functional positions, a one-size-fits-all approach won't work. The CFO of a company will often focus on price, capital expenditures and measurable return on investment (ROI). If you are a company that offers an outsourced product, for example, your email message to the CFO should explain how your solution avoids hefty up-front costs and has a built-in system for measuring the effectiveness of marketing expenditures.

To the CTO, however, the pressing issue may be how the product may abscond scarce IT resources, or how well the product integrates with the company's existing technology. And the Chief Marketing Officer may have altogether different issues—concerns with getting timely reporting from the IT staff on the effectiveness of the last marketing campaign may be top of mind. Begin by creating a laundry list of bullet points that examine your product or service from the viewpoint of each of your constituents. Then personalize your email communications, segmented by job function. Make sure you also give the marketer the financial and technical ammunition necessary to convince their respective counterparts.

Email Training Series

One of the best ways to educate your prospects and stay top-of mind is with an email-based training series. Allow the experts within your company the opportunity to help prospects and customers learn more about your industry. When prospects sign up, they receive a series of email messages at a regular interval. Inside the email is a mini-summary of the individual topic and a short case study that examines the practical application of your solution. A quiz after each lesson can provide immediate feedback on what they've learned.

Product Discussion List

An effective way to get feedback on your product or service is to engage your customers in the product development process by using an email discussion list. Allow your engineers, designers and customer service representatives to interact with your customer's in a discussion forum. After all, your customers are the ones who are using your solution to accomplish their business goals and have a vested effort in shaping the future of your offering. A moderated list allows control over what information is posted and who is able to send to the list.

Additional Information by Email

Give your prospects a way to receive additional information from your company. Give prospects access to a passwordprotected area of your website where they can select what documents they would like to receive via email. An emailbased approach can work better than simply giving prospects access to an online directory of files, because many professionals use their email inbox (and subfolders) to organize their content. Instead of relying on prospects to open a document from your website only to print it and forget it, email is a way to reach out to prospect's inbox and deliver the information directly to them. Plus, you've just created an additional reason to contact them with a personalized message.

Web Meetings and Presentations

While face-to-face meetings are indeed essential, PowerPoint presentations and informational meetings often take place in a dark room. A web meeting usually consists of an audio conference call and a PowerPoint presentation that the recipient views by going to a special website and signing in with a username and password. Use web meetings to communicate product-specific information or to better prospect different customers. Plane tickets are expensive, and waiting in line at the airport behind other weary travelers only to find out that the flight is delayed does little to promote productivity. Web meetings are especially cost effective if the potential client is in a geographically remote location where few other potential sales prospects exist.

Teach the Gatekeeper, Too!

Many hard-to-reach business prospects have excellent administrative assistants that don't always see the value of your offering. One way to break through to these 'gatekeepers' is to demonstrate how one facet of your product or service can help them do their job better. Because gatekeepers are frequently interrupted, avoid using scheduled web seminars. Instead, use an email training series delivered right to their email inbox. Offer, for example, an email-based tutorial that demonstrates how to better use email filters to prioritize incoming messages.

Sequenced Communications

According to author Seth Godin, permission marketing is like dating: "It turns strangers into friends and friends into lifetime customers". Treat your sales process as a series of interactions that will grow into a long-term, profitable customer relationship. Develop a series of sequenced communications, designed to inform, educate and convert prospects into paying customers. If a prospect downloads a whitepaper, for example, have your system automatically send a personalized email message a couple of days later, asking if they have any additional questions or need further information.

SECTION III

Retail and Industrial

CHAPTER

14

The Internet Retail

With Internet Retail being one of the fastest growing sectors in the overall retail industry, and with a strong fourth quarter in 2009, we expect retailers will continue to look to online as a next generation vehicle for growth. By contrast, during 2009 the MandA Internet Retail market was dismal. However it is beginning to show signs of recovery and we expect MandA volume to continue to accelerate over the next five years as the industry consolidates around brand name merchants.

MARKET INDICATORS—A LOOK BACK

Internet Retail sector sales have generated Compound Annual Growth Rate (CAGR) of 18.6%, from $ 34.5 billion in 2001 to $ 135.0 billion in 2009. As Internet sales grew· the growth rate declined steadily until it "fell off the cliff" in 2008.

- As a percent of total retail sales, e-commerce has grown from 1.1% of total retail sales in 2001 to 3.7% of total retail sales in 2009.

- The fourth quarter of 2009 was very strong for online retailers, with total ecommerce sales increasing 14.6% YOY from Q408; and totaling 4.3% of total retail sales in Q409.
- Stock prices for publicly traded online retailers have increased 130% from February 2009. In contrast the SandP 500 Retailing Index is up close to 70% over the same period.

MARKET INDICATORS—A LOOK FORWARD

- Forecasted sales for internet retailers are projected to progress at a "modest" 6.4% CAGR through 2013 according to Mintel Research and US Census Bureau data. Growth is projected to accelerate after a weak recovery in 2010 and 2011. This will bring yearly internet sales to 4.3% of total retail sales should total retail sales grow at their historic CAGR of 2.3%. Within the Internet Retail sector, we expect that social media and mobile shopping will be the fastest growing segments, and will be sources of considerable revenue growth as consumer purchasing habits continue to evolve.
- Traditional brick and mortar retailers will increasingly focus on online store sales as they seek revenue growth. Recently Joseph A. Bank, Marks and Spencer, Sears, and Charming Shoppes, Inc. have each re-launched their website to accommodate increased traffic and enhanced customers' shopping experience.
- Since there are few significant barriers to entry in online retail and companies continue to look for revenue growth in e-commerce, price competition will continue to increase and put increased pressures on margins.
- Strong brands will, as always, be the best protection against price competition. Furthermore, as branding importance grows, pay-per-click advertising will diminish in importance but its cost will continue to rise.

- As these trends develop, the industry will consolidate around established entities. Small players unable to compete in an increasingly competitive marketplace will exit or eke out a sub-standard existence. Mid-size players with weak brand recognition and value propositions or poor supply chain and fulfillment economics will be picked off by larger, better recognized, and stronger competitors

Internet Retail has performed well over the past several months, and is well on its way to recovery.

- As consumer spending continues to show signs of a recovery, with March's 0.6% increase, consumer expenditures have recorded growth for 6 straight months.
- The shift to internet shopping has been accelerated by current economic conditions. Price conscious consumers increasingly prefer shopping over the internet to compare prices.
- The convenience and expedited nature of shopping online also drives time-constrained consumers to the internet.
- Recent growth in the sector, combined with a strong finish to 2009, will attract additional investment from traditional and catalog retailers as management looks to increased internet retail presence as the primary vehicle for growth.
- Increased competition will continue to drive down retail prices, and contract margins. The result will be that small to mid-sized players with less brand recognition, supply chain weaknesses or poor financial performance will be acquired by stronger rivals.
- Branding will grow in importance as a defense against increasing price competition as the industry consolidates. National and large regional retailers will gain share at the expense of smaller firms.

- As this trend develops we expect that the number of substantial industry players will contract, fueling increased MandA activity over the next 5 years.

The Indian Online Retail is a rich segment waiting to be exploited. Internet is a potent medium that can serve as a unique platform for the growth of retail brands in India. The medium holds many virtues favorable for the retail industry including a higher customer penetration, increased visibility, and convenient operations. Different players in internet retailing, 5 and 10 years back (brick and mortar stores, mail-order companies, limited number of upcoming internet pure players). How did their "old" business model help them to be successful in these years of internet retailing?

- Mail-order companies: 50+ years in remotely dealing with consumers
- Advantages due to existing client base and infrastructure (logistics, CRM, etc.
- Pure players with only limited access to clients
- Online marketing (not performance marketing) helped players to keep brand awareness

Today's players in internet retailing: brick and mortar stores, mail-order companies, brands/manufacturers, internet pure players, aggregators, new venture/business models. Why is the business model of "old" players harming their internet retailing activities and why are "new" players rapidly growing in a 10+ year internet business?

- *"Old" players:* processes and IT are not matching "online" requirements
- Brands/manufacturers learning to keep direct contact to consumer (flag-ship store approach in internet)
- Leading to higher pressure on retail sector, as brand focus in moving from retail-brand to manufacturer-brand
- Key advantages for new players: speed, user-driven, IT-enabled, new shopping experience, outsourcing infrastructure, etc.

- Performance marketing as a driving factor for "new" players

RETAIL MARKETING IN INDIA IS IN RECESSION

The retail market in India is facing slowdown with the ongoing financial crisis happening across the world markets. Since the markets always have internally linked with each other, the impact of the crisis is generally shared among all. The following circumstances are creating unwelcome interruptions to the Indian retail industry. The industry hopes for the best alternations to overcome the acrimonious situations

Markets in recession worldwide and India too: The current meltdown in the world markets is shaking the globe today. Not even a single country seems to be off the hook. The high level of inflation has been a wet blanket for the global markets. The roots of the world markets are nearly pulled away with the heavy downfall of the American financial giants. Amongst many countries, India too not exempted from the impact of world financial crisis. All this is leading to a temporary recess for the markets from a regular busy schedule. However, these fluctuations are not new for global market. For the decades long, markets, across the world, have been witnessing such ups and downs. But the ultimately fact is that the market growth rate is always constantly high when comparing to such downfalls.

Economic slowdown: The Financial crisis is adding to the pressure on global economies. The International Monetary Fund (IMF) now sees the world entering a major slowdown. The recovery would depend on three key factors: commodity prices stabilizing, the crisis in the US housing sector bottoming out, and emerging economies providing a source of resilience. But, if the current crisis were to last longer, the emerging economies are more likely to be affected.

The impact on retail industry: The inflation or the economic slowdown is adversely affecting the retail industry. With the suddenly disturbed economical status, consumers are gradually losing interest on buying. And for the interested, the unbalanced income, followed by the economic slowdown, is not meeting their buying requirements. This evolution had soon disappointed the hopes of Retail industry. Anyhow, it's all a short-term crisis for the retail industry until the things turn around.

Low marketing and advertising budgets will work out: To rectify the things, right solutions are always excavated. Whether the market growth is slower or faster, its potential should not be left unused. Anyway, new and innovative solutions must be invented to answer the current market slump. Cutting down the marketing and advertising budgets will reduce the financial burden on retailing industry. Marketing and advertising are the supreme factors for the retail industry to penetrate more into retail market. Following innovative marketing and effective advertising at low prices will be a brilliant move for the present day market trends.

Challenge to get more customers at low cost: In this current meltdown, driving the customers to the retail stores seems high and dry. But, the markets always have the hidden potential despite the slump. Today, the changing market trends demand the retail industry to expand its reach to the more customer touch points so as to drive them to the retail points. 'Low investments and high returns' is now made possible with the arrival of technology enabled marketing services. The retail industry should realize that it would be at a fair advantage of including technology enabled marketing services to unfold the immense retailing opportunities.

Present communication channel is ineffective and involves high costs: The present channel for customer communication is apparently ineffective which the retail industry has been following for the decades. Moreover, it always involves high costs too. The outdated communication channels should be modified according to the changing market trends. Now, an uninterrupted marketing channel, which will be continuously tied to the shoppers, is needed to boost up the retail industry. Going beyond the traditional marketing at low prices will cut down the high costs and brings good returns.

Best alternative is Online branding and marketing through effective presence: Now it is the time to find the right alternative for the retail industry to bring down the expenses and to move up in the market. With the lacks of online searches, happening daily for the different products, online market is now creating enormous opportunities in retail business. To reach the online shoppers, online retailing is the best alternative solution for the retail industry, through which online branding can be achieved. Online branding and online marketing are the ongoing retail business trends.

INTERACTIVE MARKETING *v/s* INTERNET MARKETING

The internet has provided the global audience instant information, broad connections to billions and a revolutionary form of communication. However, for all of this seemingly effortless access to consumers, the internet has traditionally been a complex problem for marketers. Numerous organizations either do not have or maintain an appropriate interactive/*internet marketing* plan. More still simply include an isolated online component, typically a *banner advertising* campaign, in an overall *marketing plan*. And those organizations with an interactive marketing plan often face the challenge of new technology, new opportunities and campaign measurement. How do you build an interactive marketing strategy? What are the key building blocks that should be included? This toolkit, How to Develop an Interactive Marketing Strategy, will describe the basic pieces and steps that are commonly utilized when creating an interactive/internet marketing plan. To ensure that this toolkit is beneficial to a wide range of marketers, this process has been divided into four steps: Plan, Accumulate, Activate and Measure. In addition, the toolkit contains several resources, including an interactive dictionary, tips, best practices, helpful websites and recommended books. While this toolkit provides a wealth of information, it should be used as a basic outline for approaching an interactive marketing plan, rather than an exact method to use in every campaign. Keep in mind that the advantage and challenge of internet marketing is that no two campaigns are exactly alike.

As with all terminology, the descriptive words ˜interactive and ˜internet mean two, slightly different things when applied in a marketing sense. Before we review the fundamental processes and techniques within interactive marketing, let review what these two terms mean.

Interactive Marketing: Interactive Marketing refers to the evolving trend in marketing whereby marketing has moved from a transaction-based effort to a conversation. The definition of interactive marketing comes from John Deighton at Harvard, who says interactive marketing is the ability to address the customer, remember what the customer says and address the customer again in a way that illustrates that we remember what the customer has told us. Interactive marketing is not synonymous with internet marketing, although interactive marketing processes are facilitated by internet technology. The ability to remember what the customer has said is made easier when we can collect customer information online and we can communicate with our customer more easily using the speed of the internet.

Internet Marketing: Internet marketing, also referred to as online marketing or Emarketing, is marketing that uses the Internet. The interactive nature of Internet media, both in terms of instant response, and in eliciting response at all, are both unique qualities of Internet marketing. Internet marketing ties together creative and technical aspects of the internet, including design, development, advertising and sales. Internet marketing methods include search engine marketing, display advertising, email marketing, affiliate marketing, interactive advertising, blog marketing, and viral marketing.

Fundamental Interactive/Internet Marketing Terms

Affiliate Marketing is a method of promoting web businesses (merchants/advertisers) in which an affiliate (publisher) is rewarded for every visitor, subscriber, customer, and/or sale provided through his/her efforts. Banner Ad (Display Ads) "A web banner or banner ad is a form of advertising on the internet. This form of internet advertising entails embedding an advertisement into a web page. It is intended to attract traffic to a website by linking them to the web site of the advertiser.

The advertisement is constructed from an image (GIF, JPEG, PNG), JavaScript program or multimedia object employing technologies such as Java, Shockwave or Flash, often employing animation or sound to maximize presence. Images are usually in a high-aspect ratio shape (i.e. either wide and short, or tall and narrow) hence the reference to banners. *Blog* "A blog (a portmanteau of web log) is a website where entries are written in chronological order and commonly displayed in reverse chronological order. Blog can also be used as a verb, meaning to maintain or add content to a blog. Many blogs provide commentary or news on a particular subject; others function as more personal online diaries. A typical blog combines text, images, and links to other blogs, web pages, and other media related to its topic. The ability for readers to leave comments in an interactive format is an important part of many blogs.

Contextual Advertising—Contextual advertising is the term applied to advertisements appearing on websites or other media, such as content displayed in mobile phones, where the advertisements are selected and served by automated systems based on the content displayed by the user.

Cost Per Action (CPA) is considered the optimal form of buying online advertising from a direct response advertisers point of view. An advertiser only pays for the ad when an action has occurred. An action can be a product being purchased, a form being filled, etc.

Cost Per Impression—A phrase often used in online advertising and marketing related to web traffic. It is used for measuring the worth and cost of a specific e-marketing campaign. This technique is applied with web banners, text links, e-mail spam, and opt-in e-mail advertising, although opt-in e-mail advertising is more commonly charged on a Cost Per Action (CPA) basis.

Email Marketing is a form of direct marketing which uses electronic mail as a means of communicating commercial or fund raising messages to an audience. In its broadest sense, every email sent to a potential or current customer could be considered email marketing. The term is also used to refer to, sending emails with the purpose of enhancing the relationship of a merchant with its current or old customers and to encourage customer loyalty and repeat business. Sending emails with the purpose of acquiring new customers or convincing old customers to buy something immediately. Adding advertisements in emails sent by other companies to their customers.

Landing Page-Sometimes known as a lead capture page, is the page that appears when a potential customer clicks on an advertisement or a search-engine result link. The page will usually display content that is a logical *extension* of the advertisement or link, and that is optimized to feature specific keywords or phrases for indexing by search engines.

In pay per click (PPC) campaigns, the landing page will also be customized to measure the effectiveness of different advertisements. By adding a parameter to the linking URL, marketers can measure advertisement effectiveness based on relative click-through rates.

PPC-Pay per click (PPC) is an advertising model used on search engines, advertising networks, and content websites/ blogs, where advertisers only pay when a user actually clicks on an ad to visit the advertisers website.

Reciprocal Link: A reciprocal link is a mutual link between two objects, commonly between two websites in order to ensure mutual traffic.

RSS Feed: Really Simple Syndication (RSS 2.0) is a family of Web feed formats used to publish frequently updated content such as blog entries, news headlines or podcasts. An RSS document, which is called a feed,web feed, or channel, contains either a summary of content from an associated web site or the full text. RSS makes it possible for people to keep up with their favorite web sites in an automated manner that easier than checking them manually.

SEM Search Engine Marketing is a form of Internet Marketing that seeks increase a websites visibility in the Search Engine result pages using the practice of buying paid search listings.

SEO Search engine optimization is the process of improving the volume and quality of traffic to a web site from search engines via natural search results. Usually, the earlier a site is presented in the search results or the higher it ranks, the more searchers will visit that site.

Search Engine (Web) search engines provide an interface to search for information on the World Wide Web. Information may consist of web pages, images and other types of files. Some search engines also mine data available in newsgroups, databases, or open directories. Google, Yahoo! Search and Ask.com are well-known examples of search engines. Site Map-A site map (or sitemap) is a graphical representation of the architecture of a web site. It can be either a document in any form used as a planning tool for web design, or a web page that lists the pages on a web site, typically organized in hierarchical fashion. This helps visitors and search engine bots find pages on the site. Spam-Spamming is the abuse of electronic messaging systems to indiscriminately send unsolicited bulk messages. While the most widely recognized form of spam is e-mail spam, the term is applied to similar abuses in other media: instant messaging spam, Usenet newsgroup spam, Web search engine spam, and spam in blogs.

Viral marketing and viral advertising refers to marketing techniques that use pre-existing social networks to produce increases in brand awareness, through self-replicating viral processes, analogous to the spread of pathological and computer viruses. It can be word-of-mouth delivered or enhanced by the network effects of the Internet. Viral marketing is a marketing phenomenon that facilitates and encourages people to pass along a marketing message voluntarily.

Viral promotions may take the form of funny video clips, interactive Flash games, advergames, images, or even text messages.

A website is a collection of Web pages, images, videos or other digital assets that is hosted on one or several Web server(s), usually accessible via the Internet or cell phone.

CREATING AN INTERACTIVE/INTERNET MARKETING PLAN

Interactive/Internet Marketing is constantly evolving and growing at an extremely rapid pace. New opportunities and methods are being developed on an almost daily basis, which would appear to make it increasingly difficult to stay up-to-date on the latest trends. While it is important to stay nimble within an interactive marketing plan, a well-planned and focused strategy, using the most appropriate and relevant placements will ensure a successful campaign regardless of the latest marketing fads. The key to success is following a simple formula : Plan, Accumulate, Activate and Measure.

Plan

The planning stage of an effective Interactive/Internet marketing plan is a crucial, but often ignored, step to ensuring the desired outcome. For example a typical scenario might go something like this; an organization completes and implements a standard (offline) marketing plan including a reasonable purchase of banner advertising on related websites. A brochure is printed, a magazine/newspaper ad is created and at some point, someone says, â€˜just scale down the print ad to a banner ad and run with that on the local newspaper site. Then, at the completion of the campaign, a click-thru report is delivered showing that 358 people clicked your banner on the local newspaper site. But wait, we purchased 27,000 banner impressions? And how many of those people ordered a visitor guide? Do we know if any of them signed up for our email? Due to the nature and pace of interactive marketing, these important questions are often overlooked until the completion of campaign. And even then, most marketing professionals do not have enough time to analyze review the results, they simply include the same banner advertising promotion in next year marketing plan.

The key to preventing this monotonous cycle of online advertising is to establish the objectives and goals of an interactive marketing strategy prior to launching the campaign.

Ask the Right Questions: While most organizations and businesses typically already promote and maintain a website for interactive marketing campaigns, it is possible to find the need to create a new website for a campaign or promotion. With that in mind, how should you begin to build or update your website in preparation for an interactive marketing campaign?

Objectives/Goals: What is the goal of the website/ campaign? Are you trying to encourage people to visit a website, or is the goal to have them order and receive, for example, a visitor guide? Or, are you trying to increase ticket sales to an attraction or event? Each example is a common goal, however the execution of an interactive/internet marketing campaign for these goals could be vastly different. One goal may require an extensive pay per click campaign, while another goal may require the sponsorship of a local newspaper calendar of events section. A common way to measure objectives and goals is with Key Performance Indicators or KPIs. KPIs help an organization to measure progress towards their organizational goals, which can differ depending on the nature of the organization and its strategy.

Whether a KPI method or other technique is implemented for your campaign, establishing objectives and goals for an interactive marketing plan is the first step to determine the marketing vehicles and placements, the creative execution and the measurement of success for the campaign.

Accumulate: Now that the objective and goals of the interactive marketing plan have been established, the next step is the accumulation of materials and content for the campaign. A commonly undervalued area of an interactive marketing plan, the content that you deliver to the consumer is one of the only things which will distinguish your website (and campaign) from countless others. Approach the creation of content by assuming these three points:

- Consumers either do not know or do not care where they receive content/information from.
- There are hundreds of other websites that offer the same or similar content as your site.
- reate valuable and interesting content for your audience.

Once you understand these ideas you can begin to determine what content will distinguish your website in the consumer mind. The goal of content creation is to develop so called sticky content, which is information or features on a website that provides users a compelling reason to visit it frequently.

Listen: To borrow a quote from Geoff Ramsey of eMarketer, Listening means that marketers set aside their ingrained command-and-control style of delivering messages on a one-way path, and instead open their senses to what consumers are saying, doing, feeling and thinking. While the connectivity and immediacy of the internet has challenged marketers to creative more effective messages, those same attributes have also opened up a vast depository of consumer thoughts, behaviors and interests. Take the time to read and explore blogs about the travel industry or your destination. Find out what people are talking about, what they are asking each other about and what they are most interested in. If the majority of people on a specific blog are asking other people for a map of a local shopping area, then create and post that content, in this case a map, on your website. Then, let everyone know about that map and that your site is a great resource for information about that subject. Use the interactivity and honesty of blogs to your advantage. Another way to listen to the consumer is by exploring social networking sites such as MySpace, Facebook, Yahoo! Travel and Trip Advisor. What are people talking about? What are they reviewing favorably? What are people reviewing unfavorably? Additionally, more traditional research methods such as focus groups and surveys can provide valuable insight into your consumer wants and needs. The advent of social networking technology has allowed millions of people to tell the world about what they are interested in, as a marketer, you just have to take the time to listen.

Content Plan: Once the type of content has been determined, an evaluation of where that content will come from is the next step. Decide if the content already exists in some form or if you need to have content created for the campaign. The type of content selected for the campaign depends on the research and planning that you have accomplished in the previous steps. Go back to the question What is the goal? and Why do we want people to visit it (the site)? If you are creating a campaign to promote a shopping district within your destination, perhaps you have learned that users are most interested in a list of stores, directions, maps and coupons. Take those insights and create a list of what content is the most desirable.

As you start to develop your website or splash page, refer to this content chart for direction on what content to place on a page and where to place it. Make sure that the most important content is easy to find and understand, while at the same time placing the unimportant content in an unobtrusive location or removing it from the website entirely. In most cases the content on a website will consist of a majority of copy (text) and images. It is important to consider the length of the copy at this point. The majority of users do not like to read large blocks of copy online, so try to keep the text in a short, memo style format. Making text easy to read is the key to offering great online copy. At the same time, ensure that the images you are presenting with the copy are relevant and exciting. While copy and images make up the bulk of a website content, specific rich media pieces such as audio files (podcasts), videos, interactive maps and slideshows provide a smaller, but equally important source of material. Prior to launching a campaign, develop these rich media components so that interested consumers are presented with an in-depth catalog of additional content.

Activate: With a marketing plan in place and the content for the campaign completed, the next step is to activate or promote the campaign to the consumer. Again, by reviewing the original goals for the campaign you can start to determine what forms of marketing and promotion offer the most beneficial results.

Choosing an Online Marketing Vehicle: Because there are so many ways to advertise and market online, choosing the correct marketing vehicle can be a daunting challenge. Should the campaign consist of all banner advertising or should we run a search engine marketing (SEM) campaign? What about podcasting and video? Do we need to create a MySpace page too? While there is no exact template or plan for selecting online marketing vehicles, it can be generally assumed that a diversified strategy will provide the best opportunity for success, especially if the campaign is in its first year.

Common Online Marketing Components: Below are some of the more common and latest marketing vehicles available to advertisers. While this list provides a brief introduction to each opportunity, it does not represent the hundreds of marketing placements that could be used in an interactive marketing campaign.

Banner Advertising: Perhaps the most common and well-known form of online advertising, banner advertising or banner ads allow the marketer to purchase online billboards on popular or relevant sites in order to show a promotional message. The ads are typically a standard size, contain text and images and are presented in a jpeg, gif or Flash format. The main challenge associated with banner advertising is a low response rate to the advertisement. Because the majority of sites feature several banner ads on a single page, attracting a consumer attention and initiating a click can be a difficult process. Recently, enhanced targeting methods have begun to improve the low click thru rates (CTRs) typical of banner ads. Refer to the next section for more information on targeting.

SEM: Search engine marketing or SEM, is another popular form of online advertising that involves purchasing sponsored links for certain search engine keywords. As a user searches for a purchased keyword or phrase, an additional listing displaying a marketing message is displayed above or to the side of the regular or natural search results. Part of the benefit of SEM is that the consumer is actively searching for your keyword and in theory, is already interested in your product or location. While a SEM advertising campaign does feature several benefits, it can be an expensive and time-consuming project for a small marketing budget. Additionally, businesses should focus on optimizing their search engine optimization (SEO) campaign to enhance rankings in natural search results, rather than rely solely on SEM.

Email Marketing: An email marketing campaign is a cost-effective and direct way to market and communicate with consumers who have already shown an interest in your product or location. Building an email database including users who have agreed and expressly consented to receiving your marketing messages is not only a solid approach, but it is also a requirement of federal law under the CAN-SPAM act. When creating an email marketing campaign pay close attention to the design, distribution and effectiveness of each email.

Sponsorships: Similar to, and in most cases including, banner advertising, online sponsorships commonly offer the ability to integrate your content or marketing message into another website. A typical sponsorship package could include several banners, locations for copy inclusion and links to the marketer website. For example, a local CVB could sponsor the weather section of a local newspaper website in exchange for banner ad placement and the opportunity to talk about (through copy) what local attractions you can experience during sunny days.

ADVANCED ONLINE MARKETING COMPONENTS

Blogs: Since blogs are also a different form of websites, they do offer some of the same basic advertising opportunities as most websites, including banner advertising and sponsorships. Beyond basic advertising, marketers can also create blogs to further enhance SEO programs, public relations initiatives, email databases and communication outlets. Some companies, including Southwest Airlines and General Motors have begun to use blogs to not only promote their products and services, but also to open a new line of communication (a new way to listen) with the consumer. However, the same openness and communication that make blogs so beneficial is also the same challenges that many companies grapple with while running a blog. Upset consumers and instant communication do make blogs a very labor intensive marketing vehicle.

Podcasting: A commonly misused marketing term, podcasting (in the truest since of the word) refers to the distribution of audio or video shows via Apple iTunes store which are available for viewing on a portable media player (mp3 player) or iPod. Due to the popularity of the iPod and podcasting, the term is often used to refer to any type of regularly distributed audio or video show that is viewed on a portable media player. In most cases, podcasting offers the producer(s) a cost-effective way to distribute information to a large audience. Typically, podcasts are structured in a form similar to a traditional television or radio show. Using podcasting as marketing vehicles does present some challenges, including a limited audience, content creation and delivering a relevant message.

Widgets: Widgets, or gadgets, are split into two types: desktop widgets and web widgets. In either case, widgets are usually a small application that displays a form of content to a user. Common widgets could show the local weather forecast, news, images or a snapshot of your email inbox.

The difference between desktop widgets and web widgets is simply the location where they are being displayed. Desktop widgets usually require the download of a special application to run the widgets on your desktop; however the new Microsoft Vista operating system already includes this feature. By using desktop widgets a user could have a variety of information displayed without the use of a web browser. Web widgets are widgets that remain online, but can be placed on a variety of sites such as a MySpace page or blog. Conventional versions of web widgets include photo slideshows, audio players and video players. Because these widgets can be easily moved from one site to another by simply copying the source code (which runs the widget), a viral marketing effect commonly occurs with the most popular widgets. Due to the distribution of widgets, many marketers face the challenge of creating compelling content that users want to see on a daily basis. Successful widgets usually offer a service or content that the user wants, rather than a standard marketing message or commercial.

Social Networking: Websites such as MySpace, Face-book and Trip-Advisor have created communities of users with common interests and relationships. These social networking sites not only offer banner advertising and sponsorship opportunities, but also the ability to harness the collective power of these relationships to promote and inform consumers about your product. A typical execution using a social networking site would involve an organization setting up a profile and creating a page on the site. Then, the organization would use the page to promote a particular product, connect with users who like that specific product and gather additional information from those users. While using social networking sites sounds easy, like blogs, marketers should be aware of the challenges that accompany consumer opinions and instant communication. Many social networking users do not respond favorably to the proliferation of advertisers on these sites. Before using social networking a component to an interactive marketing plan, research any potential opposition to your organization on these sites. Then, create valuable and relevant content for the social networking site.

Targeting : While the internet has offered marketers several ways to target specific consumers, for example by advertising on a website with related content to a product, recent advancements in technology have enhanced the targeting of online advertising. Two of the more well-known online targeting methods are contextual and behavioral targeting.

Commonly used in conjunction with banner advertisements, contextual targeting ensures that a banner ad is only shown on pages with related content. For example, if you have an advertisement about hotels in Flagstaff and a user is reading a story about a new hotel being constructed in Sedona; contextual targeting would display your banner ad because of the relationship of the word hotel Rather than target the content, behavioral targeting presents your message to the consumer regardless of what website they are on. Behavioral targeting gathers the preferences of a consumer as they browse the web, building a profile of that person's interests. The advertising network uses that information to present your ad to a targeted consumer, regardless of what website they are currently browsing. While both forms of targeting do raise some concerns, specifically privacy of information, they offer a proven way to present a marketing message to a specific section of consumers.

Offline Activation: Including steps to promote your interactive marketing plan offline may seem ironic; however offline activation is another important piece of creating a successful campaign. Using a call to action with a specific URL or web address in print ads, radio ads and television spots is a common way to increase traffic to your interactive campaign. Be sure to also consider the other offline locations that could benefit your online campaign such as including a URL or web address on business cards, letterhead, collateral materials and promotional materials.

Measure: Once your interactive marketing plan has been launched, it is essential that the campaign be tested, measured and optimized. Without a comprehensive measurement plan even the best interactive marketing plans will not deliver the necessary results.

Establish Measurements: One of the benefits of online advertising is the vast amount of tracking and statistics that are available. Determining which statistics to track and report on depends upon the original goals of the campaign. If the goal of the interactive marketing plan is to further the branding message of your organization a possible measurement would be time spent and the click thru rate from the banner advertising.

Tracking Tools: Now that measurement metrics have been established, make sure that the proper tracking tools are in place to record the data. Tracking tools for websites and banner advertisements are common tools available for monitoring interactive marketing campaigns. Website tracking software should be a standard piece of any website development project. While such website statistics tools vary in price, service and tracking techniques any of the major website statistics companies such as Web-Trends, HBX Analytics or Google Analytics are widely accepted. Data collected by a website statistics tool is typically reporting in the form of web traffic report. These web traffic reports are then compared against the goals or key performance indicators that were previously established. In addition to website statistics tools, banner ad networks also record data from a banner advertising campaign. These reports are typically sent on a weekly or monthly basis and, in combination with website statistics tools, can provide valuable insight into the success of a banner advertising campaign. While these reports will provide a good amount of data, additional tracking tools such as unique URLs and landing pages, can impart even more detailed information about a campaign. Unique URLs could be as simple as a different domain name or as complex as a unique URL string, both of which will provide statistics on the effectiveness of a specific advertising execution. The use of landing pages or splash pages is another technique that can differentiate the amount of advertising-specific traffic versus normal website traffic.

Testing: By using a variety of tracking tools, an organization can start to develop a robust understanding of how an interactive marketing campaign is performing. Using this data, tests can be performed on specific creative, copy or emails to determine what best combination of elements returns the highest ROI, click thru rate or time spent. The most common testing technique is multivariate or A/B testing, which compares to slightly different versions of a website or email.

Tips: Now that an interactive marketing plan has been developed, take a moment to review these tips and best practices for websites, search engine marketing, email marketing

Websites

- Place the organization or website logo at the top (usually top-left) of every page and link the logo back to the homepage of the site.
- Use clear and descriptive text when links to other pages or websites, rather than click here. Not only will this provide a clear path for navigating a website, it will also enhance SEO or search engine optimization efforts.
- Do not use â€˜under construction or coming soon pages. They send a message that a site is incomplete. Only post content once it has been fully developed.
- Avoid using â€˜mystery meat navigation or icon-based navigation. Navigation that is composed of a series of symbols or images is usually difficult for users to understand.
- The majority of web browsers in use are already sufficient to view the latest web designs therefore links to download the latest browser versions are not always necessary. Avoid making users download a new browser version before visiting a site by ensuring the site is accessible to the largest audience possible.
- Distinguish links that require a file download, such as a PDF or Word document file, by including identifying text such as This is a.PDF file.
- Avoid mixing too many font typefaces, sizes and colors. The right amount of variety can create a good visual distinction, but too much can create confusion.

- Avoid using blinking text, scrolling text or sounds on the homepage; these can be more of a distraction than an enhancement.
- Create copy in short, easy-to-read segments. Avoid creating blocks of copy that are too long or too wide. Users typically scan pages, therefore pages with too much, unreadable content are usually skipped.
- Place descriptive alt tags on all images, which will provide additional information to website visitors as well as visitors who are using text only browsers.

Email Marketing

- Use your organization or brand name in the from line, which tells recipients who sent the email.
- Keep subject lines short words or less is considered ideal.
- Avoid using superfluous images, graphics, sound or video within emails. Many ISP and email client spam filters will block messages containing these elements.
- Test each email message before you send it. Use different browsers such as Internet Explorer, Firefox and Opera as well as different clients such as Outlook, AOL, Gmail and Yahoo!
- Help readers manage and connect with your messages. Include forward-to-a-friend links and printer-friendly options that are clearly labeled.

RETAIL INDUSTRY : BIG BAZAAR

Big Bazaar is a chain of shopping malls in India currently with 31 outlets, owned by the Pantaloon Group. The idea was pioneered by entrepreneur Kishore Biyani, the head of Pantaloon Retail India Ltd. The idea from the very beginning was to make Big Bazaar very comfortable for the Indian customer. That was Kishoreji's strength as a retailer. He had a lot of confidence in what he was doing, even though it defied conventional logic.

Big bazaar is not just another hypermarket. It caters to every need of your family. Where Big Bazaar scores over other stores is its value for *money* proposition for the Indian customers. At Big Bazaar, you will definitely get the best products at the best prices-that what they guarantee. With the ever increasing array of private labels, it has opened the doors into the world of fashion and general merchandise including home furnishings, utensils, crockery, cutlery, sports goods and much more at prices that will surprise you. And this is just the beginning. Big Bazaar plans to add much more to complete their customers shopping experience.

If one looks at Indian bazaars, mandis, melas, they are environments created by traders to give shoppers a sense of moment, of event, of place. They provide an inclusive environment where men and women from all castes, creeds and classes can come and shop at the same place. The founders of Big Bazaar were from the beginning very clear that they had to reflect the look and feel of Indian bazaars at their modern outlets, so that no customer would feel intimidated with the surroundings.

In India most of us are not prepared for the consumerism that is setting in this country. We underestimate how many people are going to fly and that s why our airports get crowded. We underestimate how many people will speak on the phone for how many billions of minutes and therefore our cell phone networks are always congested. But the minds responsible for the huge success of Big Bazaar have captured and understood the force of consumerism that is unfolding.

Big Bazaar all over India attract a few thousand customers on any regular day, and a lot more if they are offering something extra on each buy, which they normally are! And the sales force at Big Bazaar along with the executives is prepared for them.

Objective of Big Bazaar

The central objective for earlier businesses of Big Bazaar was to bring in stability and consolidation. They were built to enforce order. However, in the new era where nothing remains constant, the dominant theme for businesses needs to be speed and imagination.

The new macro-differentiator can be design. Design is helping companies to sell differentiated experiences and solutions that connect with the consumer emotions. Its no longer about selling products and services alone. Nor is it just about completing transactions. Every time a customer walks in, it is an opportunity to build a relationship and invite the customer to become a part of the transformational scenario. Design management is helping us position the customer at the center of every decision we take and also operate with true entrepreneurial spirit.

Target Customers

Big Bazaar targets higher and upper middle class customers because there has been growth in Indian middle class that has so far been used to buying apparel and groceries from small and cluttered neighborhood market shops is fast realizing the joys of visiting malls that have redefined the freedom to shop and entertain. Such malls are the new temples of leisure and weekend entertainment. India National Council for Applied Economic Research estimates that the nation's middle class population currently comprises about 17 million households 90 million people with annual earnings. An additional 287 million could be termed as aspirers or those that hope to join the middle class in the near term. Rising incomes, particularly in the lower and middle-income households, are impacting retail growth in India as these groups tend to spend more on upgrading and diversifying their lifestyles, eating out and moving on to processed and convenience foods.

Targeting Young Working Class

The large and growing young working population is a preferred customer segment for Big bazaar. These young people are early adopters of most modern product lines. The ongoing boom in sectors such as information technology and business process outsourcing has created a clientele with high disposable income and a increased demand for lifestyle merchandise such as watches, cosmetics and perfumes. This is a much-travelled and brand-savvy urban population. Interestingly, an estimated 40-50% of the Indian working woman salary is spent on apparel and footwear. Eating out, mobile phones and accessories make up the other leading spending options. Big Bazaar specifically *target* young, working professionals, home makers who are primary decision maker.

Value for Money

All our lines of business are consumer centric and I believe that if we are to be in the larger consumer space, we would need to keep changing, evolving and accordingly be flexible in our business plans. Consumers are the same everywhere; we are only bound by our social systems. Their desires, greeds and needs are similar. The value for money proposition is so ingrained in the Indian consumers mind that he needs to be shown true value all the time. Therefore, all our current and future businesses would necessarily have the common denominator as the consumer. All our alliances and relationships with many company's have been built, keeping the synergies of business and consumer offerings in mind.

Image

Nothing captures the sprit of Big Bazaar better than this one liner. It is a simple statement and yet it positioned at the top of Indian customers mind. It shows that big bazaar was built on the foundation of entrepreneurship and simplicity. They believe in service and value for the customers. They consider that it is their only duty to keep customer in mind at every step, they go that extra mile and buy directly from source in bulk so that they can get best rates by keeping the margin low Big Bazaar is constantly on the lookout for finding new ways and means to improve the current state of affairs. Thus, innovation is a very important aspect of their working strategy. The other very important philosophy is that of Indian-ness. All the concepts and formats as well as the way of doing things are very Indian. The way Big Bazaar is designed and the way the whole concept has developed reflects a sense of Indian-ness.

Merchandise

Main objective of the store layout is to maximize the interface between customers and merchandise. It provides easy accessibility to the customers to view the offerings of the store. Layout of the store has been strategically designed in order to make effective use of merchandise and passage to draw customers attention on store's offerings

Location

Big bazaar is located has 31 outlets in India, big bazaar locates its outlet near the commercial area and residential complexs so that they can cover all their target customers Eg : their outlet in phoenix mill, lowerparel mumbai, is located near commercial areas so that the working class people can drop in and shop house hold items after office hrs. On the other hand their outlets in single is a bit different from what we would see at say, high street Phoenix in Mumbai. For instance isn't air conditioned: instead, there are air coolers installed inside the store,also there are many shoppers there on days as an weekends. Unlike office going people in big cities, people in smaller towns do not restrict their shopping to weekends. The choice of location of Big Bazaar in many ways captures the essence of what they were doing-they adapt themselves to the habits tastes and preferences according to the location. One of the distinct feature of their location is that it is easily accessible and they try to locate their outlet in such a location where they can reach a large customer base.

Services

Big Bazaar provides a wide range of services to its customers like Trial rooms, elevators, car parking, security, baggage counter, trolleys so that one could shop easily They even provide them with after sale services in case of buying electronic items. One of the major service provided by them is one stop shop as one could get a whole range of items under one shop and at the most reasonable price. They always have their outlets in such a location where it is easy to commute. They have also given major emphasis to convince for customers in which layout has played a major role. The layout of the store is so effective that customers find their way out of what they want. Big Bazaar provides good employee service i.e their salesmen are always redy to provide help. Employee service is often neglected as part of good retail marketing but customer and employee interaction can be used as the significant tool for retail marketing.

NIVEA : THE USE OF THE MARKETING MIX IN PRODUCT LAUNCH

NIVEA is an established name in high quality skin and beauty care products. It is part of a range of brands produced and sold by Beiersdorf. Beiersdorf, founded in 1882, has grown to be a global company specialising in skin and beauty care. In the UK, Beiersdorf's continuing goal is to have its products as close as possible to its consumers, regardless of where they live. Its aims are to understand its consumers in its many different markets and delight them with innovative products for their skin and beauty care needs. This strengthens the trust and appeal of Beiersdorf brands. The business prides itself on being consumer-led and this focus has helped it to grow NIVEA into one of the largest skin care brands in the world. Beiersdorf continuing programme of market research showed a gap in the market. This led to the launch of NIVEA VISAGEÂ. Young in 2005 as part of the NIVEA VISAGE range offering a comprehensive selection of products aimed at young women. It carries the strength of the NIVEA brand image to the target market of girls aged 13-19.

Market Orientation and Product Orientation

The market can be developed by creating a good product/ range and introducing it to the market (product-orientated approach) or by finding a gap in the market and developing a product to fill it (market-orientated approach). Having identified a gap in the market, Beiersdorf launched NIVEA VISAGE Young using an effective *balance* of the right product, price, promotion and place. This is known as the marketing mix or four Ps. It is vital that a company gets the balance of these four elements correct so that a product will achieve its critical success factors. Beiersdorf needed to develop a mix that suited the product and the target market as well as meeting its own business objectives. The company re-launched the NIVEA VISAGE Young range in June 2007 further optimizing its position in the market. Optimized means the product had a new formula, new design, new packaging and a new name.

Product : The first stage in building an effective mix is to understand the market. NIVEA uses market research to target key market segments which identifies groups of people with the same characteristics such as age/gender/attitude/lifestyle. The knowledge and understanding from the research helps in the development of new products. NIVEA carries out its market research with consumers in a number of different ways. These include:

- using focus groups to listen to consumers directly.
- gathering data from consumers through a variety of different research techniques.
- product testing with consumers in different markets.

How Research Improved the Product

- *Beiersdorf*'s market research identified that younger consumers wanted more specialised face care aimed at their own age group that offered a beautifying benefit, rather than a solution to skin problems. NIVEA VISAGE Young is a skin care range targeted at girls who do not want medicated products but want a regime for their normal skin.
- Competitor products tend to be problem focused and offer medicated solutions. This gives NIVEA competitive advantage. NIVEA VISAGE Young provides a unique bridge between the teenage market and the adult market.

Beiersdorf tested the improved products on a sample group from its target audience before finalizing the range for re-launch. This testing resulted in a number of changes to existing products. Improvements included:

- changing the formula of some products. For example, it removed alcohol from one product and used natural sea salts and minerals in others
- introducing two completely new products
- a new modern pack design with a flower pattern and softer colors to appeal to younger women
- changing product descriptions and introducing larger pack sizes.

Corporate responsibility: Some of these changes reflect NIVEA's commitment to the environment. Its corporate responsibility approach aims to:

- reduce packaging and waste-by using larger pack sizes
- use more natural products by including minerals and sea salts in the formula
- increase opportunities for recycling-by using recyclable plastic in its containers.

Price Lots of factors affect the end price of a product, for example, the costs of production or the business need to maximize profits or sales.

Pricing strategies: There are several pricing strategies that a business can use:

- cost based pricing this can either simply cover costs or include an element of profit. It focuses on the product and does not take account of consumers.
- penetration price an initial low price to ensure that there is a high volume of purchases and market share is quickly won. This strategy encourages consumers to develop a habit of buying.
- price skimming an initial high price for a unique product encouraging those who want to be first to buy to pay a premium revenue before a competitor product reaches the market. price. This strategy helps a business to gain maximum.

On re-launch the price for NIVEA VISAGE Young was slightly higher than previously. This reflected its new formulations, packaging and extended product range. However, the company also had to take into account that the target market was both teenage girls and mums buying the product for their daughters. This meant that the price had to offer value for money or it would be out of reach of its target market.

Price leader: As NIVEA VISAGE Young is one of the leading skin care ranges meeting the beautifying needs of this market segment, it is effectively the price leader. This means that it sets the price level that competitors will follow or undercut. NIVEA needs to regularly review prices should a competitor enter the market at the market growth point of the product life cycle to ensure that its pricing remains competitive. The pricing strategy for NIVEA is not the same as that of the retailers. It sells products to retailers at one price. However, retailers have the freedom to use other strategies for sales promotion. These take account of the competitive nature of the high street. They may use:

- *loss leader*: the retailer sells for less than it cost to attract large volume of sales, for example by supermarkets.
- discounting alongside other special offers, such as ˜Buy one, get one free" (BOGOF) or ˜two for one".

Place: Place refers to:

- how the product arrives at the point of sale. This means a business must think about what distribution strategies it will use.
- where a product is sold. This includes retail outlets like supermarkets or high street shops. It also includes other ways in which businesses make products directly available to their target market, for example, through direct mail or the Internet.

Distribution channels: The main channels for the product are retail outlets where consumers sales stock beauty products, such as ASDA, Tesco and Sainsbury. expect to find skin care ranges. Around 65% of NIVEA VISAGE Young are through large high street shops such as Boots and Superdrug. Superdrug is particularly important for the young-end market. The other 35% of sales mainly comes from large grocery chains. Research also shows that the majority of purchasers are actually made by mums, buying for teenagers. Mums are more likely to buy the product from supermarkets whilst doing their grocery shopping. NIVEA distributes through a range of outlets that are cost effective but that also reach the highest number of consumers. Its distribution strategies also consider the environmental impact of transport.

- It uses a central distribution point in the UK. Products arrive from European production plants using contract vehicles for efficiency for onward delivery to retail stores.
- Beiersdorf does not sell direct to smaller retailers as the volume of products sold would not be cost effective to deliver but it uses wholesalers for these smaller accounts.
- It does not sell directly through its website as the costs of producing small orders would be too high. However, the retailers, like Tesco, feature and sell the NIVEA products in their online stores.

Promotion: Promotion is how the business tells customers that products are available and persuades them to buy. Promotion is either above-the-line or below-the-line. Above-the-line promotion is directly paid for, for example TV or newspaper advertising. Below-the-line is where the business uses other promotional methods to get the product message across. Promotional activities include:

- Events or trade fairs help to launch a product to a wide audience. Events may be business to consumer (B2C) whereas trade fairs are business to business (B2B).
- Direct mail can reach a large number of people but is not easy to target specific consumers cost-effectively.
- Public relations (PR) includes the different ways a business can communicate with its stakeholders, through, for example, newspaper press releases. Other PR activities include sponsorship of high profile events like Formula 1 or the World Cup, as well as donations to or participation in charity events.
- Branding a strong and consistent brand identity differentiates the product and helps consumers to

understand and trust the product. This aims to keep consumers buying the product long-term.

- Sales promotions, for example competitions or sampling, encourage consumers to buy products in the short-term.

NIVEA realises that a one way message, using TV or the press, is not as effective as talking directly to its target group of consumers. Therefore NIVEA does not plan to use any above-the-line promotion for NIVEA VISAGE Young.

Consumer-led promotion: The promotion of NIVEA VISAGE Young is consumer-led. Using various below-the-line routes, NIVEA identifies ways of talking to teenagers (and their mums) directly.

- A key part of the strategy is the use of product samples. These allow customers to touch, feel, smell and try the products. Over a million samples of NIVEA VISAGE Young products will be given away during 2008. These samples will be available through the website, samples in stores or in goody bags given out at VISAGE road shows up and down the country.
- NIVEA VISAGE Young launched an interactive online magazine called FYI (Fun, Young and Independent) to raise awareness of the brand. The concept behind the magazine is to give teenage girls the confidence to become young women and to enjoy their new-found independence. Communication channels are original and engaging to enable teenagers to identify with NIVEA VISAGE Young. The magazine focuses on first time experiences relating to NIVEA VISAGE Young being their first skincare routine. It is promoted using the Hit40UK chart show and the TMF digital TV channel.
- In connection with FYI, NIVEA VISAGE Young has recognized the power of social network sites for this young audience and also has pages on MySpace, Facebook and Bebo. The company is using the power of new media as part of the mix to grow awareness amongst the target audience.

NIVEA VISAGE Young is a skincare range in the UK market designed to enhance the skin and beauty of the teenage consumer rather than being medicated to treat skin problems. As such, it has created a clear position in the market. This shows that NIVEA understands its consumers and has produced this differentiated product range in order to meet their needs. To bring the range to market, the business has put together a marketing mix. This mix balances the four elements of product, price, place and promotion. The mix uses traditional methods of place, such as distribution through the high street, alongside more modern methods of promotion, such as through social networking sites. It makes sure that the message of NIVEA VISAGE Young reaches the right people in the right way.

CHAPTER

15

Internet Marketing for Industrial Sector

THE UNIQUE SELLING PROPOSITION (USP)

The starting point of a marketing campaign often revolves around defining a point of differentiation. What is it about your product or service that sets it apart from the competition? Often, this has already been defined at a higher brand level and you just need to re-iterate it in a succinct way on your landing page. If not, this is your first task. Try to break down your offering to its most basic level, to describe the specific benefit your customers will get by choosing your product/service.

- A classic example comes from Domino's Pizza: "You get fresh, hot pizza delivered to your door in 30 minutes or less-or it's free".
- A well crafted USP sets clear expectations for your customers and allows them to understand why they should care.

- On your landing page, the USP should be delivered using a combination of the following page elements:
- The primary headline: the Domino's example above is a perfect illustration of a page headline.

1. Sub header

Sometimes you will need a secondary headline (typically smaller in size) that provides some clarification about the primary headline. Most commonly, this is used to allow the primary headline to be very short and punchy.

2. The Benefits

Following on directly from the USP is a more detailed description of your offer's benefits and features. By crafting an effective headline you gained the attention of your customer, and now you have to provide a little more detail to the offer to answer any questions they may have. Try to focus on answering the question "What will this do for me?", as this will help you to write copy that speaks directly to your customers questions.

It's important to strike a balance here and not get into so much detail that your landing page feels like it's full of text. Write a brief one paragraph summary and 3-5 bullet points for clarity. Come back to this section many times and edit the copy to remove any bloated or unnecessary verbiage.

3. The Hero Shot

The adage "a picture is worth a thousand words" is especially true in the short attention span world of the landing page. The hero shot is the visual representation of your offer and can help people to gain a better understanding of what it is or what it looks like. It will most commonly be one of these types of visual element:

- A photograph of your product/service-preferably shown in it's context of use (see point 4 below)
- A diagram illustrating how it fits into the realm of an existing problem (like a series of steps)
- A chart comparing it to the competition

- A large graphic simply stating the numerical aspect of the offer-200% Bonus, FREE.

4. Context of Use

You should aim to showcase your product or service being used in real life. The idea here is to get your customers to empathize and place themselves in a scenario where they are using it. There are many ways in which to achieve this, including:

- *A photo*: Consider an example of a collapsible step ladder. A standard white-background photo of the item would work for the hero shot, but to add extra effect you could provide supplementary photos of someone unfolding it, using it to reach somewhere high, and placing it neatly into a small cupboard afterward.
- *Video*: While the camera never lies, video is an even more compelling way to showcase your product. Think of the common Shamwow and Slapchop commercials currently running. While cheesy, they impart a sense of need by illustrating direct benefits to everyday life.
- *Testimonials*: Show that you already have customers, but keep them real.
- *Client lists*: By listing known brand names that are using your service provides an implied sense of context and adds to the feeling of trust.

5. Request for data

It's common-especially in the B2B marketplace-for the main purpose of your landing page to be lead generation. Usually this will involve asking the visitor for their Name and Email in exchange for some sort of freebie (we'll be covering this in Thursday's post). If you are requesting data from your customers, keep the form as short as possible and include a privacy statement near the button or email address field.

TIP: There is some thought and opinion on the placement of lead generation forms that suggests placing them on the right-hand side of the page yields higher conversions. This is likely due to the way westerners read from left to right. As such, placing the form on the left is akin to asking for something before explaining the benefits involved.

6. The Backup Plan

Not all visitors will become paying customers after the first kiss. To give you the opportunity for a little extra foreplay, leave a non-committal escape route from the page. This is what's known as a Safety Net, and its purpose is to capture the attention of someone who is interested but not ready to buy. Examples include:

- *Follow us on Twitter*: Once someone is following you on Twitter they can be exposed to your other marketing and brand messages, which may entice them to buy in the future.
- *Remind Me*: Provide a way for them to be reminded (via email) at a predetermined time in the future (1 day, 1 week, 1 month, specific date etc.) and be sure to place a trust statement beside it that explicitly states that you will not contact them at any other time.
- *A Free Takeaway*: Provide a link to a free downloadable brochure (without having to complete a form).
- *Bookmark This Page*: A classic technique that isn't likely to yield great results as people don't really check their bookmarks a a matter of process. It does however enable someone to find you again if they want to deal with you later on-especially important for standalone landing pages that are reached via an Ad they may never see again.

7. The Call to Action (CTA)

The final part of your landing page is the all important Call To Action or CTA. This is the statement or copy that instructs your visitor to take a specific action. Often it will be the button on a form, or a large graphical button that takes your new customer through to a final destination somewhere on your main website. It's critical that the CTA is very obvious and is written in a way that describes what clicking on it will actually do.

SEO TIPS FOR INDUSTRIAL MARKETERS

Search Engine Optimization (SEO) can help your company's Web pages rise higher in the search engine results for specific keyword searches. Done correctly, SEO can help you attract motivated prospects to your Web site in real time as they search online for products and services like those you offer.

Engaging in some level of SEO will be of benefit to most companies. Your level of involvement depends on your goals, expertise and resources. Some simple yet effective SEO techniques can be performed with limited expertise and resources, while other, more complex techniques require SEO experts and technical skills.

1. Identify Keywords

The first step in SEO is to identify the keywords and search terms most relevant to your company, products and services and that users are typing into search engines to look for products and services like yours. This way, you can tailor the content of your Web pages to include these keywords, helping your pages rank higher on search engines.

Here are some good techniques for discovering keywords:

- Conduct internal brainstorming sessions
- Ask customers how they describe your products and services
- Review competitor Web sites and the keywords they use
- Review Web server log files for search terms used to find your site
- Use commercially available keyword research tools, such as Wordtracker or the Google Keyword Tool

2. Integrate Keywords into Page Copy

Once you have a list of keywords, weave them into the copy of your Web pages. A single page should be optimized only for one or two keywords. Use keywords in the headline of the page and in the first paragraph, and repeat them as appropriate on the page, but make sure the use of keywords is natural and the copy flows and reads easily. Otherwise, you will confuse or turn off readers who might abandon your site, which will defeat your SEO efforts.

3. Add Internal Links

Search engines use software programs called spiders that roam the Web and follow links to find pages to index in the search engine database. By adding links between the pages on your Web site, you make it easier for search engines to find and index your pages. When creating links between pages, use keywords for the text. Instead of "click here" or "more information," try writing "centrifugal pumps" or "properties of oscillating pumps".

4. Build a Site Map

A site map containing HTML links to all of the major pages on your Web site makes it easier for a search engine to find and index your Web pages in its database. A site map is also a great usability and navigation feature, helping visitors understand the breadth and depth of your Web site and find what they are looking for. Be sure to update your site map when you add or delete pages from your Web site.

5. Use HTML Navigation

HTML navigation is another one of those internal linking techniques that make it easier for search engines to find and index your Web pages. Navigation based on images or drop-down navigation menus coded in Java script is difficult for search engines to follow. Re-programming navigation menus to straight HTML will take time and money. If you can't do this, you should at least repeat the navigation as text links at the bottom of your Web pages in the footer area.

6. Seek Incoming Links to Your Site

Link popularity refers to the SEO technique of getting other relevant Web sites to link to yours. It is used by major search engines to determine the importance of a Web page, under the philosophy that the most important Web pages will have the most links pointing to them. Managing a link strategy can be resource intensive. It's more important to get quality incoming links than a high quantity of irrelevant links. You can get links by submitting articles and press releases to industry directories and Web sites; asking partners, distributors and trade associations to link to your Web site; and commenting on industry blogs.

7. Keep Web Content Updated and Relevant

The quality of the content on your Web site is important. The higher quality and more relevant your content, the more likely external Web sites will link to yours and search engines will find and index the fresh content. Write and publish articles and white papers on your Web site, post press releases, or start a blog.

8. Download the White Paper: "Search Engine Optimization for the Industrial Marketer"

This white paper, written by GlobalSpec's SEO experts, will help you understand how SEO can fit into your marketing strategy, describing in more detail various SEO techniques, and helping you weigh an investment in SEO vs. other marketing programs helping you make the best use of your marketing budget to achieve your objectives.

Improve Internet Marketing

E-mail remains a popular and effective B2B marketing tactic. But as a marketer, you must fight for your audience's attention. Inboxes are overflowing and people are quick to delete anything that isn't of immediate interest or might be considered spam. Use these ten tips to make your e-mail marketing more effective.

1. *Identify yourself*—make sure your company and brand appear in the e-mail 'From' line so your recipients know who the e-mail is coming from. If the e-mail is sent by an individual, unless that individual is well-known to recipients, make sure to include the company name as well.

2. *Write compelling subject lines*—Short, benefit-oriented subject lines will interest your audience: "New pumps work twice as fast" or "White paper demonstrates laser advancements". Your subject line is the most important element in enticing your recipients to pay attention to your e-mail. Don't just dash one off. Instead, consider testing different subject lines with segments of your audience to see what message resonates best.
3. *Use the preview pane*—many people use their e-mail program's preview pane to see what an e-mail is about before deciding to open it. Put the most important information and a call to action in the top 300-500 pixels of your e-mail to grab the interest of your audience. Don't waste that space with large images or an overpowering header.
4. *Provide relevant content*—the most important thing you can do to improve e-mail effectiveness is to provide content that is so interesting to your audience that they look forward to every e-mail you send. First and foremost, provide content that helps them do their jobs. Think in terms of how-to articles, best practices (such as this top ten tips article), educational Webinars, case studies, application ideas, downloads, free trials. Once you have established relevancy and trust, you can mix in some e-mails that promote your products and services or even are funny and entertaining.
5. *Add multiple calls-to-action*—Some people like to click buttons, others look for text links. Make sure you use both and sprinkle them throughout your e-mail, without overwhelming your reader. The whole idea is to get recipients to take advantage of your offer: download the white paper, register for the Webinar, read the article, etc. Use these same action phrases on your buttons and link text.
6. *Use images wisely*—Images are a great way to add visual interest and relevancy to your e-mails. Go beyond your company logo and consider adding thumbnails of white paper covers, product images,

photographs of interview subjects and more. But be sure to use images sparingly-many of your e-mail recipients will have images turned off, so make sure that they don't interfere with the text being displayed. On a side note, if you send HTML e-mails, make sure you also produce a text-only version for recipients who indicate that preference.

TIPS FOR GROWING YOUR OPT-IN e-MAIL LIST

E-mail marketing to your in-house list is an effective, affordable and measurable marketing tactic. According to results of the GlobalSpec "Trends in Industrial Marketing 2010" survey, more than 70 percent of industrial marketers plan to use e-mail marketing to in-house lists in 2010, and e-mail marketing is one of the top five sources of leads for companies in the industrial sector.

To get the most out of your e-mail marketing efforts, you should focus on growing your opt-in list of subscribers. Opt-in means that subscribers are choosing to receive your e-mail marketing communications by registering and providing their e-mail address to you.

The primary strategy in growing your list is to use every opportunity available to you to ask people to opt-in to your e-mail communications. Follow the tips below to increase the number of subscribers who receive your e-mails, which in turn can increase brand awareness, lead generation and sales opportunities for your company.

Include Sign-up Forms on Your Website

Every page on your Web site should promote your e-mail communications. Try an eye-catching graphic and headline with a link to your registration page. Place it in various locations on Web pages and track which pages and locations work best for converting subscribers. Alternatively, you can try adding just a simple form on each page that allows a visitor to put in their e-mail address and instantly subscribe.

Use Viral Features in Your E-mails

Add a "Forward to a Friend" feature to your

communications that allows current subscribers to forward your e-mail to others by adding e-mail addresses into a form. If you don't have the capability to add that feature (almost all e-mail marketing service providers offer it), you can put "Please forward" in the subject line or headline.

Create a Compelling Subscription Page

If you provide links from your Web pages to an e-mail subscription page, make sure that page "sells" your e-mail communications. Here are specific tips for the subscription page:

- Describe exactly what subscribers are opting-in for: how often you will send e-mails, what they will contain, and the benefits for subscribers.
- Ask for the minimal amount of information on your registration form. A few fields should do it: name (so you can personalize e-mails), e-mail address, and preference for HTML or text version (yes, you should offer both). You can include other fields on your form, but make them optional. Later on, if you begin a relationship with a subscriber, you can capture more information.
- Add an offer to help drive subscriptions. Offer your just-published white paper, a recorded Webinar, a discount off a purchase, free shipping or anything else that will motivate visitors to become subscribers.

EIGHT TIPS FOR BETTER BLOGGING

Blogs are becoming an increasingly important part of the marketing mix for industrial companies. 26 percent are currently making use of a company blog and 35 percent are planning to implement a blog in 2010, according to the GlobalSpec 2010 Marketing Trends Survey. Blogs can help you establish a thought leadership position, increase brand recognition, improve search engine rankings, foster good relationships with customers and prospects, and create opportunities for leads and sales. But many attempts at blogging start out healthy and end up withering. Whether your company is already blogging or planning to get started, follow these tips to help ensure success.

1. *Define your strategy:* As with any marketing program, your blogging efforts should be driven by a strategy. What are the goals you hope to achieve by blogging? It could be thought leadership, brand building, or customer relationships. Who is your primary audience? Define who you are writing for and their needs. You need this strategy in place because it will guide your other decisions along the way.
2. *Establish a voice and tone:* Voice and tone are related not to what is being written, but how it is being written. Blog entries tend to be written in a less formal, more conversational style, offering an opportunity for the writer's (company's) personality or attitude to show. Some blogs are written from a position of authority, some are more analytical, and others may be inquisitive in nature. Establish the voice and tone that are right for your blog and communicate this policy to anyone who writes for your blog.
3. *Recruit writers:* Because you should post new content to your blog frequently, you may want to consider assembling a team of employees to participate. It can be difficult for one person to do all the writing for a blog—although one person probably should serve as an overall editor to ensure consistency of voice and tone, as well as adherence to strategy. Try recruiting fellow employees to contribute to the blog. Executives, engineers, customer service representatives, sales people and others all have an area of expertise that may be of interest to your audience. Be sure to let others know they don't have to be expert writers or compose long articles. A blog entry could be, for example, a single paragraph with a comment and link to an interesting article.
4. *Develop an editorial calendar:* One of the biggest reasons blogs fail is due to the lack of regular content updates. For this reason, you should develop an

editorial calendar that can help to keep you on track. It is also valuable if you use a team of contributors, so they understand their commitment as well. It's also a good idea to keep a library of extra content on hand that you can publish in the event you miss a calendar deadline. You should post to your blog as frequently as possible, but anything less than once a week and your blog is no longer the topical, current flow of information and interactive dialog with your audience it was intended to be.

5. *Be interesting:* Ultimately, this may be the most important tip of all. If you are interesting, you will engage your readers, foster discussion, grow your audience, and meet your goals. What makes a blog interesting? In the business-to-business world, interest equals usefulness. Help your audience perform their jobs better by providing insightful analysis and commentary on industry issues, technical challenges, and other work-related matters. Offer links to white papers, instructional videos, product applications and important articles. Issue invitations to educational Webinars. Also, sprinkle in lighter fare for a change of pace: games, contests, humor.
6. *Increase visibility for your blog:* A blog is only useful if your audience knows about it. One advantage of frequently updated blogs is that search engines like fresh content. Use keywords in your posts when they fit naturally with what you are writing, add keyword-based links to blog entries, and link to your blog from your company Web site. Also, link to your blog from your e-newsletter, from directories such as GlobalSpec, and even in your e-mail signature. You should get a unique URL for your blog, such as blog.companyname.com or companyname.com/blog.
7. *Encourage audience comments:* Blogs are meant to be interactive. Encourage your audience to leave comments by taking a stand and writing persuasively about key issues. Ask your audience for their opinions by posing a question—that way you prompt

a response. When you get comments and questions, respond to them on the blog. Always respond respectfully—even when you get negative comments. Don't get into arguments with your readers.

8. *Track your results:* We began and ended this list with tips that apply to every marketing program, from starting with a strategy to tracking results. Like other online marketing programs, a blog is built for measurement. Look for upward trends in the number of visits to your blog, page views, times spent on the blog, and comments from your readers. Keep writing to your blog and promoting it and you'll soon see results.

SECTION IV

Case Studies

CASE STUDY—I

McDONALD'S

With 31,500 locations in 119 countries, and serving nearly 47 million customers daily, McDonald's is the world's largest chain of fast food restaurants. Few are strangers to the brand that primarily sells hamburgers, cheeseburgers, chicken products, french fries, breakfast items, soft drinks, milkshakes, desserts and more recently, salads, wraps and fruit.

Build Website and Promote w/Internet Marketing Blitz in 10 Days!

In late spring 2007, McDonald's was preparing to launch a tasty new line of premium burgers to their Southern California market. The "Angus Third Pounders" are made with 100 percent USDA-inspected Angus beef and would come in 3 varieties. All eyes would be on Southern California to gauge their success. Ten days before the launch, McDonald's decided to take their campaign online. They wanted an interactive Flash website built and a solid online marketing campaign to help promote it.

Make an Interactive Website that Encourages Coupon Download

With little time to spare, eVisibility assembled their A-team to work non-stop, building out an interactive Flash website with the added ability to download a coupon for the new burger. The team also needed to develop a strong Internet marketing campaign to support not only the new website, but all the offline media as well. eVisibility would have to work closely with the McDonald's advertising agency to ensure the website's look and feel supported the message that was being created offline. They quickly got busy creating a keyword list made up of words and terms that fans, old and new, might use to search for the new burger. The end goal: To deliver 50,000 visits in month 1 with 4,000 downloaded coupons.

One of the Most Successful Product Launches in McDonald's History!

In 9 days, eVisibility successfully delivered a fully interactive Flash website that brought the McDonald's offline campaign to the online world. The downloadable coupon feature was a big success! In the first month 59,000 visitors came to the website downloading 29,000 coupons. By month 2 the website had 120,000 hits and just over 56,000 coupons downloaded. Today the burger continues to be a hit in Southern California and other regions throughout North America.

Issue for Discussion

What encouraged the customers to download coupons?

CASE STUDY—2

Q-INDUSTRIES

Q-Industries is an interactive agency that designs and builds online brands, websites and advanced Internet applications. Founded in 1999, clients range from startups to Fortune 500 companies.

Shifting Gears in a Highly Competitive PPC Market

Initially, Q-Industries ran their highly competitive paid search campaigns in-house, but failed to get their desired leads. Fed up with the significant amount of time and money invested, with nothing to show, they turned to eVisibility.

Analyze, Create, Build, Launch and Automate

To analyze existing campaign's historical performance data in order to identify and improve poor performing areas. To create a highly targeted campaign and improve segmentation in order to better reach key clients. Build a better targeted keyword list and remove keywords that do not lead to conversions.

Create and test ad text to increase relevance, traffic, and ad positioning. Identify and promote "core keywords" that drive relevant traffic. Launch ads at specific hours of the day to further target relevant traffic.

Develop, Optimize, Implement and Link

With eVisibility's Paid Search expertise and proprietary software ClickPro, Q-Industries was able to achieve results that surpassed their expectations:

- Increased monthly ROI
- Increase in keyword positioning
- Increased Click Through Rate
- Decreased monthly spend

Improved ROI-24% to 280% in No Time Flat

Q-Industries Paid Search campaign was fully launched in July of 2007, the same month we started work on the campaign. Once the launch was complete

Q-Industries quickly saw the benefits of their revamped Paid Search campaign. They were able to break sales records each month while decreasing their total Paid Search spending. This significantly improved return on investment from 24% to 280%.

Issue for Discussion

How to increase relevant traffic for internet marketing?

CASE STUDY—3

LEI FINANCIAL

Product: LEI financial is a nationwide financial services company specializing in niche-mortgage products.

Problem

Although very successful online, LEI financial had a cost per lead for online leads nearing $ 350 which was about 9x greater than what was profitable for the company.

Objective

To develop niche landing sites online that gear toward a specific loan product or visitor demographic with the overall goal of bringing the cost per lead down to $ 55.

Strategy

For the paid search campaign, to find niches and demographics that main competitors where not looking at. Specifically a combination of geo-targeted campaigns running toward niche loan products for that client. For the Organic campaign, to increase their nationwide exposure and acquire more free traffic.

Results

Over a period of 3 months, eVisibility got the cost per lead down for the paid search campaign to under $ 50, without losing any quality in conversion on leads. eVisibility was able to get top national Organic Search rankings, including: #8 for the word mortgage on MSN; #5 for California Mortgage Brokers in Google.

Issue for Discussion

How the organization increased eVisibility?

CASE STUDY—4

ONLINE STORE SALES SUCCESS

Our client had an online store. They were spending $ 15,000 each month on pay per click advertising. This resulted in about $ 225,000 per month in sales. They didn't know which clicks were leading to sales because they didn't track the clicks. There rankings in the natural listings was minimal because they hadn't done keyword research on what visitors were using to try to find a site like theirs. They weren't able to quantify results because their web statistics program only showed very general traffic information. They were also doing a an irregular email newsletter even though they had more than 32,000 emails in their database.

Analysis of the Situation

In the natural listings we suspected they were being penalized by the search engines for duplicate content. The search engines frown on this because they feel this is trying to fool them. Google will often give a site like this something called "Supplemental Results", which means that the search engines know the page exists but doesn't have any content in their database. We also suspected their email newsletter was being blocked by many spam blockers because the names of the products they sold were often on used in spam emails.

Implementation of a Solution

For the pay per click advertising we started tracking the clicks down to the individual terms and the actual results that came from them. We were able to delete terms that were not getting enough sales and increase the bids on ones that brought sales. For the natural listings we did keyword research and focused on the main keywords on the content for the home page and in the META tags. We also found that visitors search on product names rather than manufacturers, so in the Title tag for the page we switched and put the product name before the manufacturer. With the newsletter, we used a good mix of graphics and content to appease the spam blockers, as well as put the product names in graphics so they wouldn't be blocked. In order to analyze of the site's traffic, we implemented a powerful web statistics program.

Results of Our Work

Through our tactics, our client was able to move up to #4 on Google for their main search term, which got a lot of traffic. With pay per click, they went from $ .62 per click to $ .43. They decrease their budget to $ 10,000 per month, yet was able to increase their traffice by 33 percent. Through our optimization of their pay per click, their cost per conversion to sale decreased by at least 45 percent. The deliverability of their newsletter increased as well. Within an year, their sales increased to over $ 600,000 per month.

Issue for Discussion

What tactics were applied to increase the traffic?

CASE STUDY—5

WEB SITE REDESIGN AND SEARCH ENGINE MARKETING

Our client sells custom-made pieces of machinery to help other companies get greater visibility at major events. They had two people working part-time to manufacture and sell their products.

Analysis of the Situation

The client had a working web site that was somewhat disjointed. Because of budget limitations, they were only able to optimize their site for a few key phrases with their former marketing company. They needed more focused phrases to market, and to have more pages optimized for the search engines. They had started a pay per click campaign with limited results to make up for the leads they were missing in the free results of the major search engines.

Implementation of a Solution

We redesigned their logo and web site to make it look more professional. We shortened their contact form shorter so visitors wouldn't be more likely to fill it out. We also optimized their site to get more visitors so they would get more visitors through the natural search engine results, as well as took off some pages that the search engines considered illegal. We took off some of their outgoing links so that visitors wouldn't leave their site. With their pay per click strategy we increased the number of keywords they were bidding on and added conversion tracking so they'd know which phrases were working best for them.

The Results of Our Work

Within the first month of the implementation of the plan, their web site traffic was up more than 10 percent with more qualified visitors. Their ranking on the major search engines went up on more than 90 percent of their phrases. Within the last year their traffic has increased more than 50 percent. Sales have tripled since we have started working with them, which allowed one of the owners to leave his old job to work full-time with his business.

Issue for Discussion

What solution was implemented on SEM?

CASE STUDY—6

CUSTOM PROGRAMMING SUCCESS

Our client owns a flyer delivery service for real estate professionals. Her clients had to have drop off the flyers at the printers, where she would pick them up herself. She was driving all over town through bad traffic to pick up print jobs.

Analysis of the Situation

The client had been trying for three years to get her web site to work effectively. She had experienced frustration in finding someone who understood her problem and offered a good solution. She knew that having a usable web site would help her spend less time in the car and more time serving her customers and making sales. And because she used an invoicing system, she had thousands in accounts receivable from slow-paying customers.

Implementation of a Solution

We developed a process where her customers uploaded their flyers through the site and the print jobs were automatically sent to a local Kinkos for printing, eliminating the need for her and clients to drive to the print shop. We negotiated on behalf of the client to reduce the printing price by almost 66 percent. We also had Kinkos deliver the printing to our client.

The Results of Our Work

By implementing our process, the client was able to save herself many hours in the car driving back and forth to the printers. She was also able to make more money on the printing. The CTO of Kinko was impressed that no one else in the U.S. was using this system. Our client was also able to greatly reduce her accounts receivables as a result of taking credit cards.

Issue for Discussion

What steps were implemented to get rid of frustration?

CASE STUDY—7

LARGE PRODUCT INTERNET MARKETING

Our client a large item online, which they also advertised on TV, radio, and direct sales. They were spending about $ 20,000 per month in pay per click advertising, and were paying about $ 98 per lead. At their peak, they got 407 leads in one month through pay per click.

Analysis of the Situation

In their pay per click they were bidding too much on the major keywords and were sending all their visitors to their home page. They needed to bid on more phrases and then send them to landing pages within their site. We helped them establish that they would make $ 300 on each lead they got because the net profit on each sale was $ 15,000 and they converted 1 out of 50 online leads to sales.

Implementation of a Solution

We created a dozen or more landing pages on their site that were also optimized for the natual search engine results. Created a list of more than 1,500 keywords for them to bid on. These phrases had less traffic than the major keywords but had a higher likelihood of converting to sales. They also doubled their monthly budget.

Results of Our Work

Through our tactics, our client raised their monthly budget to more than $ 80,000 per month because of increased number of leads and sales. Their monthly leads went to over 1,700 per month and their cost per lead went down to $ 42 per lead. Overall, the Return on Investment went up, over 380 percent from when we first started doing their pay per click. And this doesn't include the amount of traffic they were able to get through the natural search results

Issue for Discussion

What was the organization strategy to increase SEM?

CASE STUDY—8

ZOKA COFFEE ROASTER

Challenge: Grow internet and café sales, build solid social media strategy, improve reputation management and create devoted fan base.

Background: The Zoka Coffee Roaster and Tea Company is an award-winning independent producer of artisan coffee and tea products in the Pacific Northwest. ZokaCoffee.com had a small following of blog readership and almost no social media presence.

When Portent Interactive started working with the Zoka Coffee Roaster and Tea Company in 2009, Zoka Coffee CEO Jeff Babcock understood his product had a narrow, but loyal following of coffee connoisseurs and he knew he needed to get the word out to people who have never heard of Zoka. The solution? Use social media tools to consolidate a fan base, create buzz and drive traffic from key influencers.

Step One: Eye-catching Design

After Portent finished the Search Engine Optimization (SEO) and redesign of the Zoka Coffee website, it was time to bring the same eye-pleasing design to the Zoka Coffee page on Facebook. Portent started by highlighting Zoka's unique personality with a new, eye-catching profile image.

Using the maximum profile picture size (200 x 600 pixels), the new page image highlights the product, while displaying a little history of the company. One unique aspect of the profile picture design is that the Zoka Coffee logo fits in a 200 x 200 pixel box, which transfers seamlessly as the thumbnail on the Zoka Coffee page wall. This is important because if the logo in the profile picture is larger than 200 x 200 pixels, it will be cut off in the thumbnail image.

Instead of directing new visitors directly to the wall of the Zoka Coffee page, Portent created a new landing tab to capture a conversion opportunity from new customers. Designed as a miniature webpage, the Zoka Coffee welcome tab directs Facebook users new to the page to other resources like café locations and the online store.

Step Two: Join the Conversation

Portent launched the new page design on Facebook in Feb. 2010, two-weeks after the strategic process was complete. The improved design increased page views on the Zoka Coffee website and lead to an immediate increase in followers and fan participation.

Shortly after, the Portent social team went to work on implementing a complex social media strategy. Using social mediums like Twitter, Facebook, and the Portent social team identified key influencers in the coffee community and created interactive updates and tweets to gain feedback from followers.

Step Three: Growing the fan base

Portent quickly realized that paid search within Facebook offered an inexpensive opportunity to grow the fan base, while offering sales opportunities. After launching the Facebook Pay Per Click (PPC) campaign, the traffic spiked within a month.

Portent also implemented contests and giveaways on Twitter and Facebook, as well as implemented a successful bi-monthly email newsletter. Most notably, the Where on Earth is Zoka Coffee Photo Contest asked fans to guess the location of selection of travel photos on the Facebook page wall. The contest gained roughly 100 interactions and increased followers by 14% in three days.

Why it worked: The contest used travel images from Zoka, which correlated very well to the company's brand and demographic of affluent, worldly coffee drinkers. It also prompted interaction because with every new comment, the contest broadened its reach as it became visible to all of the friends of the commenter who were not yet become a fan of Zoka Coffee on Facebook. The grand prize of a Zoka Coffee gift basket didn't hurt either.

Results

Zoka Coffee's Twitter and Facebook traffic grew over 800% over the first 3 months. The Zoka Coffee page on Facebook is one of the top five referring sites to the Zoka webpage, and receives mentions from many predominant coffee news sources including the Seattle Times and the Seattle Weekly.

Issue for Discussion

How social media strategy helped the organization to increase sales?

CASE STUDY—9

ADJUSTING LINODE'S PPC CAMPAIGN TO INCREASE CONVERSIONS

The Challenge

Turn around a paid search campaign that was seeing very little conversions and paying far too high a price for the few it did manage to bring in.

Background

Linode is a Virtual Private Server (VPS) hosting company that offers customers packages with different amounts of server space depending on their needs. When Linode started its paid search campaign, they were getting very poor conversion rates. Costs for the campaign were running high and very few leads were coming in. In fact, the average cost per lead was running at nearly $ 1,200 and the company averaged 2-3 leads per month from paid search. Seeing these issues, they decided to come to Portent for help.

Making Much Needed Changes to PPC

The PPC team got to work right away with a complete restructure of Linode's PPC campaign. Originally, every ad was pulling from one giant list of keywords with no campaigns to differentiate between significant niche terms. Portent reviewed historical performance on each and every keyword and separated them into nine campaigns, each with several ad groups. In addition, Portent also initiated geo-targeting, limiting ad impressions to Linode's top 10 converting countries that had a primarily English-speaking constituency. After the initial restructure, the PPC team continued daily monitoring-adjusting keyword bids, campaign budgets, ads, and ad scheduling to optimize the account's performance.

The Results

After just a few weeks with Portent, Linode saw drastic improvements in their paid search performance. Click-through Rate (CTR) rose by nearly 600%, the Conversion Rate increased 128 times over, and the Cost per Conversion dropped to just over $ 200 per lead-a reduction of nearly $ 1,000 per lead! Portent's ability to narrow Linode's PPC focus resulted in a smarter and more optimized campaign

Issue for Discussion

What strategy they adopted to increase conversion rate?

CASE STUDY—10

SALTWORKS BUILDS SALES, REDUCES AD COSTS

Challenge: In short, more bang for the buck. Saltworks is one of the Internet's premiere sellers of retail and wholesale gourmet and bath salts. Sales were good, but owner Mark Zoske felt they could be better. His challenge: Greater marketing efficiency and ROI. Saltworks needed to increase sales while decreasing high pay-per-click advertising costs on Google, Overture and other pay-per-click services. He called Portent Interactive to help get his internet marketing program on track.

Portent's Strategy: Less PPC, More SEO

Portent used their proprietary keyword mining toolset to find the words and phrases most used by potential customers who searched for gourmet and bath salt products. They also began tracking the return on investment generated by each online advertisement. After a short review period, Portent recommended a scaled-back pay-per-click campaign that focused only on revenue-generating phrases.

Portent also recommended a natural search engine optimization campaign: Changes to site code and structure would help Saltworks move up in the search rankings. An improved content plan would build site content, too.

Finally, Portent performed a usability review. The results refined the Saltworks.us site, providing a better customer experience and higher conversion rates.

The Results: Higher Sales, Lower Costs

Search engine optimization has increased relevant search traffic by 50%. Saltworks has doubled the number of relevant first-place rankings on Google, MSN and Yahoo. Improvements include moving from #30 to #4 on Google for 'bath salts', moving from unranked to #1 for 'bulk dead sea salt' and moving from unranked to #2 for 'sea salts'.

These new rankings improved the flow of interested, qualified customers to Saltworks.us. At the same time, site refinements doubled conversion rates.

Portent's refined bidding strategy cut pay-per-click costs by 1/2, saving the company thousands of dollars per month. Saltworks total sales have increased by over 230%, with a 27% increase in total number of orders compared to 2004.

Issue for Discussion

Why they wanted to increase SEO?

CASE STUDY—11
MONTAGE RESORT AND SPA, LAGUNA BEACH

Montage Resort and Spa, which opened in February 2003, is a 262-room ultra-luxury resort located in Laguna Beach, California, serving both affluent leisure travelers and group business clientele.

The Challenge

As the flagship property for a new luxury hotel brand, Montage Resort and Spa, Laguna Beach, initially approached E-site Marketing to design a Website and develop and implement a fully integrated, strategic online marketing program that would:

- Establish and promote brand awareness for a newly-formed, ultra-luxury hotel company/brand.
- Position the flagship property online during critical stages of the resort's opening phase, as well as into the future.
- Generate and increase qualified leads, conversion potential and significant revenue sources to meet ambitious online sales goals.

The Solution

E-site Marketing developed a comprehensive Internet marketing program to include a diverse range of online and e-commerce solutions that would initially establish the Montage brand online and evolve to maximize awareness and generate direct revenues.

- Design, development, launch and continual enhancements of an innovative Website that intimately reflects the branding, image and attributes of the exclusive property and translates the luxurious and elegant experience of visiting the property within the actual Website visit. Innovative features include:
  - o E-Commerce Functionality:

        - E-commerce Store (www.montageshops.com)
        - Online Catalogue
        - Online Concierge
    - o Mini-Sites: Spa, Meetings, Weddings (which are independently marketed and optimized)
    - o Online RFP/Interactive Proposal Service (IPS) Integration
    - o Extensive CRM/PHP Data Collection
- Integrated Email Marketing program and customized Email Campaigns: (including a flash-based, robust bi-yearly e-newsletter): www.montageimpressions.com)
- Customized Search Engine Optimization and Marketing Program
- Customized Interactive Media and Linkage Partnership Program

The Results

- Direct revenue generated via the Website increased 35% from 2005 to 2006. 44% of this revenue was generated by Search Engine based visitors to the Website.
- Montage Shops (www.montageshops.com) revenue increased 17% from 2005 to 2006.
- Actual room nights generated via the online booking engine increased 61% from 2005 to 2006.
- Online Request for Proposals (RFPs) increased 96% from 2005 to 2006 due to strategic push marketing on Website.
- As a result of the Internet Marketing program implemented, search engine traffic increased over 100% in the 1st year of the program.
- The Website is the recipient of the prestigious HSMAI Golden Click Award and the Web Marketing Association's Standard of Excellence Award.
- The Montage Studio website is the recipient of the Web Marketing Association's Best Restaurant Website Award for 2006

Issue for Discussion

How to develop integrated strategic online marketing plan?

CASE STUDY—12

SEO AND SOCIAL MEDIA CASE STUDY

Situation

This online games and puzzles website is dedicated to providing readers with intriguing content that engages and exercises the brain. Founded by a board-certified neurologist, the site's goal is to help its readers have fun while exercising their brain.

Shortly after the website launched in the summer of 2006, this site engaged TopRank Marketing to increase the number of visitors.

Solution

To help increase visibility within the search engines and to increase monthly visitors to the website, TopRank Marketing's first step was to implement a search engine optimization program.

TopRank conducted a technical analysis of the site, keyword analysis, and made recommendations for content optimization to include optimized title tags, meta descriptions, and on-page copy. As well, the TopRank Marketing team created a new site design that sung to its true focus of providing the audience with new and entertaining online puzzles.

In addition to a search marketing program, TopRank Marketing outlined a social media marketing strategy to increase visibility of the client's brand online.

Results

As a result of TopRank Marketing's search marketing and social media marketing efforts, more than 40% of the site's overall traffic comes from the search engines while over 30% of the traffic comes from the client's online network of gaming sites and promotional marketing channels. Since starting work with TopRank Marketing in June of 2006, *unique visitors have grown by 4,400%.*

This online puzzles web site continues to develop intriguing and fresh content to engage visitors and keeps them coming back for more. Because of this content, the has achieved over *300,000 page views each month.*

Issue for Discussion

What measures should be adopted to increase number of visitors at the web-site?

CASE STUDY—13

SEO AND ONLINE PR

Situation

Powder-Solutions opened its operational doors in February 2007 as one of only two American distributors of a newly created BFM® fitting within the bulk powder industry. BFM® is a unique industrial pipe connector designed to provide safe, sanitary and efficient connections for the transportation and movement of powder within bulk powder processing plants.

Powder-Solutions engaged TopRank Marketing to help develop the company's website and launch a strategic online marketing program that would increase visitors as well as sales inquiries for the company.

Solution

To help build brand awareness and drive traffic to powder-solutions.com, TopRank Marketing implemented the following search engine optimization (SEO) tactics:

- Website development and technical assessment
- Keyword research and content optimization
- Content promotion and link building
- Web analytics and conversion tracking

In addition to SEO, the TopRank Marketing team has helped Powder-Solutions concept and deploy content marketing campaigns and targeted email marketing to help build brand awareness. To help humanize the PowderSolutions brand, and communicate the safety hazards the bulk powder industry faced, the TopRank Marketing team designed a creative concept, The Powder Doctor, to relate to the target market.

Results

As a result of TopRank Marketing's SEO efforts, PowderSolutions has seen website traffic increase more than 700% in its niche market. Additionally, with the launch of its creative campaign, The Powder Doctor, organic traffic to powdersolutions.com has more than doubled. Organic search, combined with the creative concept leveraged for online PR and email marketing campaigns, have helped to increase bottom line sales for the company by 83%.

Issue for Discussion

What steps are required to develop a website?

CASE STUDY—14

B2B INTERNET MARKETING

KoMarketing Associates works with businesses large and small. We are confident that we can craft a success story working together with you.

While the details are sensitive, the picture painted below is of successful client engagements. We are pleased to provide references to help you with your decision to work with KoMarketing Associates. Below are some of the success stories at KoMarketing Associates:

The Problem

KoMarketing was challenged with transforming the existing pay-per-click marketing campaign of a mid-size software firm to increase the total number of quality leads generated while reducing the total monthly advertising budget. As part of that challenge, we had to create a way to track each lead and measure both quantity and quality improvement.

The Steps Taken

When we took over the management of Pay Per Click (PPC) campaigns for this software company, we spent time in an initial discovery phase to define the goals, objectives, and guidelines for the program. We then worked with the client's management team to take the following steps:

1. *Lead Definition*—The first step was to determine what would constitute a lead. The software industry typically struggles to separate people looking for general information from actual qualified prospects looking to make a purchase. In this case, a form requesting an evaluation copy of the software was tagged to represent a lead. There were also geographical constraints, where the client was only looking for leads from North America and a few additional selected countries.
2. *Bid for ROI, Not Position*—We shifted the focus of the PPC efforts from "ego bidding" (staying in the number 1 ad spot just because the ad is in a higher than the competition), to bidding based on ROI criteria. Management was reluctant to move to this strategy, but we all agreed to try the new strategy and tactics and measure the results. We quickly found our sweet spot in ad positions 3 to 5.
3. *Campaign Re-Structuring and Expansion*—In order to more efficiently manage the portfolio of keywords, we created an additional 15 campaigns and over 40 new Ad Groups in Google. This allowed us to bucket keywords logically, target ad copy more effectively, and create a structure that anyone could step into and manage.
4. *Keyword Expansion*—We expanded the keyword selection from a few hundred words to over 3,000. This involved adding new terms based on technical specifications, expanding two-word terms into 3-word and 4-word combinations, and ensuring that keywords used broad, phrase, and exact match types.
5. *Leveraging Negative Keywords*—In order to control costs, ensure that ads were shown to the most-

qualified searchers, and to manage Google's keyword quality scoring algorithm, we added in negative keywords to prevent ads from being displayed for less-qualified keyword queries. Using a wide range of negative keywords, from "free", to "open source" to words containing platform-specific words, we generated a higher Click Through Rate, higher conversion rate, and improved the Quality Score for ads in Google AdWords, which helped allow us to bid less for keywords without sacrificing ad position.

6. *Ad Copy Improvement and Version Testing*—Ad copy had remained stagnant for approximately two years, and needed to be reviewed and refreshed. We worked with the client to write technical ad copy to highlight features/benefits in order to better qualify prospects before they clicked on the ad. Multiple versions of ads were created, along with a test plan for further refinements, and these ad versions were served simultaneously to gauge both user interest and conversion response.
7. *Additional Search Engines*—The client was only using Google AdWords when we began working with them. We added Yahoo! Sponsored Search and Business.com to the media mix. This expansion served to reach a larger number of qualified prospects simply by reaching a larger overall market base. We used the same logic on these search engines as we did with Google AdWords to duplicate the strong results.
8. *Landing Page Creation and Optimization*—We created specific landing pages for high-volume keywords to improve conversion rates and capture well-qualified leads. Incremental steps were taken in creating and optimizing the landing pages, starting with basic copy modifications, then moving to testing product images, navigational elements, and adding contact form fields to the pages.
9. *Tracking and Analytics*—KoMarketing incorporated web analytics to track individual keyword performance beyond simple conversion tracking

codes. We advised the client to send leads to a CRM database-SalesForce.com, with the search engine and keyword identified. The company was then able to follow their search advertising spend through the sales process. By linking sales data back to keywords, ad text, and search engines, a feedback loop was established to continually modify and improve the campaigns each month.

The Results

- As a result of our efforts, the number of leads per month increased from an average of 150 to an average of 190, with some months as high as 245 leads.
- The quality of those leads also improved, with a higher percentage resulting in an end sale.
- The total monthly click charge was lowered by an average of $ 3,000 per month, and the cost per lead dropped from $ 110 to the mid-$ 60 range.

KoMarketing has been overwhelmingly successful in assisting this software company in achieving its marketing goals, and the company continues to be a client today.

Issue for Discussion

What objective and guidelines are required to increase the traffic?

CASE STUDY—15

1ST CLASS CLEANING

THE company was looking to increase its leads and sales providing services primarily to residential consumers in the highly competitive New York Metropolitan area. Prior to hiring Optimum7, the client was frustrated because whether he attempted Search Engine Optimization (SEO), Pay per Click (PPC) or Email Marketing with other firms, the results just were poor compared to expectations.

A website analysis was conducted and the following factors were identified:

- Poor onsite SEO elements including page titles and descriptions and no dynamic sitemap.
- Insufficient content/Stale Content.
- Few Backlinks with no quality.
- No prominent call to actions on the site

Poor Website Design

In brief, Optimum7 needed to address these issues almost as if this was a brand new website as there was little in the way of positive SEO elements.

Based on the client's budget, as well as short, medium and long term considerations, it was concluded that Optimum7 SEO Local PLUS was the best solution to address the main issue of poor leads primarily due to poor traffic. PPC was ruled out based on budgetary issues as well as the understanding that it was only warranted if the client needed to have the phone ring within days rather than a few months.

Challenges

The main challenge is one of the math; i.e. already big numbers. Optimum7's compensation is pad for in large measure on a Pay for Performance Basis. Specifically, the amount for our fees varies based on the percentage increase in organic site visits. So, were starting with a number of 40,000 so large percentage increases are obviously more challenging. However, based upon preliminary keyword research, we felt confident that we can achieve significant results that will meet and exceed the profit goals of both companies.

Solution Implementation

All Optimum7 SEO implementation begins with extensive keyword research and competitive research. The client was requested and provided the list of the top 25 terms that he felt were the most important. This was used as valuable input as a part of the research process. The following is an outline of the initial processes that were followed:

Research

- Get CPanel/FTP Access from Client
- Review Site Structure and Elements
- Advanced Keyword Research
- Keyword Research on Industry and the Competition

Niche Terms Research

- Top 10-20 keywords organized from list, and list sub-keywords from tools
- Competition Back link research for top 10-20 keywords

Finalize Keywords

- Provide Client with Keyword List. Have Client identify any/all irrelevant/negative keywords.
- Determine Link Saturation, Quality and Anchor Texts
- Setup Link velocity monitoring for Client and Competition
- Blog Research

Plan Social Bookmarking strategy and review existing accounts

We then moved forward to Onsite Optimization which obviously involves strictly on-page elements that serve as the foundation for all future onsite and offsite optimization. Here are those processes focused upon onsite optimization:

Initial on site Optimization

- Continuing Keyword Research
- Article Topic Research
- On Site Article Creation-10 articles per month for this client
- RSS Feed Updating and Pingback
- Specific Article Pages and Optimization
- Press Releases-2 per year for this client

- Viral Video Implementation and Submission
- Meta Tag Testing
- Blog Development, if applicable

Ongoing on site Optimization

- Continuing Keyword Research
- Article Topic Research
- On Site Article Creation-30 articles per month plus additional content assigned to client for Optimum7 Implementation
- RSS Feed Updating and Pingback
- Specific Article Pages and Optimization
- Press Releases-4 per year for this client
- Viral Video Implementation and Submission
- Meta Tag Testing
- Blog Development, if applicable

With ongoing onsite optimization moving smoothly we proceeded to the 2nd major track of SEO, Offsite Optimization. All offsite optimization is geared towards generating high quality and high quantities of highly relevant, naturally occurring backlinks. Backlinks are one-way links that originate outside of the project website linking to/pointing to relevant content on the client's website. Quality Backlinks are the single most important differentiator that Google uses to actually rank websites keyword for keyword. The fuel for all backlinks at Optimum7 is CONTENT; articles, blog posts, press releases, videos, podcasts and more. The following outlines the processes involved offsite SEO.

Off site Optimization

- Social Media accounts setup
- Video/Podcast creation and development if applicable
- Google Local Submissions/Google Maps
- Essential Directory Submission

Off site ongoing Optimization

- Great Content Generation for Great Link Quality Generation
- Article Syndication
- Backlink research and implementation
- Viral Video Syndication
- Press Release Syndication
- Social Bookmarking Submissions and Popularity
- Social Media Backlinking

Results

Optimum7 is focused on results based on the processes just outlined. The most important data will be reviewed here as follows:

- Organic Traffic from searches
- Number of Keywords used to actually land on the site
- Backlink Growth

Issue for Discussion

How to analyze the PPC model of Internet marketing?

CASE STUDY—16

BEAUTY SCHOOLS OF AMERICA

Background

Beauty Schools of America (BSA) is one of the leading educational institutions for beauty and spa professionals. The primary focus of their marketing strategy for 20 years had been through traditional channels such as TV, print, and radio. They knew that a well-executed online marketing campaign would take their business to the next level but with a competitive landscape and limited budget, they were tentative as to the approach. BSA interviewed several Internet marketing agencies and chose IMI for our ability to bring a fully integrated strategy to the table.

The Goal

To drastically increase enrollment lead generation through online marketing channels at the lowest cost possible.

The Strategy

With an outdated website and limited ability to track enrollment through the web, it immediately became apparent that BSA needed a fresh start and complete solution. A multilingual campaign using both English and Spanish was needed to reach their targeted demographic. Internet Marketing Inc. developed a strategy within the their given budget that would prove to maximize enrollment well beyond their expectations. The strategy included the following:

- Website Design and Development
- Search Engine Optimization
- Landing Page Design and Optimization
- Pay Per Click Advertising
- Display Banner Design
- Social Media and Facebook Advertising
- Online Reputation Management
- Internal Lead Testing

The Results

Prior to hiring IMI, BSA was only generating approximately 20 enrollment leads per month through their website. We designed a new website and landing pages and rolled out an aggressive online marketing strategy that has resulted in the consistent generation of well over 1,000 leads per month.

We have also taken it a step further. To ensure that our plan comes full circle and has a direct positive impact on BSA's business, we wanted to ensure that the leads generated were resulting in actual enrollment. We performed lead testing using a survey system and found that 80% of the interested potential students were either not contacted in a timely manner or were very disappointed with the level of communication and service. Through improved lead quality and better internal enrollment procedures, IMI helped BSA drastically improve customer satisfaction which resulted in further increases in enrollment and ROI.

How We Put it All Together

Phase One: Design and Develop a New Website and Landing Page

We started by creating a foundation for the campaign which would ensure proper conversions. BSA needed a new SEO friendly website with an improved appearance, a robust Content Management System, an improved registration system and lead database, and landing pages to support the PPC campaigns. We created BSA.edu in both English and Spanish. The new site has experienced increased conversions, increased time on site, and praise from students all over the world.

Phase Two: Launch SEO and PPC

As we approached the launch date for the website, we started the research phase for both the SEO and PPC campaigns. Upon launch, we began the full SEO process and activated the PPC campaigns. IMI used A/B split testing for PPC landing page optimization and found that the page using video converted at the highest rate. Throughout the course of the PPC campaign, IMI has successfully reduced the Cost Per Acquisition (CPA) by 45%. Prior to launching SEO, BSA only ranked for a handful of brand related keywords and only received a few hundred visitors per month to their website. Our robust SEO strategy that has been performed in both English and Spanish, has resulted in 230 keywords now ranking on the first page in Google. BSA's website traffic from organic keywords has more than doubled. Overall website traffic has increased by more than five times.

Phase Three: Launch Social Media, Facebook Advertising, and Online Reputation Management

To further reach BSA's demographic, IMI developed a social media engagement strategy that includes blogging, video, Facebook interaction, and Facebook Ads. By using Facebook and YouTube, BSA has been able to share valuable content with their audience and keep in touch with current and potential students. The Facebook Ads contribute approximately 20% of the overall enrollment lead generation. BSA had a complaint on RipOffReport.com ranking number four in Google for their brand name. This denigrating content was receiving a lot of traffic and most likely having a negative impact on enrollment. By using our proprietary Online Reputation Management strategies, IMI was able to push the RipOffReport.com article off the first page of Google.

Phase Four: Lead Testing

At IMI, our goal is to grow our clients' businesses and provide a tangible return on investment. Generating over 1,000 leads per month is a powerful result but we wanted to ensure that those leads were translating into increased enrollment. We implemented a survey system and discovered that 80% of the leads were not being properly handled. Those people that had been contacted by enrollment were not satisfied with the experience. This discovery helped BSA improve their lead handling procedures which further increased ROI.

Issue for Discussion

Why and How to launch SEO and PPC?

Bibliography

Anderson, Simon P., Jean J. Gabszewicz. 2005. "The Media and Advertising: A Tale of Two-Sided Markets". *CEPR Discussion Paper No. 5223*. Armstrong, Mark. 2006. "Competition in Two-Sided Markets". *RAND Journal of Economics,* 37(3)

Arango, Tim. 2008. "Cable Firms Join Forces to Attract Focused Ads," *New York Times* (March 10).

Bennett, Tricia (2010, Jan 12). Cloud CRM: Ready, Steady,. http://www.crmbuyer.com/story

C-H Park and Y-G Kim, "A framework for dynamic CRM: linking marketing with information strategy". *Business Process Management Journal* vol. 9 no. 5 (2003).

Chandra, Satish, and Ted J. Strickland (2004) Technological differences between CRM and eCRM, Issues in Information Systems, http://www.iacis.org

Clarke III, Irvine and Theresa B. Flaherty (eds) (2005), *Advances in Electronic Marketing.*

ComScore Press Release. 2008. "U.S. Search Engines Rankings". (November 26), at http://www.marketwatch.com

Duboff, Robert S. 2007. *ROI for Marketing: Balancing Accountability with Long-Term Needs.* New York: Association of National Advertisers.

Edelman B., Michael Ostrovsky, and Michael Schwarz. 2007. "Internet Advertising and the Generalized Price Auction: Selling Billions of Dollars Worth of Keywords". *American Economic Review,* 97(1).

Elliott, Stuart. 2006. "At the Four A's, a Focus on Getting Stronger". *New York Times* (April 3), at European Commission. 2008. *Opinion on Data Protection Issues Related to Search Engines,* April.

Evans, David and Richard Schmalensee, 2005. *Paying with Plastic, 2nd Edition: The Digital Revolution in Buying and Borrowing.* Cambridge: The MIT Press.

———, 2009. "Platform Failure". Available at SSRN, http://ssrn.com/abstract

Evans, David S., 2008. "The Economics of the Online Advertising Industry," *Review of Network Economics,* 7(3)

———, 2009. "How Catalysts Ignite: The Economics of Platform-Based Start-Ups".

Forrester Report, "B2B US Interactive Marketing Forecast, 2009-2014" http://bit.ly/akM4E

Geysken *et. al.,* "The market valuation of internet channel addition," *Journal of Marketing,* Vol. 66 (2002).

GlobalSpec's: "Trends in Industrial Marketing 2010". http://www.globalspec.com/advertising/e-marketing-newsletter "information technology", Oxford English Dictionary (2 ed.), Oxford University Press, 1989, http://dictionary.oed.com/, retrieved 20 November 2010

Goldsmith, R.E., and Bridges, E. (2000). E-tailing versus retailing: Using attitudes to predict online buying behavior. *Quarterly Journal of Electronic Commerce.*

Hallerman, David. 2008. "US Online Advertising: Resilient in a Rough Economy: Summary". March, available at eMarketer.com.

Helft, Miguel. 2008".Google's New Tool Is Meant for Marketers". *The New York Times.* (August 6), at http://www.nytimes.com.

History of Pay Per Click Advertising and Yahoo! Sponsored Search," 2007. November 1. http://www.semvironment.com

http://en.wikipedia.org/wiki/ECRM-cite_ref-27*Camponovo et al., "Mobile customer relationship management: an explorative investigation of the Italian consumer market," Proceedings of 4th International Conference on Mobile Business 11-13 july, Sydney (2005).*

http://en.wikipedia.org/wiki/Information_technology-cite_ref-3 http://en.wikipedia.org/wiki/Information_technology-cite_ref-gartner.com_5-0"*Gartner Says Worldwide IT Services Revenue Declined 5.3 Percent in 2009", Gartner,* http://www.gartner.com

http://searchcrm.techtarget.com/tip/Four-steps-for-an-effective-mobile-CRM-implementation.

http://www.destinationcrm.com/Articles/Web Exclusives/Viewpoints/CRM-Customer-Relationship-Mobile.

http://www.mediabuzz.com.sg/asian-emarketing/

http://www.prweb.com/Online-Marketing

http://www.nytimes.com/2008/03/10/technology/html

http://www.ebizq.net/topics/bpm/features

http://www.awprofessional.com/articles/article

http://www.codeproject.com/KB/architecture/Dude

http://web.inter.nl.net/users/T.Koppelaars

http://www.iseing.org/emcis/CDROM

http://www.destinationcrm.com/Categories/Enterprise-CRM

http://www.pcworld.com/businesscenter/article

http://www.destinationcrm.com/Articles/Columns

Internet Marketing-How, When, Where?. Daily Mirror.

http://print.dailymirror.lk/business/127.

Jaakko Sinisalo *et. al.* (2007). "Mobile customer relationship management: underlying issues and challenges" (in *(English)*). *Business Process Management Journal* 13 (6). *doi:10.1108/14637150710834541.*

Kaye, Barabara K and Norman Medoff. 2001. *Just A Click Away: Advertising on the Internet.* Massachusetts: Allyn and Bacon.

Lakshmi Goel and Elham Mousavidin, "vCRM: Virtual Customer Relationship Management," *Database for Advances in Information Systems* vol. 38 no. 4 (2007).

Lauren Keller Johnson, "New Views on Digital CRM," *Sloan Management Review* fall (2002): 10.

Marketing Sherpa Report. 2008. "Banner Ad Size and Click Rate: Bigger a Bit Better, But It is the Click that Counts," September 16.

Microsoft Advertising Industry News. 2008. "Spending on Behavioral Targeting Predicted to Increase," September 8 http://advertising.microsoft.com

Morais, Shanti A. (2010) eCRM: Striking the Balance Between Business and Privacy Issues.

Nenad Jukic *et. al.*, "Implementing Polyinstantiation as a Strategy for Electronic Commerce Customer Relationship Management," *International Journal of Electronic Commerce* Vol. 7, No. 2 (2002-3).

Pope, Daniel. 1983. *Making of Modern Advertising*. New York, NY: Basic Books.

Rayner, Andrew (April 21, 2010). *"Put the E-mphasis on Local Internet Marketing and reach first page on Google". http://www.prlog.org/10638959-put-the-mphasis-on-local-internet-marketing-and-reach-first-page-on-google.html.*

Reponen, Tapio(2003) *Information Technology-Enabled Global Customer Service http://en.wikipedia.org/wiki/ECRM-cite_ref-Sinisalo_1-0* Jaakko Sinisalo *et. al.* (2007). "Mobile customer relationship management: underlying issues and challenges" (in (English)). *Business Process Management Journal* 13 (6).

Rochet, Jean-Charles and Jean. Tirole. 2003. "Platform Competition in Two-Sided Markets". *Journal of the European Economic Association*, 1(4).

Russel S. Winer, "A Framework for Customer Relationship Management," *California Management Review* vol. 43 no. 4 (2001).

Shin, Namchul, (2005), *Strategies for Generating E-Business Returns on Investment*.

Silk, Alvin J., Lisa R. Klein and Ernst R. Berndt. 2001. "The Emerging Position of the Internet as an Advertising Medium".

Sindell, Kathleen, Ph.D.,(2000) *Loyalty Marketing for the Internet Age: How to Identify, Attract, Serve, and Retain Customers in an E-commerce Environment* Downes, L., and Mui, C. (1998). *Unleashing the killer app:Digital strategies for market dominance. Boston: Harvard Business School Press.*

Story, Louise and comScore (March 10, 2008). *"They Know More Than You Think"* (JPEG). *The New York Times. http://www.nytimes.com/imagepages/2008/03/10/technology/20080310_PRIVACY_GRAPHIC.html.* in Story, Louise (March 10, 2008). *"To Aim Ads, Web Is Keeping Closer Eye on*

You". The New York Times (The New York Times Company). *http://www.nytimes.com/2008/03/10/technology/10privacy.html.*

T. Coltman, "Why build a Customer Relationship Management Capability?", *Journal of Strategic Information Systems* 16 (2007).

The Medium is the Massages. 2002. *Adweek,* July 29.

Turban *et. al., Information Technology for Management: Transforming Organizations in the Digital Economy,* 6th ed.

U.S. Department of Commerce. 2008. *Quarterly Retail E-Commerce Sales 3rd Quarter 2008,* Press Release.

Valerie A. Zeithaml *et. al.,* "The Customer Pyramid: Creating and Serving Profitable Customers," *California Management Review,* Vol. 43, No. 4. (2001).

Varian, Hal R. 2007. "Position Auctions". *International Journal of Industrial Organization* 25(6) Winter:

Yahoo Press Release, 2007. *"Yahoo!'s New "SmartAds" Meld Brand and Direct Response Advertising".* (July 2).

Yujong Hwang and Dan, J. Kim, "Customer Self-service Systems: The Effect of Perceived Web quality with service contents on enjoyment, anxiety, and e-trust," *Decision Support Systems* 43 (2007).

Index